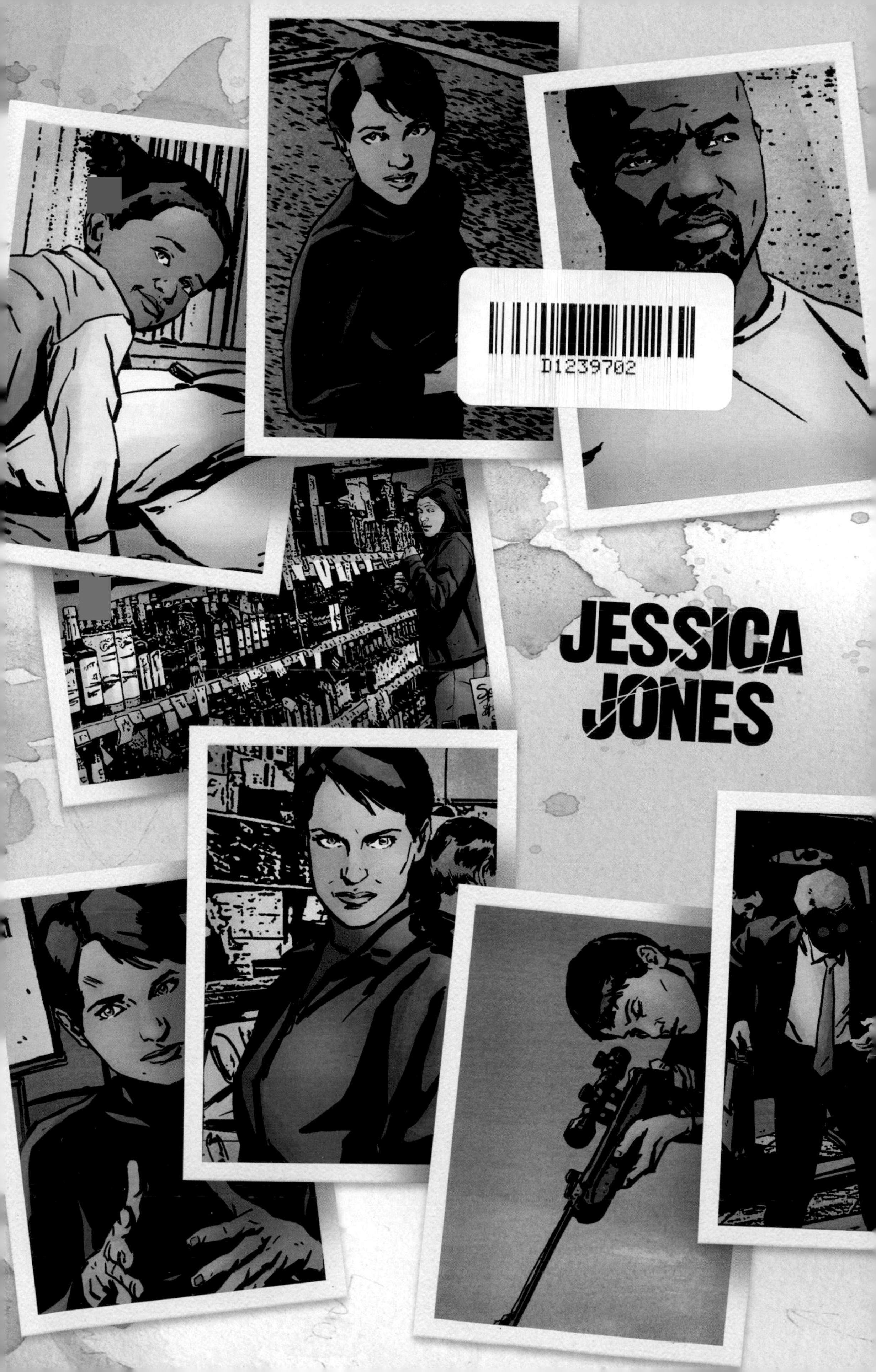
JESSICA
JONES

ALIAS INVESTIGATIONS
NEW YORK, NY

JESSICA RECENTLY FAKED A FALL FROM GRACE TO HELP CAPTAIN MARVEL LURE AN ANTI-SUPER-HERO GROUP OUT OF HIDING — A FALL SO CONVINCING IT ALIENATED HER FROM THE SUPER HERO COMMUNITY...AND HER HUSBAND, LUKE CAGE.

THE STUNT WAS SUCCESSFUL, AND CAPTAIN MARVEL AND JESSICA WERE ABLE TO CAPTURE THE LEADER OF THE GROUP BEFORE SHE COULD HARM ANYONE ELSE — BUT THEY WEREN'T IN TIME TO KEEP LUKE FROM DISCOVERING WHERE JESSICA HAD HIDDEN THEIR DAUGHTER.

CAN JESSICA SALVAGE HER PERSONAL LIFE? OR IS IT TOO LATE?

JESSICA JONES VOL. 2: THE SECRETS OF MARIA HILL. Contains material originally published in magazine form as JESSICA JONES #7-12. First printing 2017. ISBN# 978-1-302-90636-8. Published by MARVEL WORLDWIDE, INC., a subsidiary of MARVEL ENTERTAINMENT, LLC. OFFICE OF PUBLICATION: 135 West 50th Street, New York, NY 10020. Copyright © 2017 MARVEL No similarity between any of the names, characters, persons, and/or institutions in this magazine with those of any living or dead person or institution is intended, and any such similarity which may exist is purely coincidental. **Printed in Canada.** DAN BUCKLEY, President, Marvel Entertainment; JOE QUESADA, Chief Creative Officer; TOM BREVOORT, SVP of Publishing; DAVID BOGART, SVP of Business Affairs & Operations, Publishing & Partnership; C.B. CEBULSKI, VP of Brand Management & Development, Asia; DAVID GABRIEL, SVP of Sales & Marketing, Publishing; JEFF YOUNGQUIST, VP of Production & Special Projects; DAN CARR, Executive Director of Publishing Technology; ALEX MORALES, Director of Publishing Operations; SUSAN CRESPI, Production Manager; STAN LEE, Chairman Emeritus. For information regarding advertising in Marvel Comics or on Marvel.com, please contact Vit DeBellis, Integrated Sales Manager, at vdebellis@marvel.com. For Marvel subscription inquiries, please call 888-511-5480. **Manufactured between 10/6/2017 and 11/7/2017 by SOLISCO PRINTERS, SCOTT, QC, CANADA.**

10 9 8 7 6 5 4 3 2 1

Jessica Jones, a former costumed super hero, is now the owner and sole employee of Alias Investigations--a small private investigative firm.

But dark secrets from her super hero past haunt her, affecting her relationships and happiness.

JESSICA JONES

The Secrets of Maria Hill

Writer: **Brian Michael Bendis**
Artist: **Michael Gaydos**
Color Artist: **Matt Hollingsworth**
Flashback Artist/Colorist: **Javier Pulido**

Letterer: **VC's Cory Petit**
Cover Art: **David Mack**

Assistant Editor: **Alanna Smith**
Editor: **Tom Brevoort**

Based on characters created by **Brian Michael Bendis** & **Michael Gaydos**

Collection Editor: **Jennifer Grünwald** • Assistant Editor: **Caitlin O'Connell**
Associate Managing Editor: **Kateri Woody** • Editor, Special Projects: **Mark D. Beazley**
VP Production & Special Projects: **Jeff Youngquist** • SVP Print, Sales & Marketing: **David Gabriel**
Book Designer: **Jay Bowen**

Editor in Chief: **Axel Alonso** • Chief Creative Officer: **Joe Quesada**
President: **Dan Buckley** • Executive Producer: **Alan Fine**

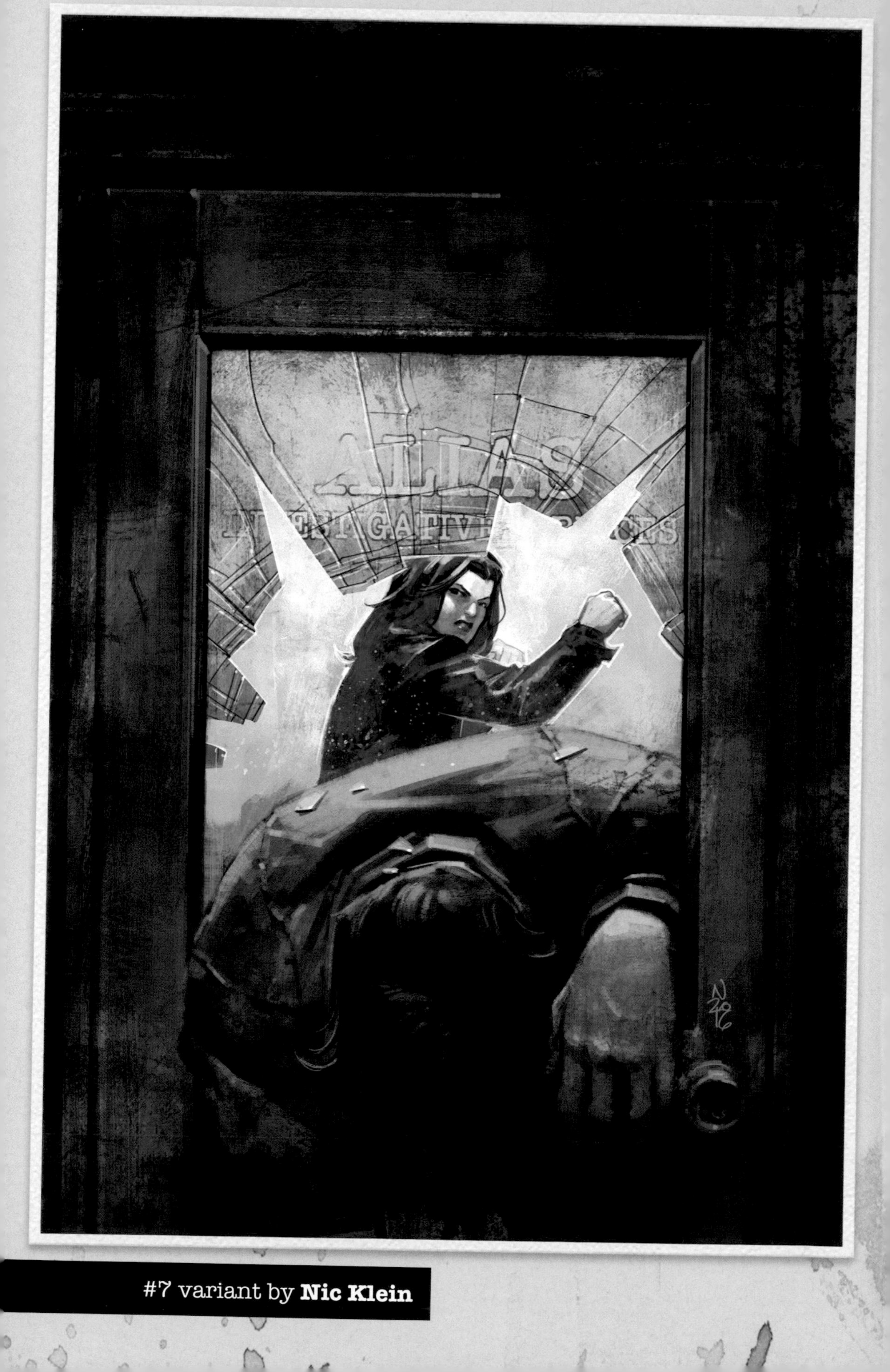
ALIAS

#7 variant by **Nic Klein**

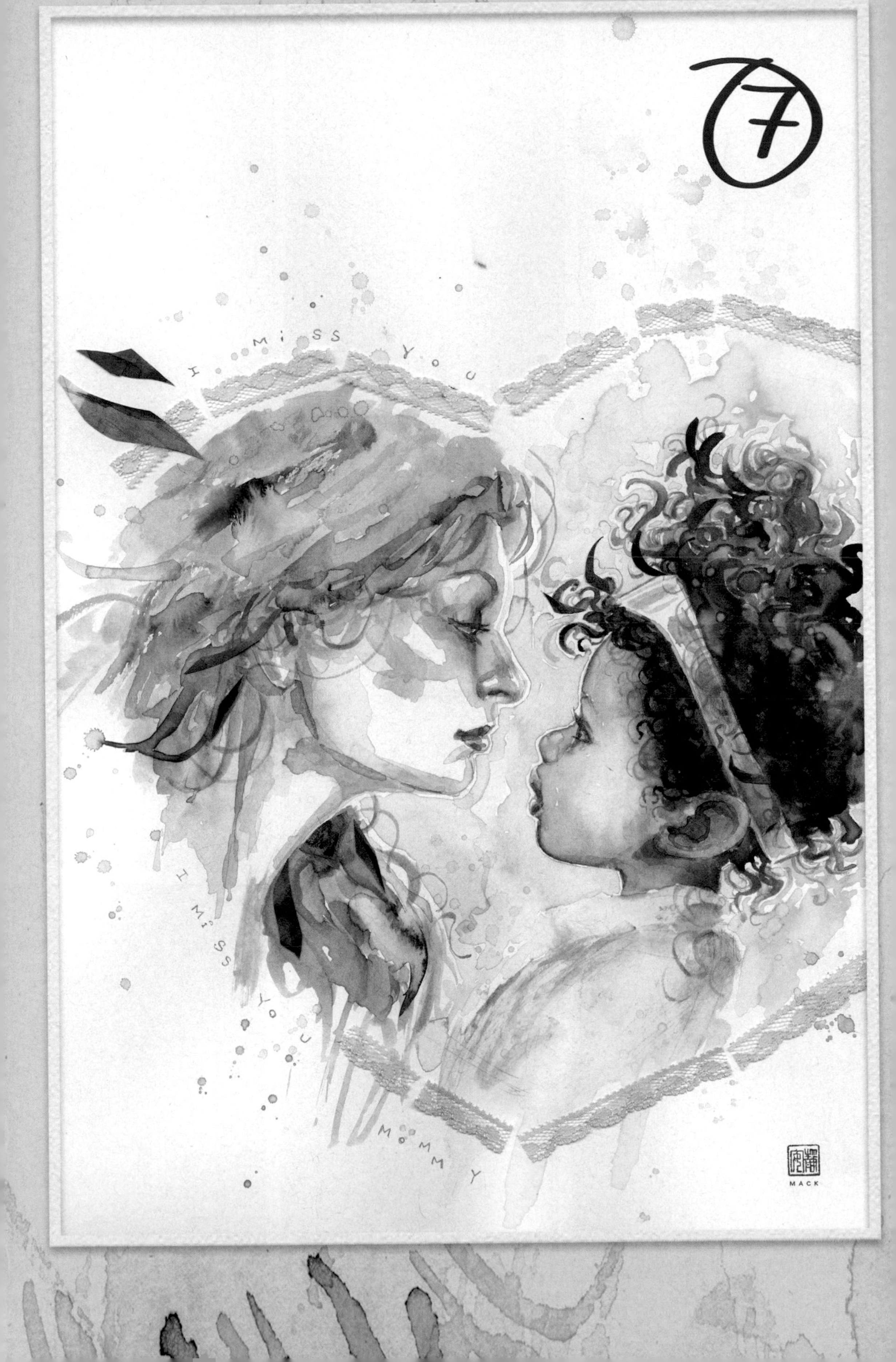
7
I MiSS YOU
I MiSS YOU
MOMMY
MACK

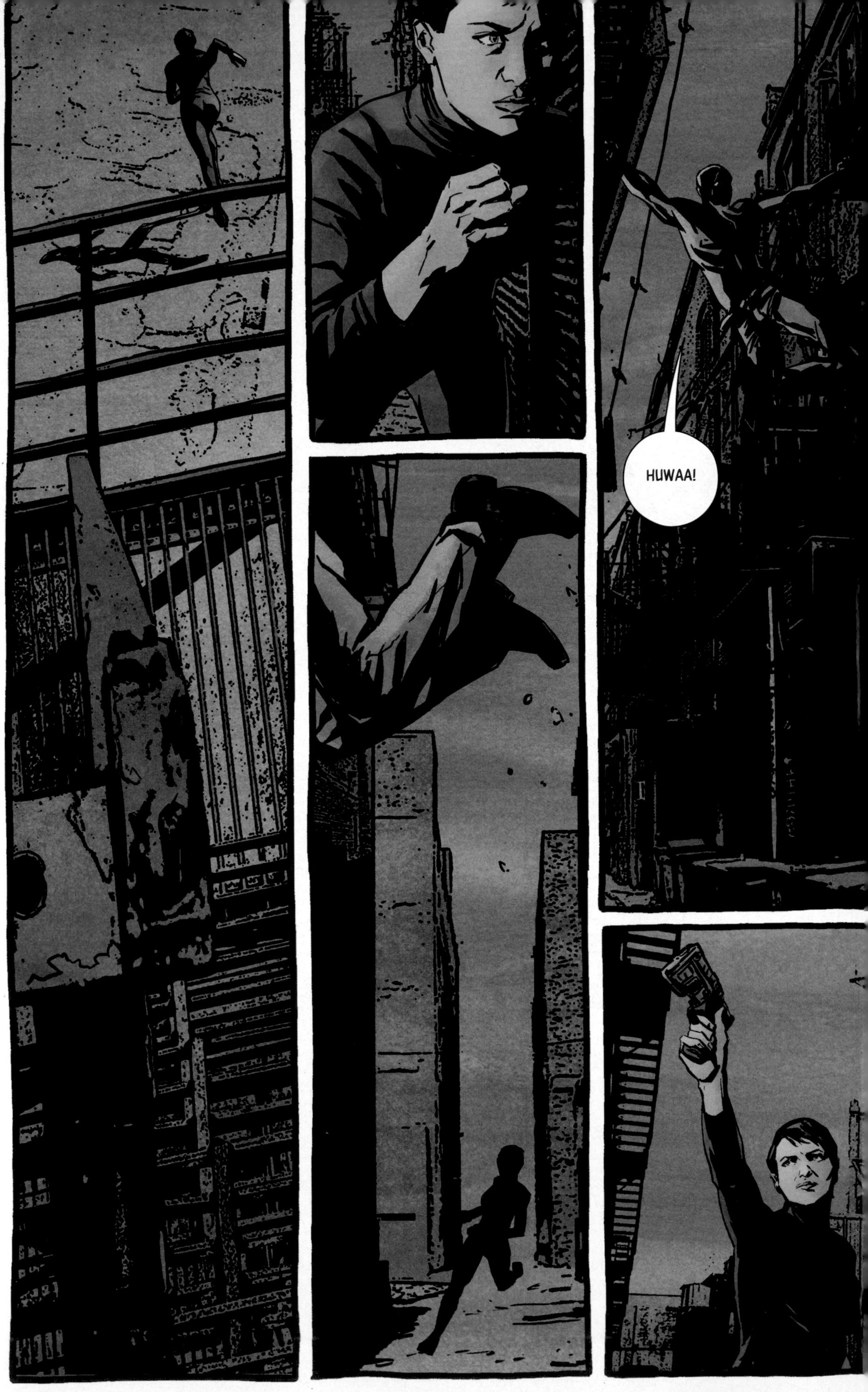
HUWAA!

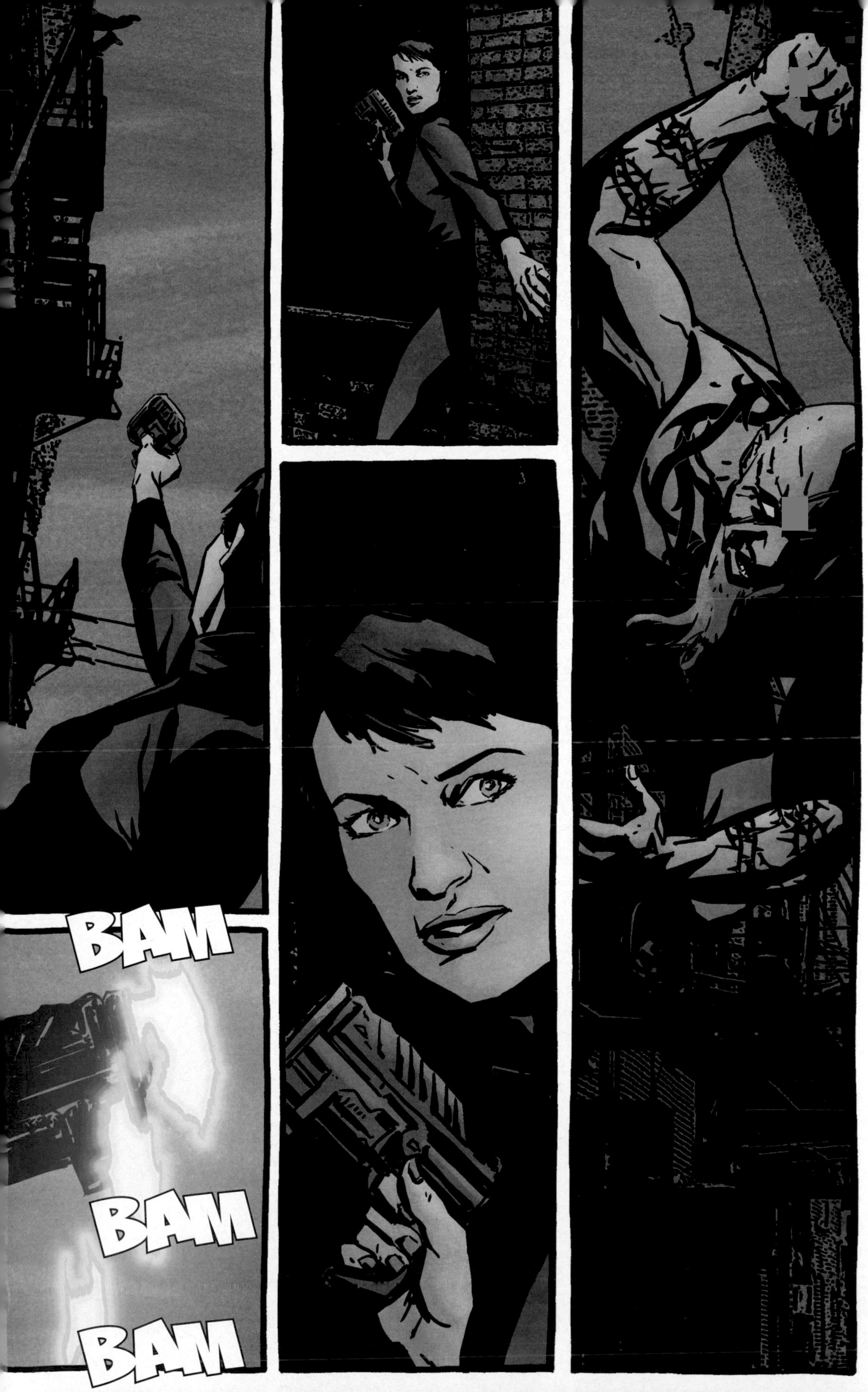
BAM
BAM
BAM

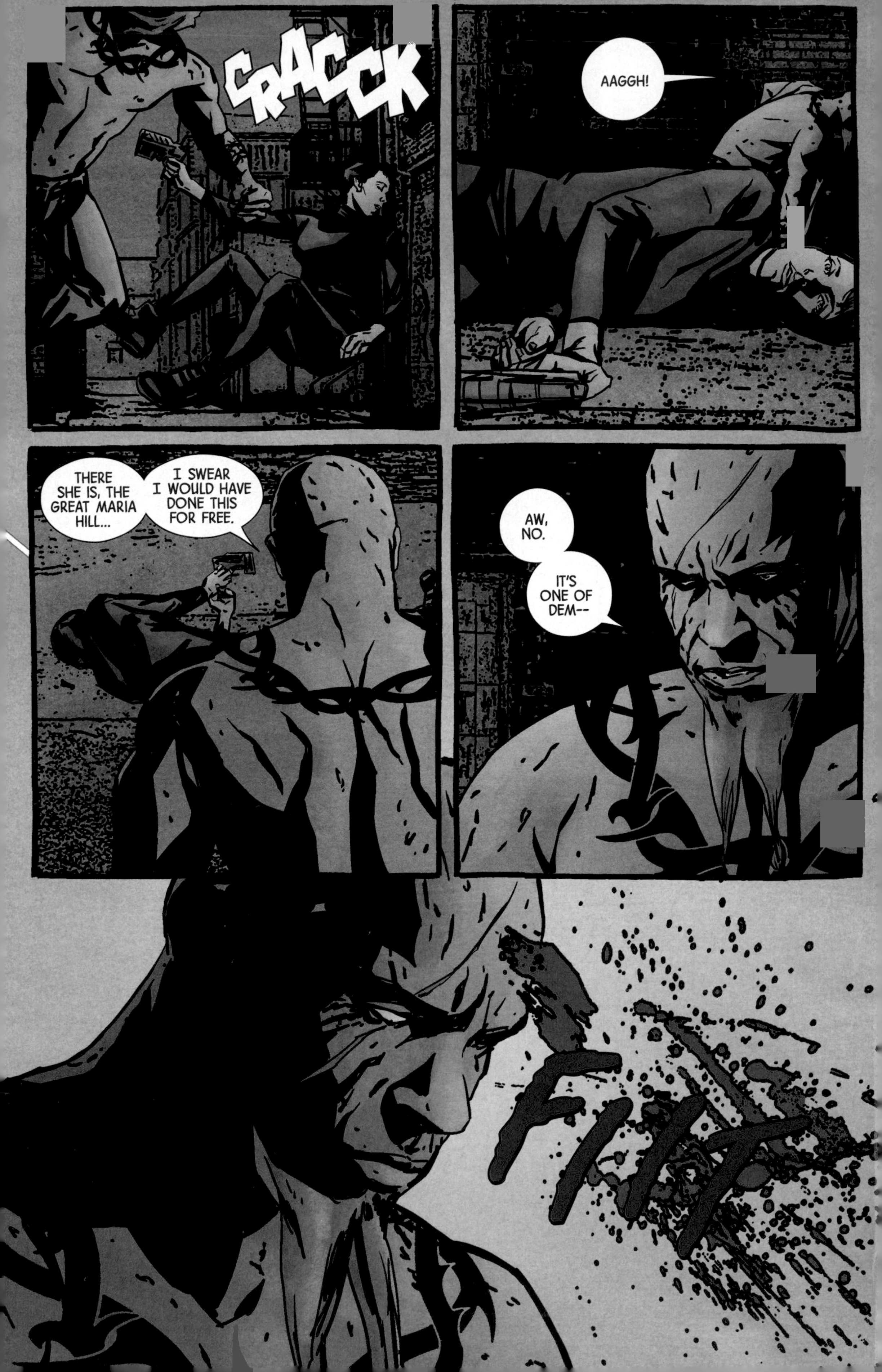
CRACCK
AAGGH!
THERE SHE IS, THE GREAT MARIA HILL...
I SWEAR I WOULD HAVE DONE THIS FOR FREE.
AW, NO.
IT'S ONE OF DEM--
FITT

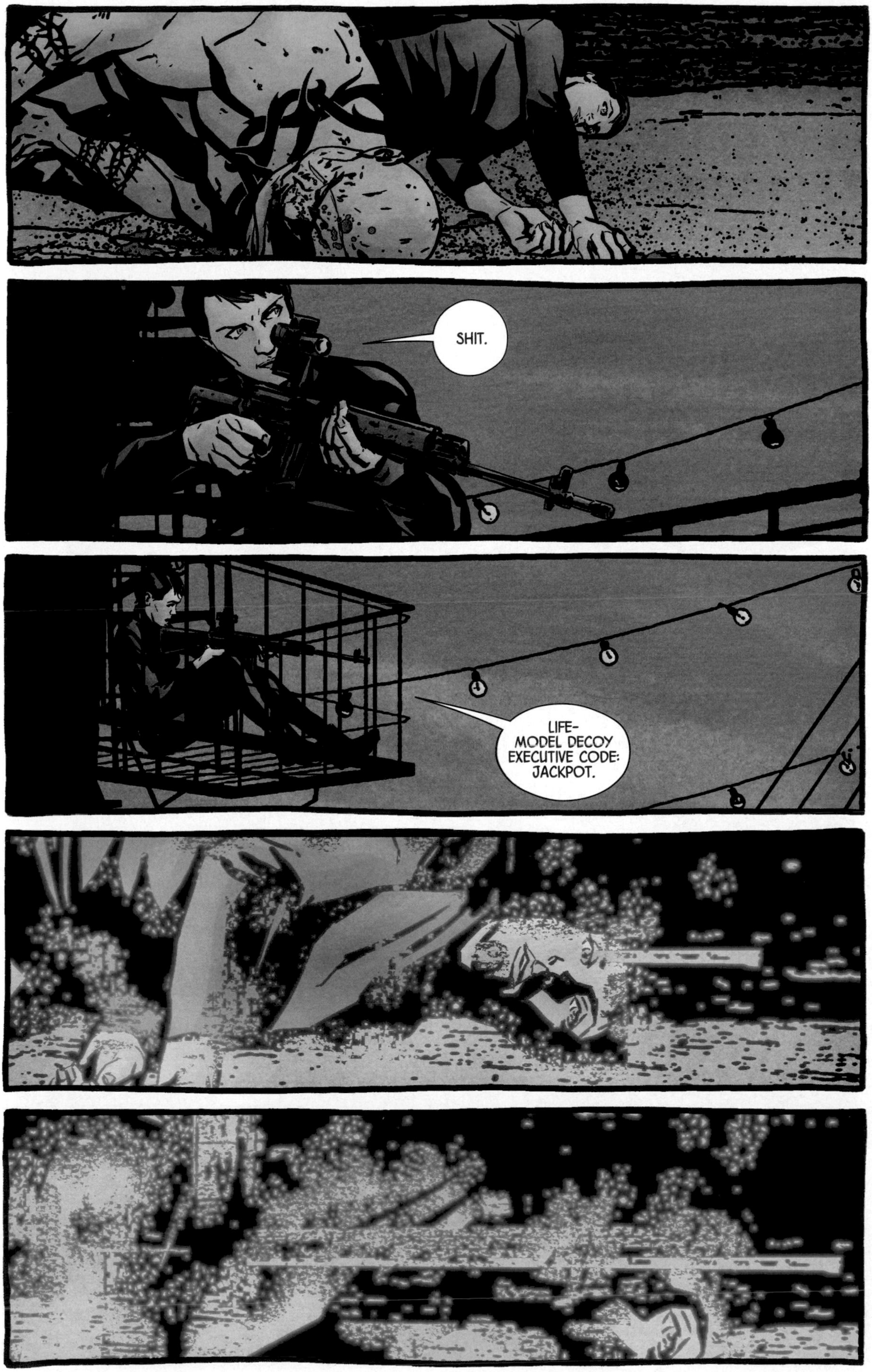
SHIT.
LIFE-MODEL DECOY EXECUTIVE CODE: JACKPOT.

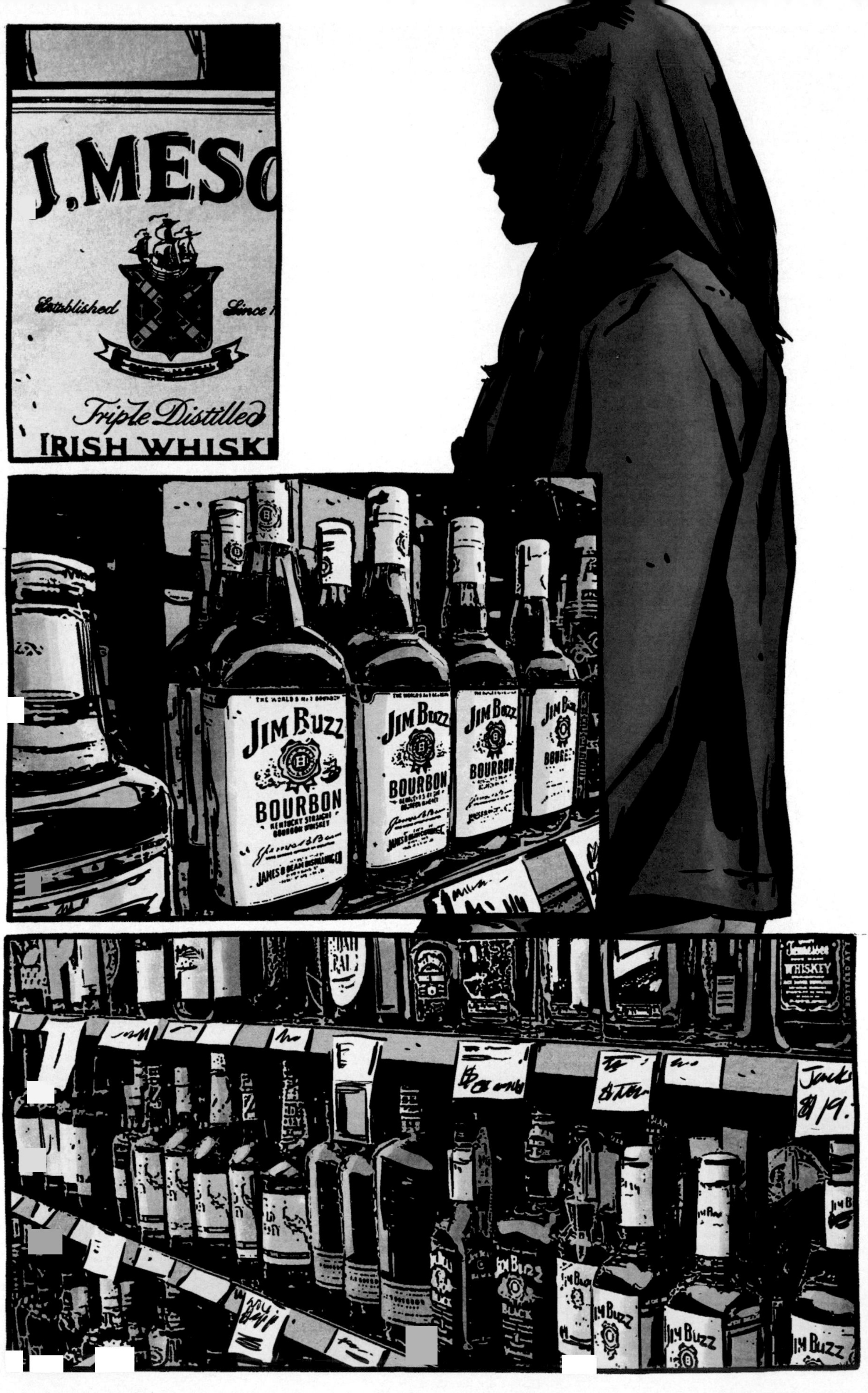
Established
Triple Distilled
JIM BUZZ
BOURBON
WHISKEY

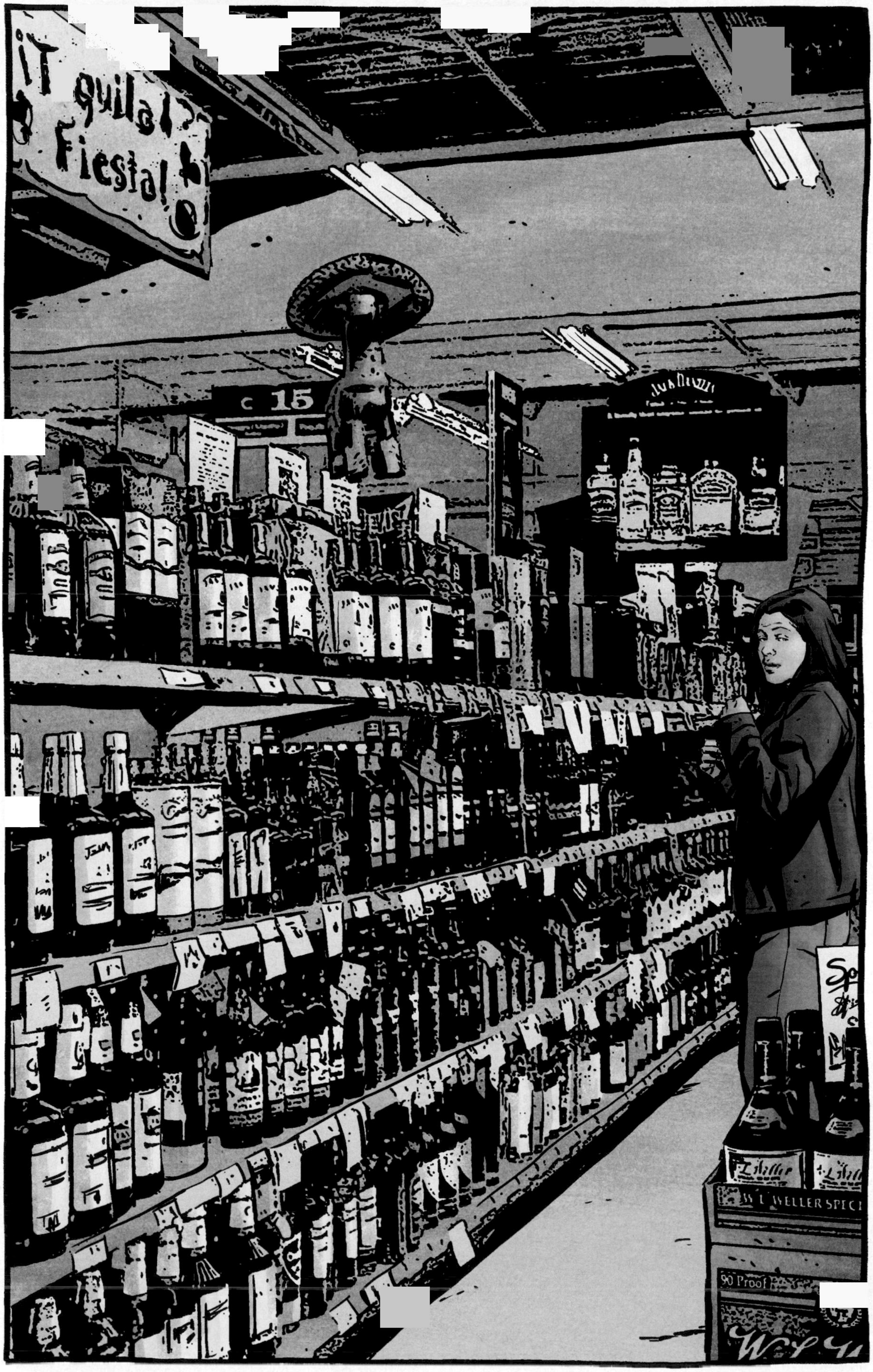
Fiesta!
C 15
90 Proof

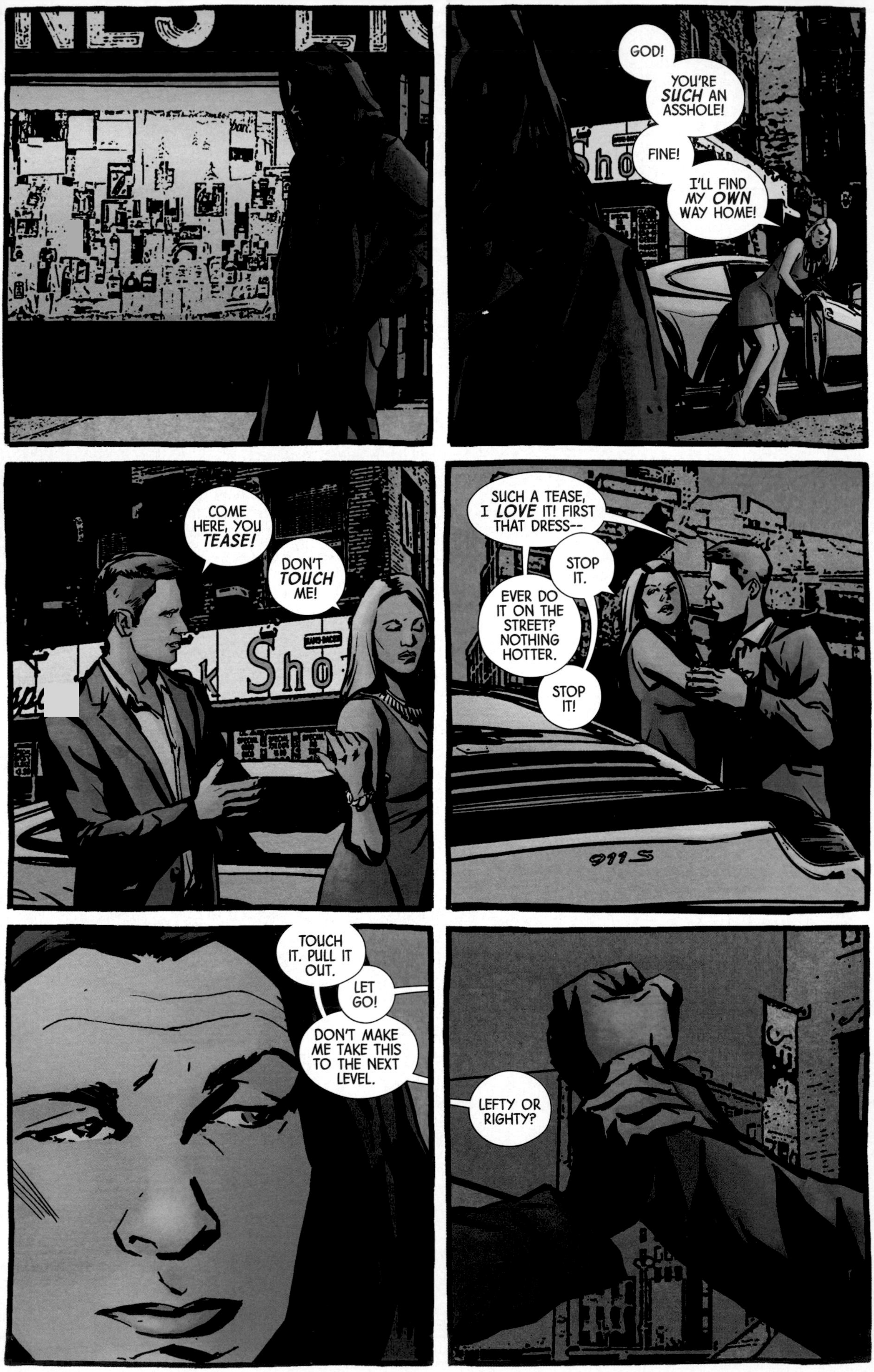

GOD!
YOU'RE SUCH AN ASSHOLE!
FINE!
I'LL FIND MY OWN WAY HOME!
COME HERE, YOU TEASE!
DON'T TOUCH ME!
Sho
SUCH A TEASE, I LOVE IT! FIRST THAT DRESS--
STOP IT.
EVER DO IT ON THE STREET? NOTHING HOTTER.
STOP IT!
911 S
TOUCH IT. PULL IT OUT.
LET GO!
DON'T MAKE ME TAKE THIS TO THE NEXT LEVEL.
LEFTY OR RIGHTY?

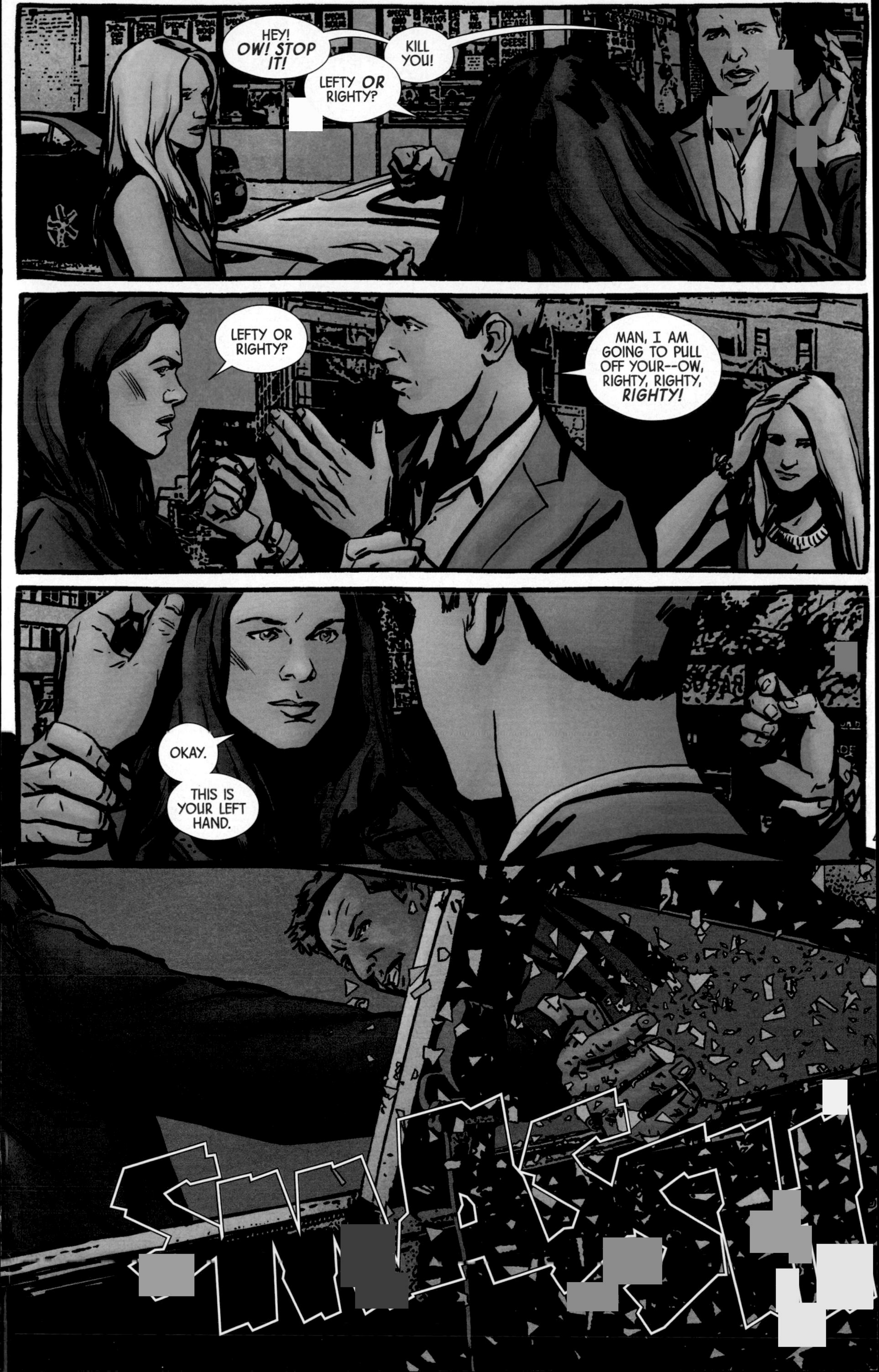
HEY! OW! STOP IT!
KILL YOU!
LEFTY OR RIGHTY?
LEFTY OR RIGHTY?
MAN, I AM GOING TO PULL OFF YOUR--OW, RIGHTY, RIGHTY, RIGHTY!
OKAY.
THIS IS YOUR LEFT HAND.

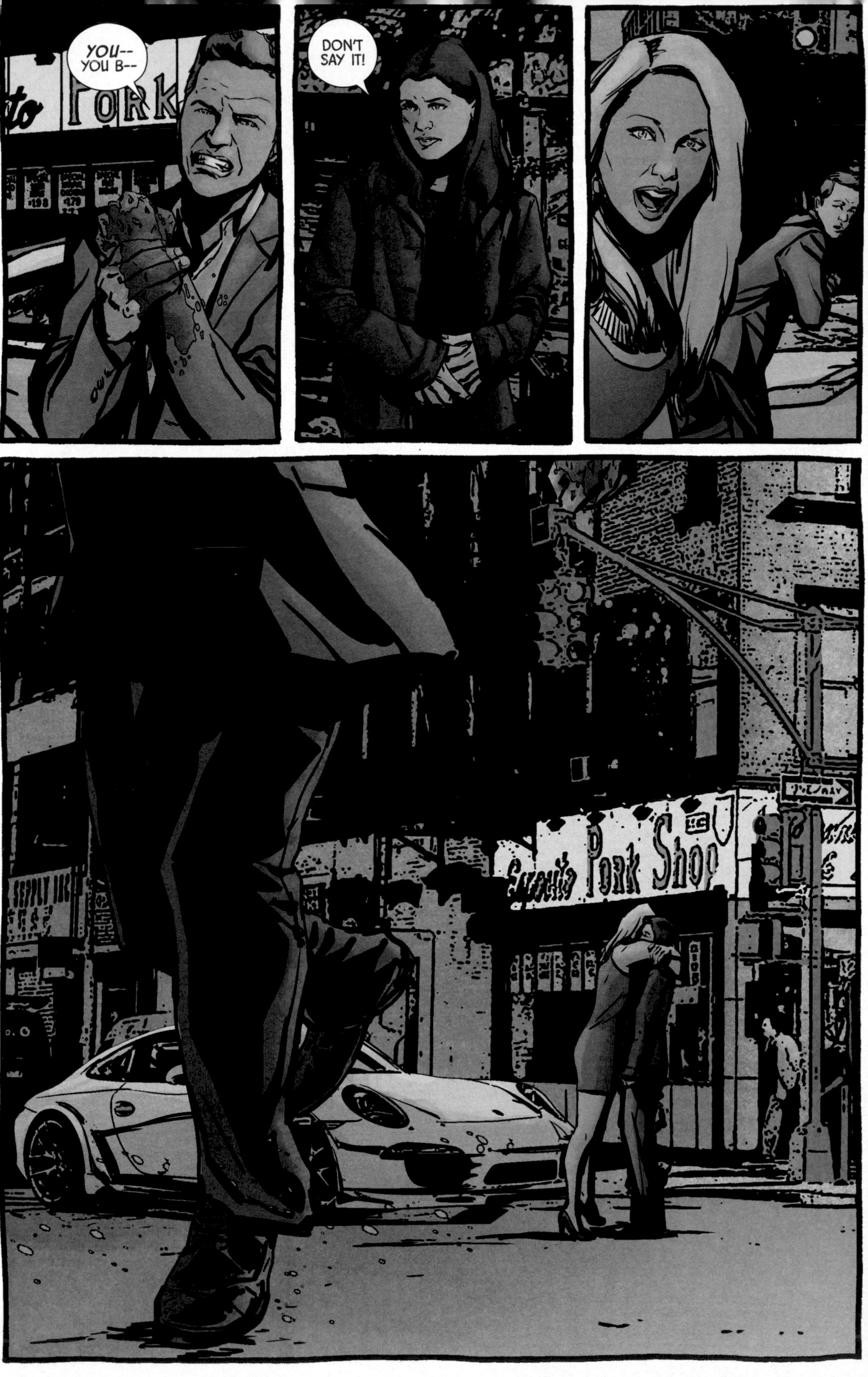
YOU--
YOU B--
DON'T SAY IT!
Pork Shop

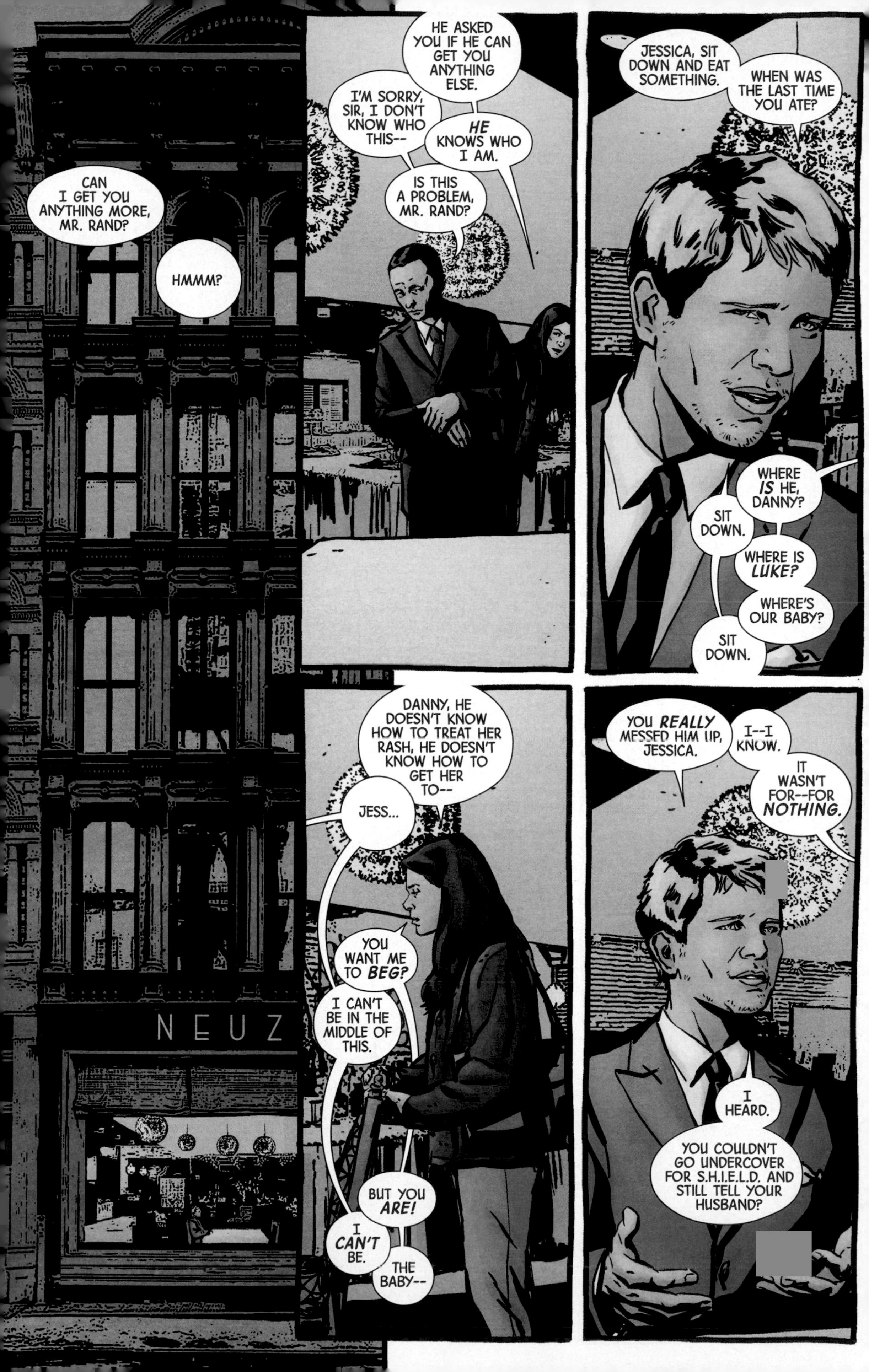
CAN I GET YOU ANYTHING MORE, MR. RAND?
HMMM?
NEUZ
HE ASKED YOU IF HE CAN GET YOU ANYTHING ELSE.
I'M SORRY, SIR, I DON'T KNOW WHO THIS--
HE KNOWS WHO I AM.
IS THIS A PROBLEM, MR. RAND?
JESSICA, SIT DOWN AND EAT SOMETHING.
WHEN WAS THE LAST TIME YOU ATE?
WHERE IS HE, DANNY?
SIT DOWN.
WHERE IS LUKE?
WHERE'S OUR BABY?
SIT DOWN.
DANNY, HE DOESN'T KNOW HOW TO TREAT HER RASH, HE DOESN'T KNOW HOW TO GET HER TO--
JESS...
YOU WANT ME TO BEG?
I CAN'T BE IN THE MIDDLE OF THIS.
BUT YOU ARE!
I CAN'T BE.
THE BABY--
YOU REALLY MESSED HIM UP, JESSICA.
I--I KNOW.
IT WASN'T FOR--FOR NOTHING.
I HEARD.
YOU COULDN'T GO UNDERCOVER FOR S.H.I.E.L.D. AND STILL TELL YOUR HUSBAND?

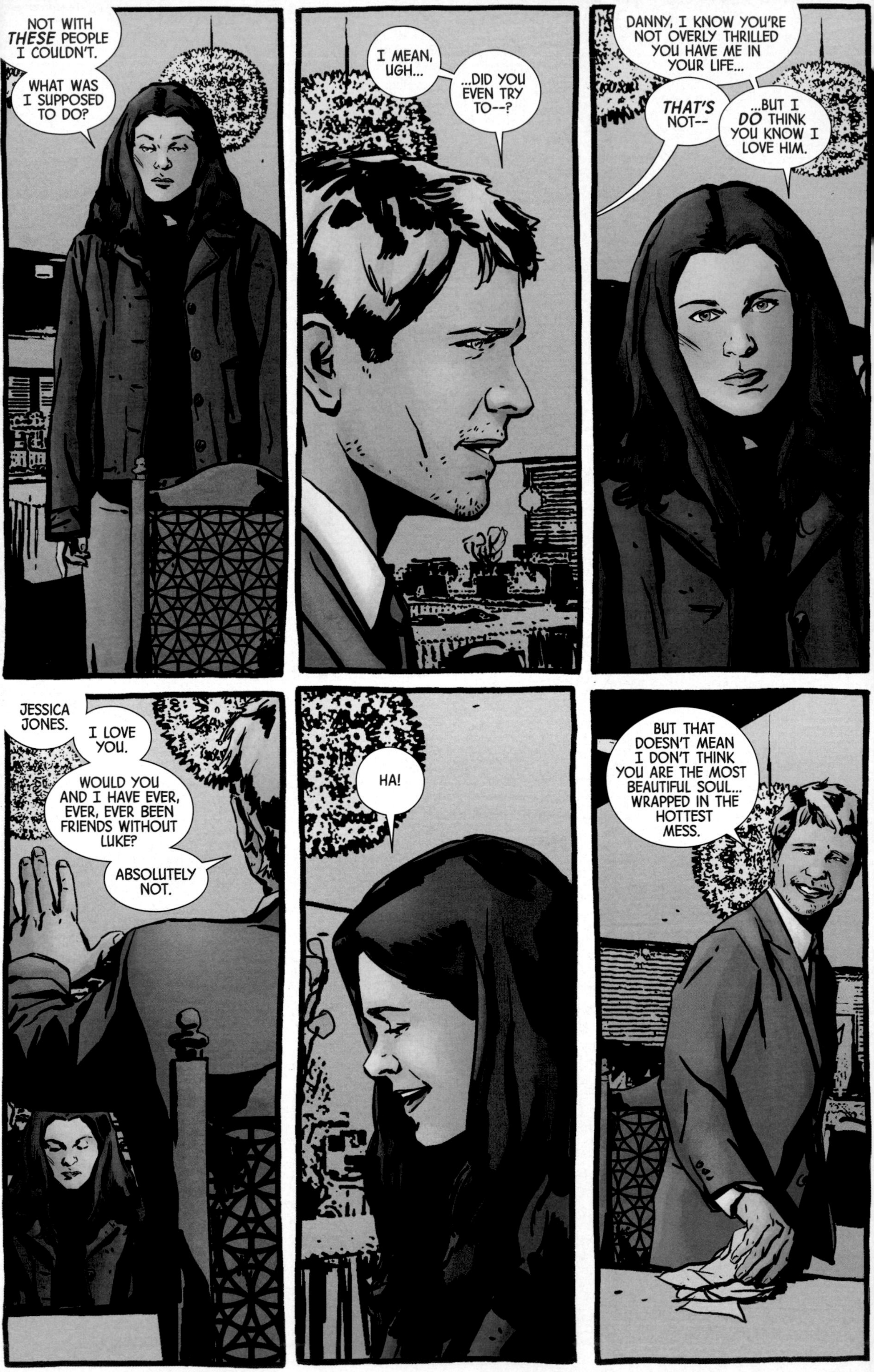
NOT WITH *THESE* PEOPLE I COULDN'T.
WHAT WAS I SUPPOSED TO DO?
I MEAN, UGH...
...DID YOU EVEN TRY TO--?
DANNY, I KNOW YOU'RE NOT OVERLY THRILLED YOU HAVE ME IN YOUR LIFE...
THAT'S NOT--
...BUT I *DO* THINK YOU KNOW I LOVE HIM.
JESSICA JONES.
I LOVE YOU.
WOULD YOU AND I HAVE EVER, EVER, EVER BEEN FRIENDS WITHOUT LUKE?
ABSOLUTELY NOT.
HA!
BUT THAT DOESN'T MEAN I DON'T THINK YOU ARE THE MOST BEAUTIFUL SOUL... WRAPPED IN THE HOTTEST MESS.

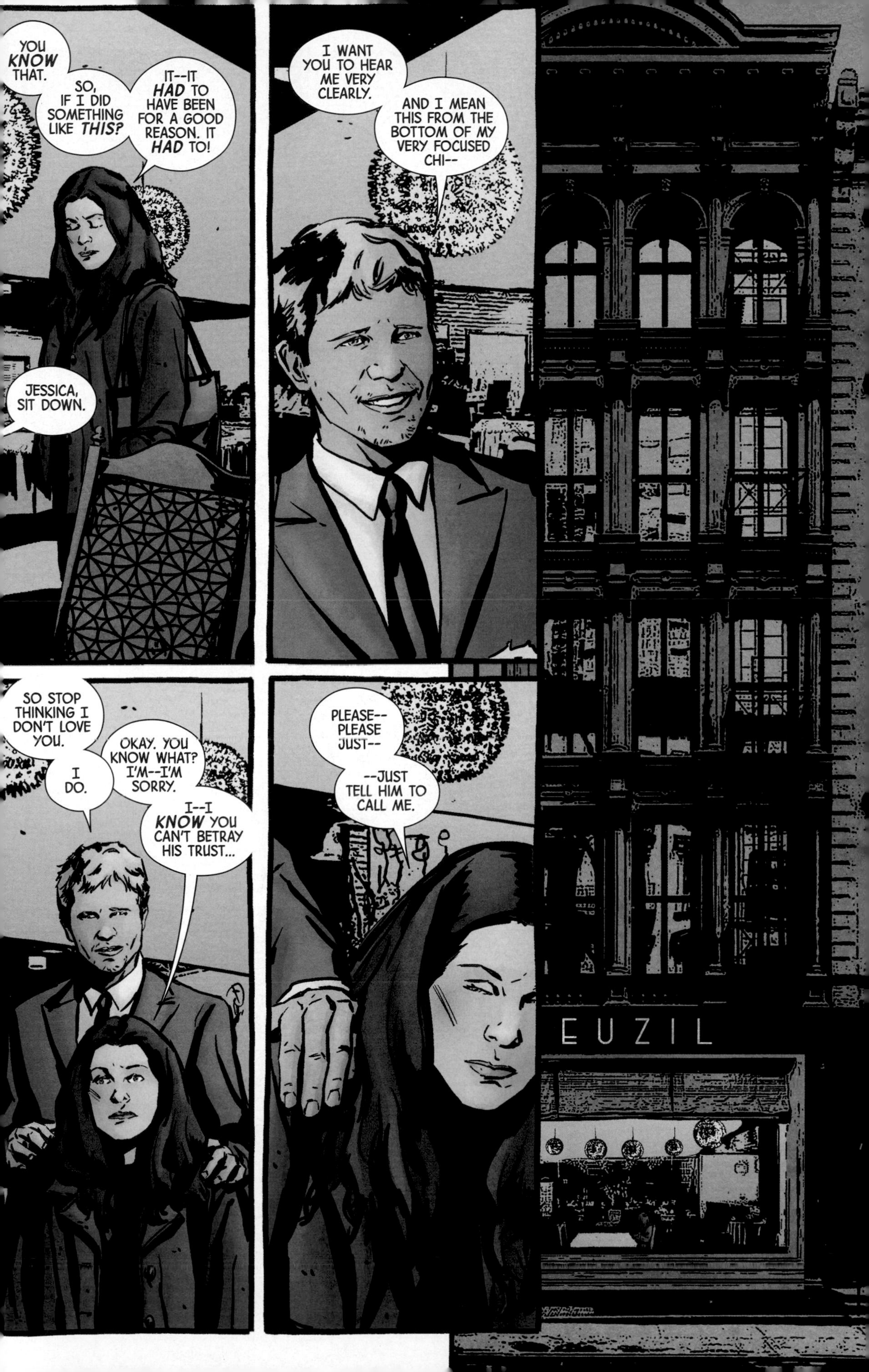

YOU KNOW THAT.
SO, IF I DID SOMETHING LIKE THIS?
IT--IT HAD TO HAVE BEEN FOR A GOOD REASON. IT HAD TO!
JESSICA, SIT DOWN.
I WANT YOU TO HEAR ME VERY CLEARLY.
AND I MEAN THIS FROM THE BOTTOM OF MY VERY FOCUSED CHI--
SO STOP THINKING I DON'T LOVE YOU.
I DO.
OKAY. YOU KNOW WHAT? I'M--I'M SORRY.
I--I KNOW YOU CAN'T BETRAY HIS TRUST...
PLEASE-- PLEASE JUST--
--JUST TELL HIM TO CALL ME.
EUZIL

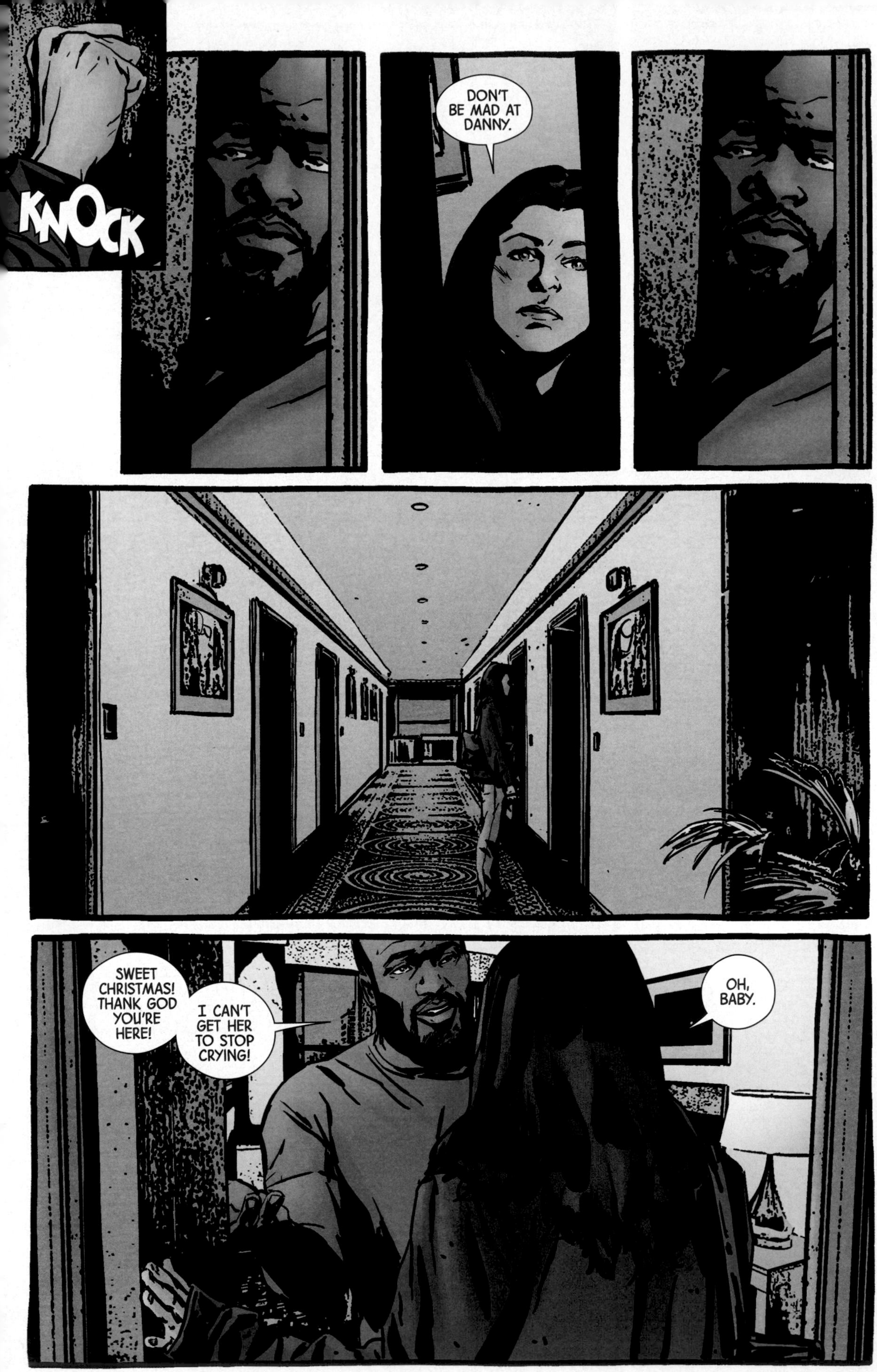
KNOCK
DON'T BE MAD AT DANNY.
SWEET CHRISTMAS! THANK GOD YOU'RE HERE!
I CAN'T GET HER TO STOP CRYING!
OH, BABY.

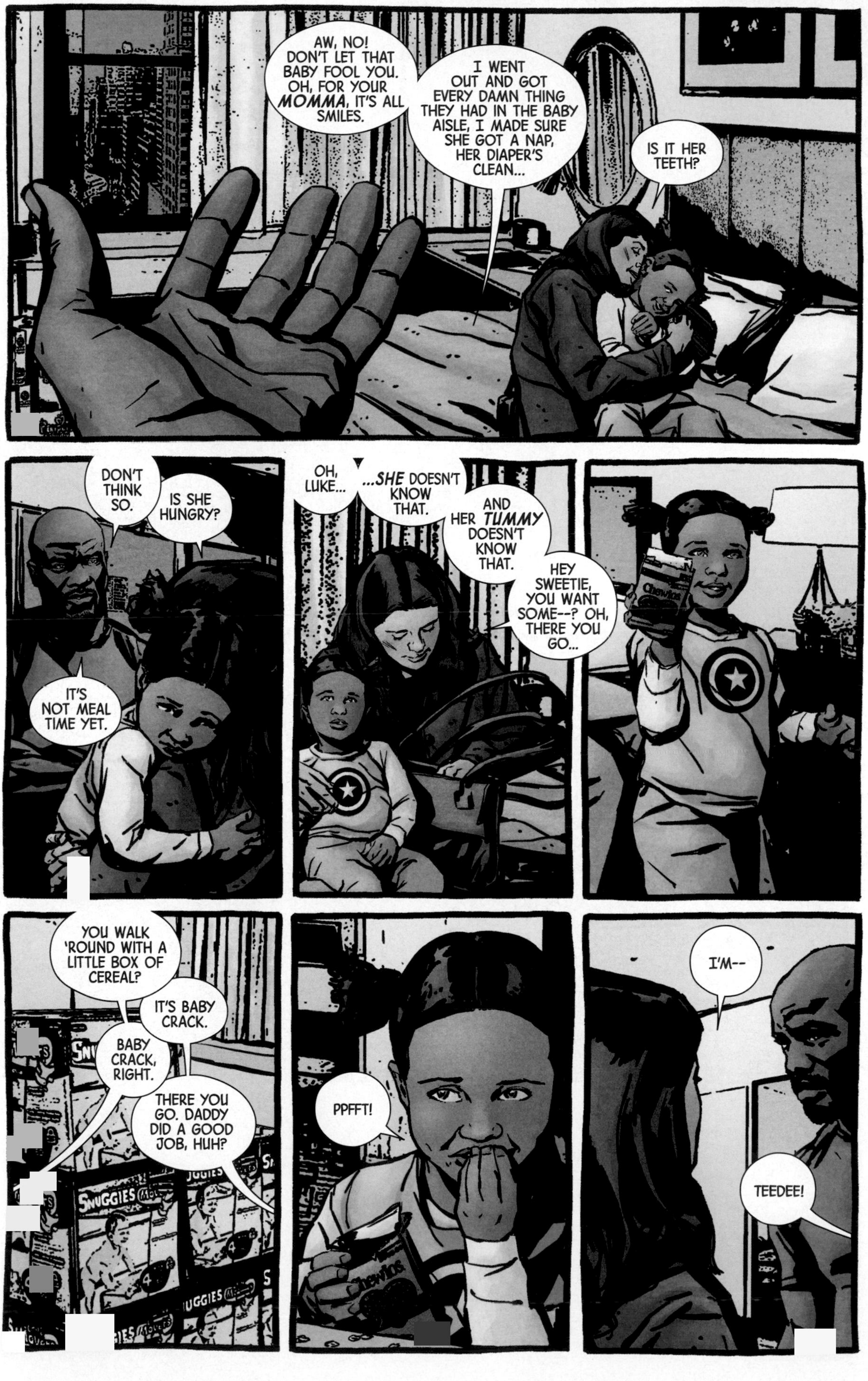
AW, NO! DON'T LET THAT BABY FOOL YOU. OH, FOR YOUR MOMMA, IT'S ALL SMILES.
I WENT OUT AND GOT EVERY DAMN THING THEY HAD IN THE BABY AISLE, I MADE SURE SHE GOT A NAP, HER DIAPER'S CLEAN...
IS IT HER TEETH?
DON'T THINK SO.
IS SHE HUNGRY?
IT'S NOT MEAL TIME YET.
OH, LUKE...
...SHE DOESN'T KNOW THAT.
AND HER TUMMY DOESN'T KNOW THAT.
HEY SWEETIE, YOU WANT SOME--? OH, THERE YOU GO...
Chewios
YOU WALK 'ROUND WITH A LITTLE BOX OF CEREAL?
IT'S BABY CRACK.
BABY CRACK, RIGHT.
THERE YOU GO. DADDY DID A GOOD JOB, HUH?
SNUGGIES
PPFFT!
Chewios
I'M--
TEEDEE!

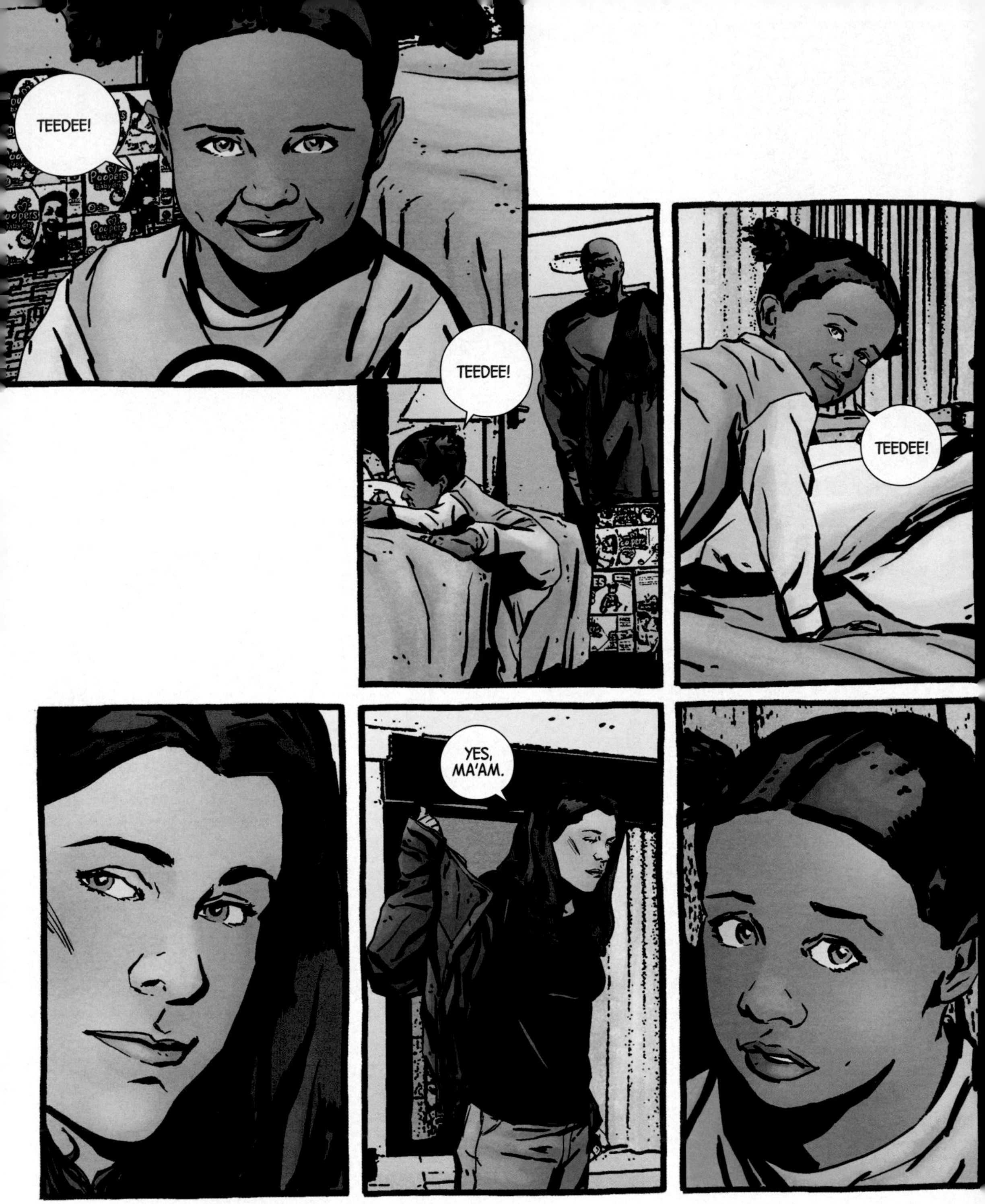
TEEDEE!
TEEDEE!
TEEDEE!
YES, MA'AM.

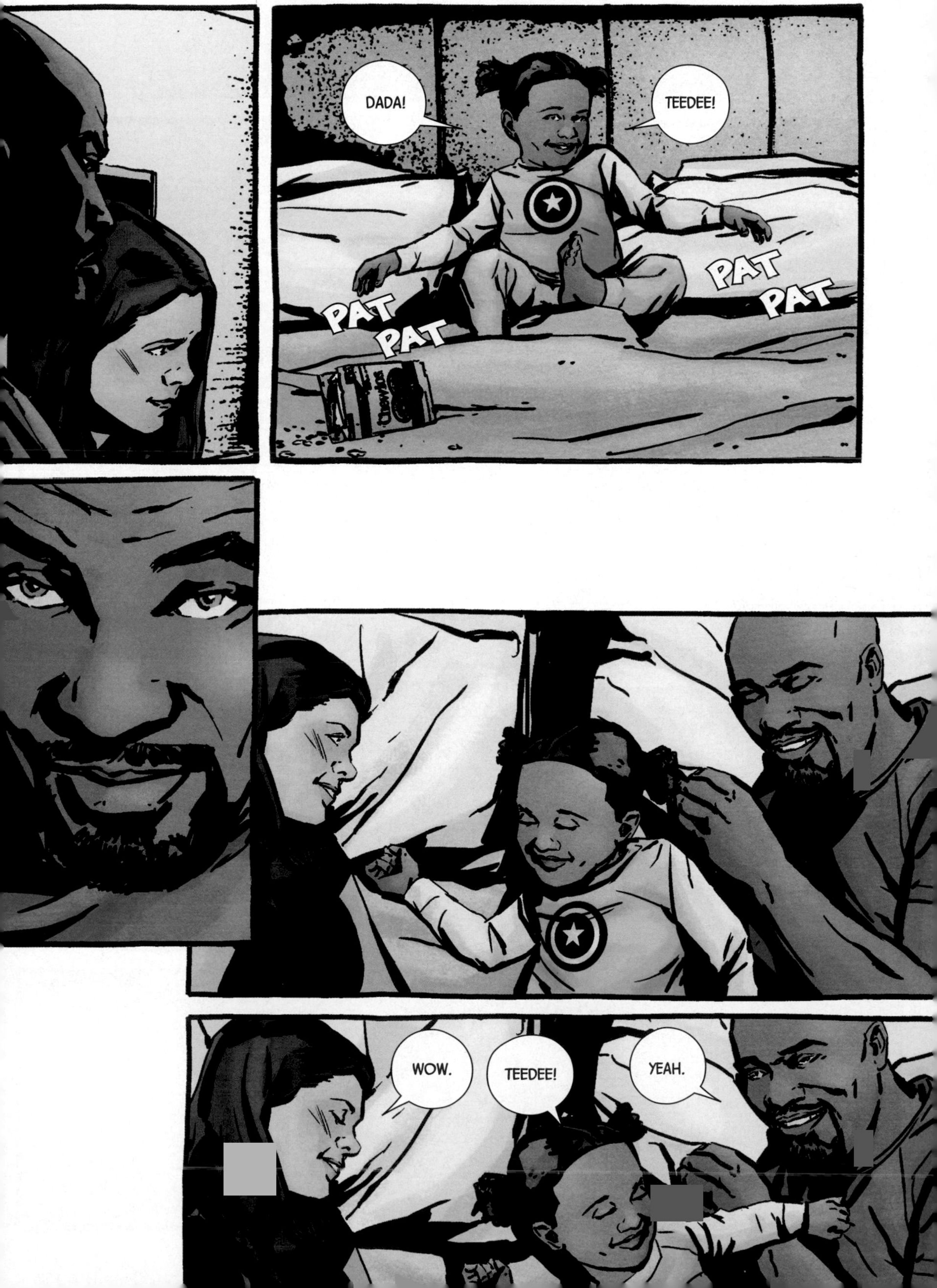
DADA!
TEEDEE!
PAT
PAT
PAT
PAT
WOW.
TEEDEE!
YEAH.

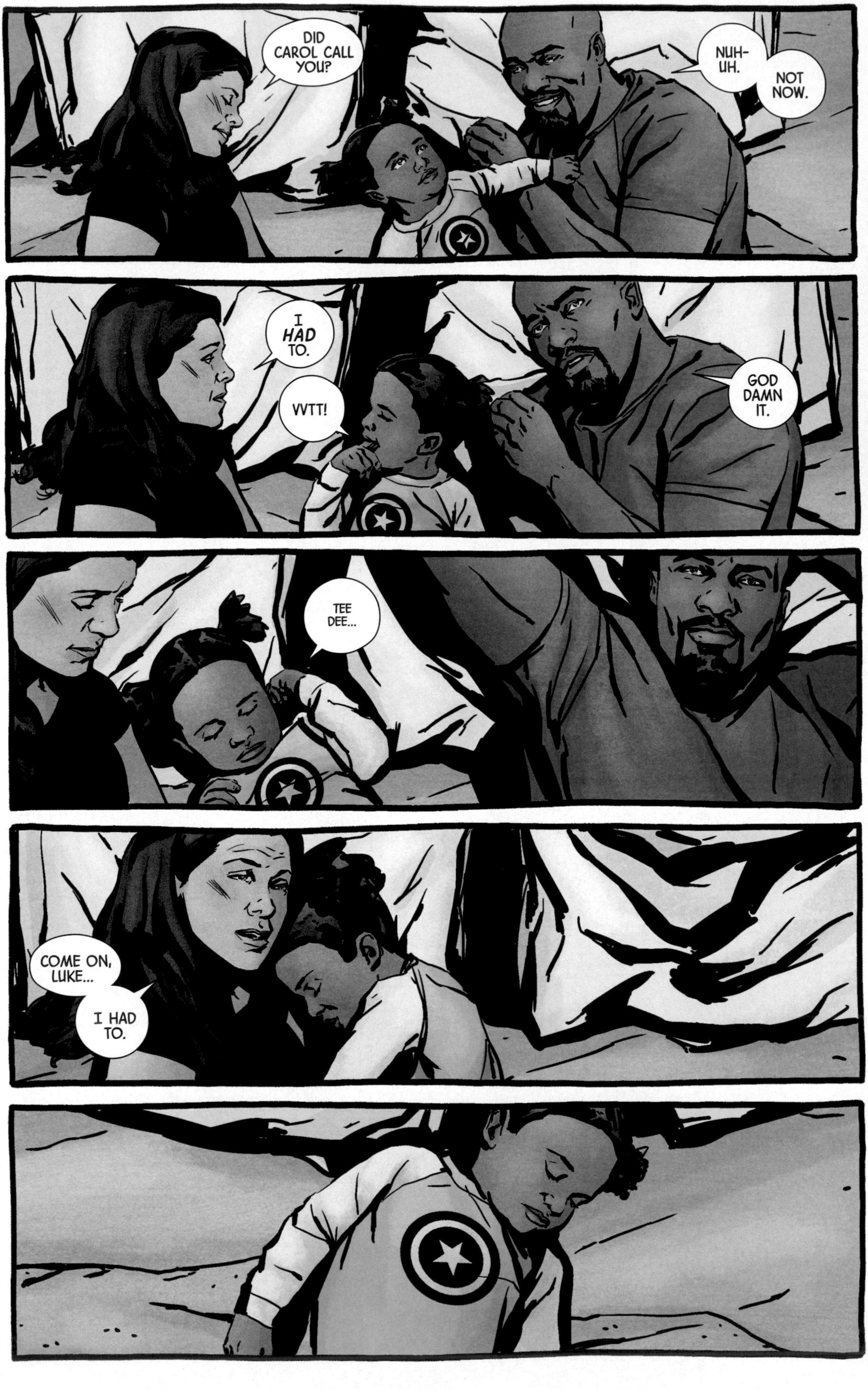
DID CAROL CALL YOU?
NUH-UH.
NOT NOW.
I *HAD* TO.
VVTT!
GOD DAMN IT.
TEE DEE...
COME ON, LUKE...
I HAD TO.

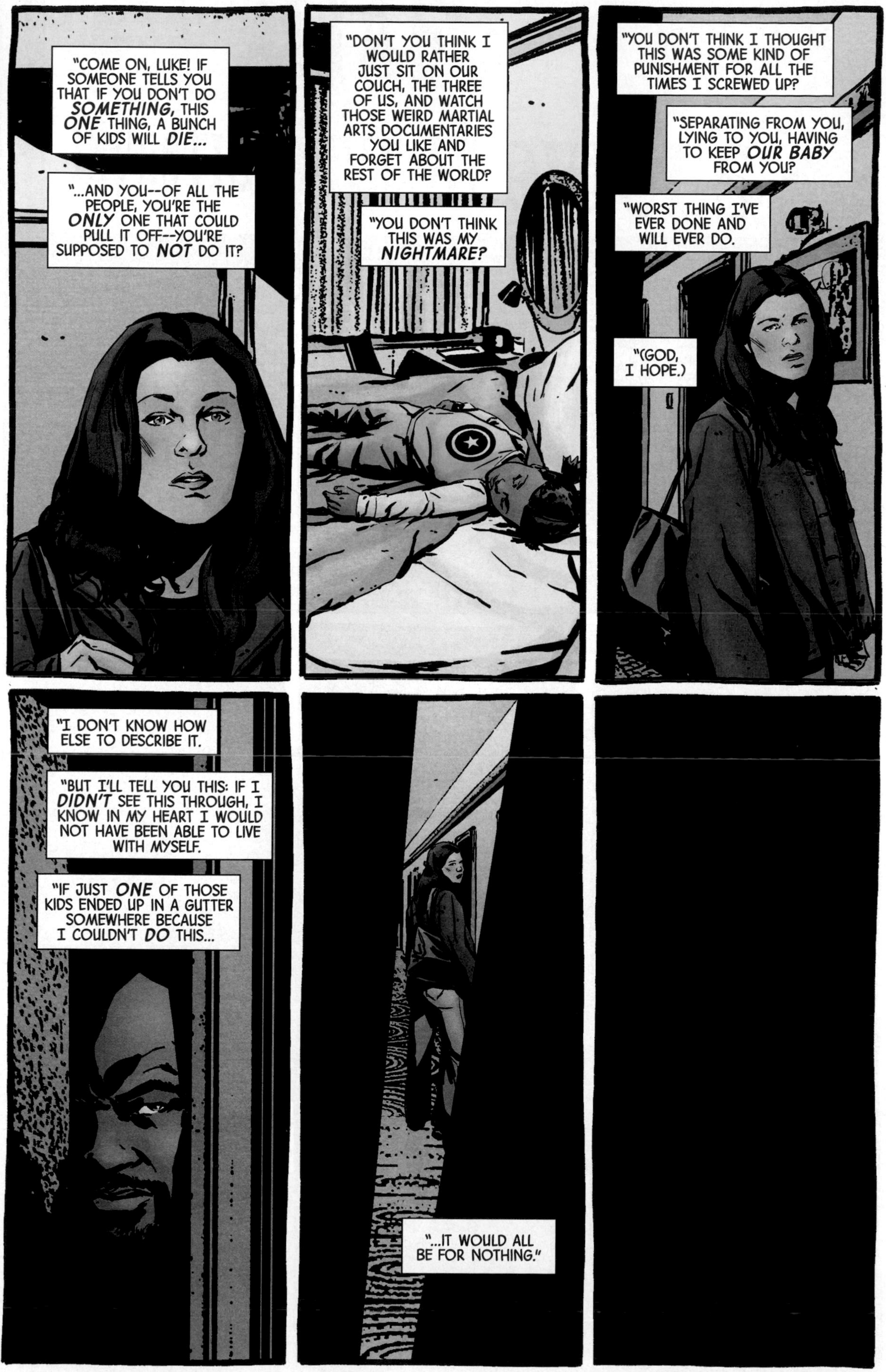
"COME ON, LUKE! IF SOMEONE TELLS YOU THAT IF YOU DON'T DO SOMETHING, THIS ONE THING, A BUNCH OF KIDS WILL DIE...
"...AND YOU--OF ALL THE PEOPLE, YOU'RE THE ONLY ONE THAT COULD PULL IT OFF--YOU'RE SUPPOSED TO NOT DO IT?
"DON'T YOU THINK I WOULD RATHER JUST SIT ON OUR COUCH, THE THREE OF US, AND WATCH THOSE WEIRD MARTIAL ARTS DOCUMENTARIES YOU LIKE AND FORGET ABOUT THE REST OF THE WORLD?
"YOU DON'T THINK THIS WAS MY NIGHTMARE?
"YOU DON'T THINK I THOUGHT THIS WAS SOME KIND OF PUNISHMENT FOR ALL THE TIMES I SCREWED UP?
"SEPARATING FROM YOU, LYING TO YOU, HAVING TO KEEP OUR BABY FROM YOU?
"WORST THING I'VE EVER DONE AND WILL EVER DO.
"(GOD, I HOPE.)
"I DON'T KNOW HOW ELSE TO DESCRIBE IT.
"BUT I'LL TELL YOU THIS: IF I DIDN'T SEE THIS THROUGH, I KNOW IN MY HEART I WOULD NOT HAVE BEEN ABLE TO LIVE WITH MYSELF.
"IF JUST ONE OF THOSE KIDS ENDED UP IN A GUTTER SOMEWHERE BECAUSE I COULDN'T DO THIS...
"...IT WOULD ALL BE FOR NOTHING."

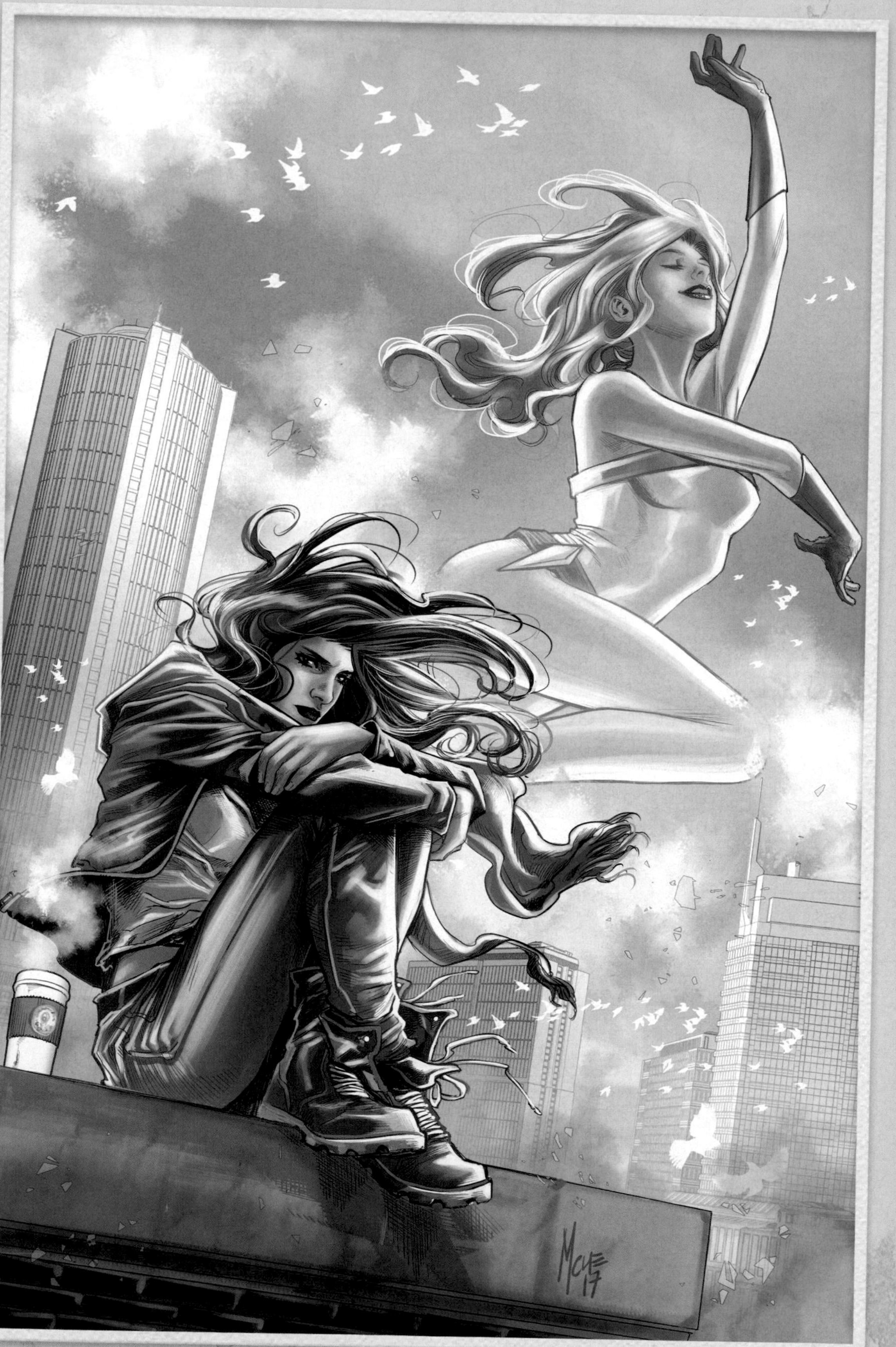

#8 variant by **Marco Checchetto**

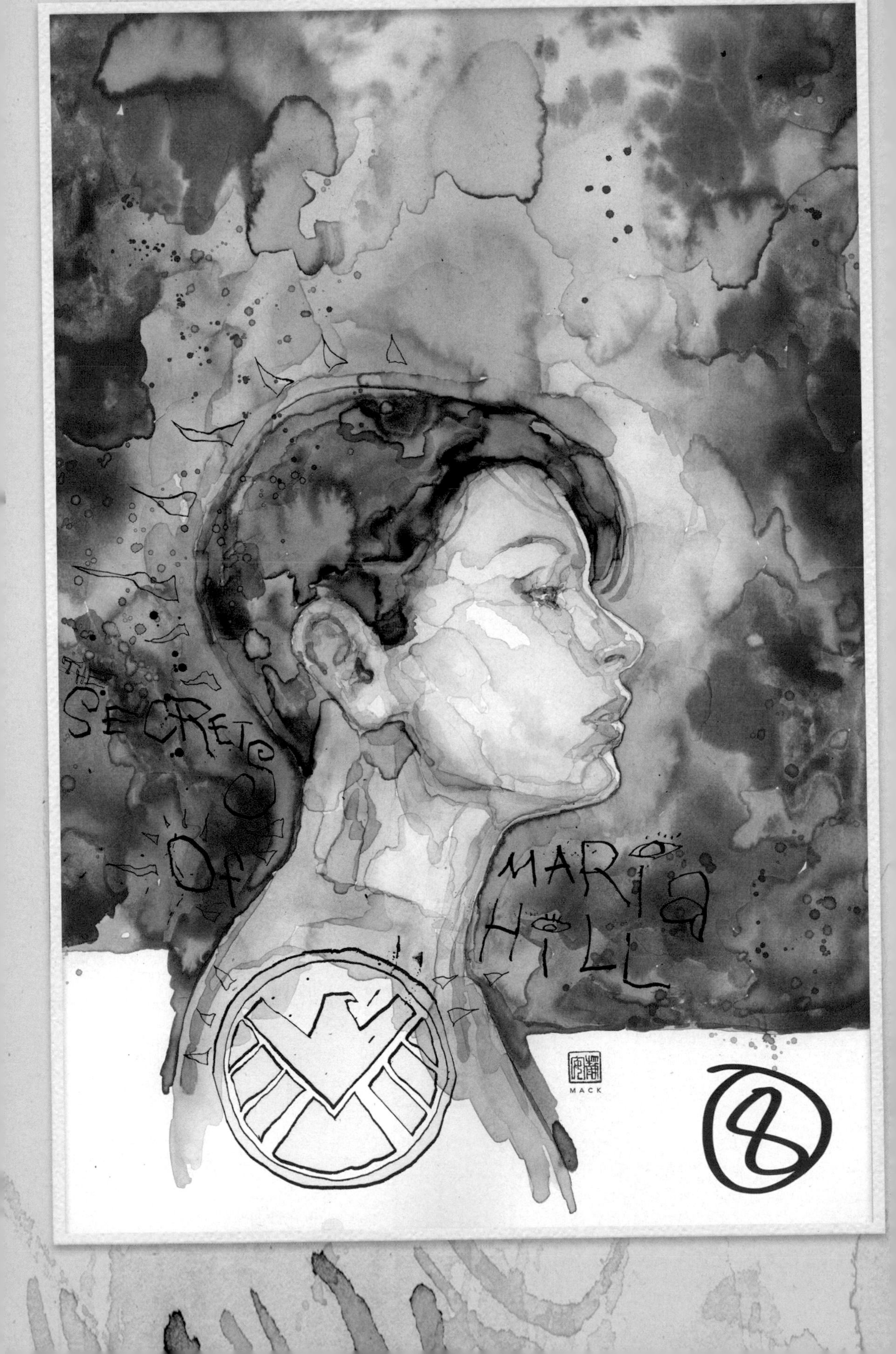
THE SECRETS OF MARIA HILL
MACK
8

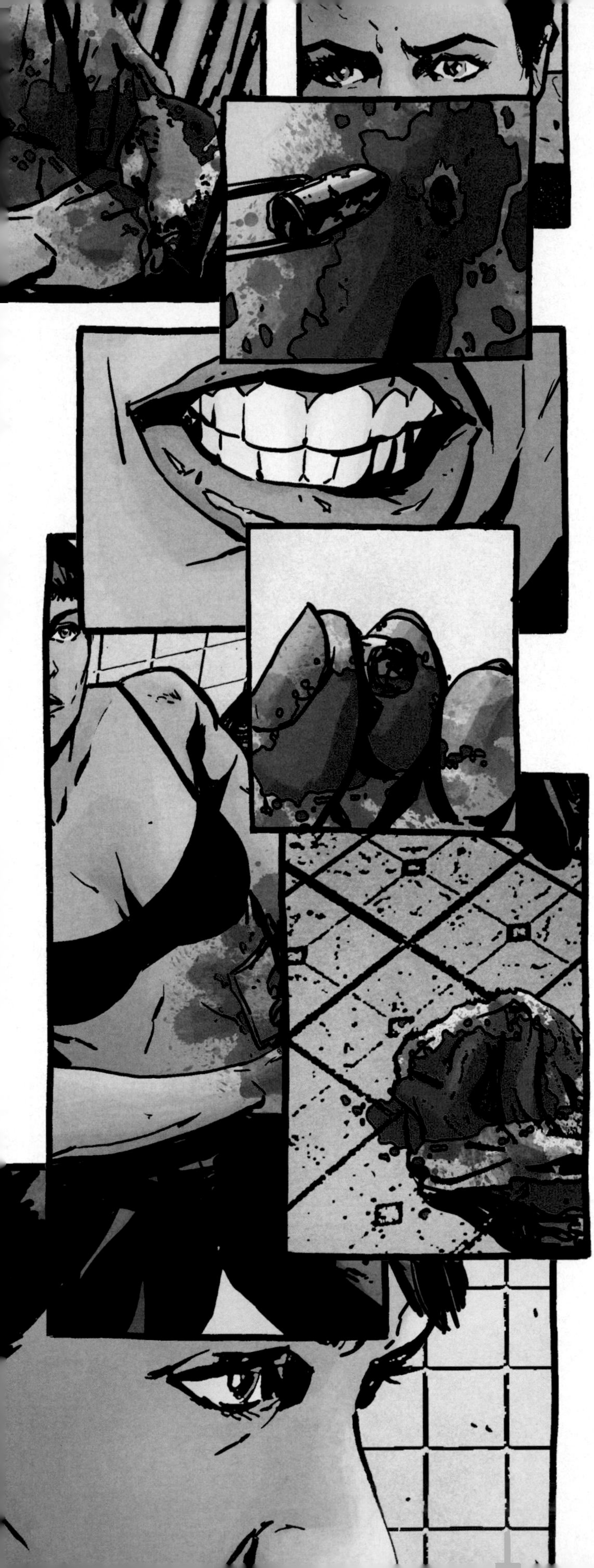

SO HERE'S HOW ***MY*** BRAIN WORKS.

DOES IT SAY TO ME, ***"OH MY GOD!*** THERE'S A WOMAN BLEEDING IN MY BATHROOM!"?

NO. BECAUSE THE WOMAN BLEEDING ALL OVER MY BATHROOM TILE IS ***MARIA HILL.***

WHO, UP UNTIL RECENTLY, WAS AN AGENT OF S.H.I.E.L.D.

A SPY. A ***PROFESSIONAL*** SPY. WHAT WE CIVILIANS WOULD CALL A PROFESSIONAL ***LIAR.***

ACTUALLY, SHE WAS THE HEAD OF ALL THE AGENTS OF S.H.I.E.L.D., WHICH MEANS SHE WAS PROBABLY THE ***BEST*** AGENT OF S.H.I.E.L.D.

THE BEST LIAR ***EVER.***

THINK ABOUT WHAT ***THAT*** JOB IS. THINK ABOUT WHAT KIND OF PERSON WOULD ***WANT*** THE JOB AS HEAD OF S.H.I.E.L.D.

A JOB THAT DEMANDS YOU TREAT AGENTS, OTHER HUMAN BEINGS, LIKE PUPPETS TO MANEUVER AND PLAY CHESS WITH.

LIFE-AND-DEATH CHESS.

SO, HERE SHE IS... MASTER SPY, MASTER LIAR. MASTER MANIPULATOR.

SOCIOPATH.

IN MY BATHROOM. UNINVITED.

AND I'M NOT HAVING IT.

I DON'T BELIEVE ANYTHING YOU SAY, LADY.

I DON'T EVEN BELIEVE SHE'S NO LONGER HEAD OF S.H.I.E.L.D.

HOW DO I KNOW THAT'S TRUE? BECAUSE I ***HEARD*** IT?

THAT COULD BE SOME STORY PUT OUT THERE TO FLUSH OUT SOME TRIPLE COUNTER AGENT AND SHE'S PROBABLY HERE TO USE ME TO SET UP SOMETHING TO BLACKMAIL SOMEONE SO SOMEONE ACCIDENTALLY POISONS THE RED SKULL'S COUSIN AND I END UP ROTTING TO DEATH IN A LATVERIAN PRISON.

I DON'T BELIEVE THAT'S HER BLOOD.

SHE PROBABLY ***DID*** THAT TO HERSELF.

TOOK SOME PAINKILLERS AND THEN JABBED HERSELF TO MAKE ME BELIEVE SHE'S BEEN ATTACKED.

AND HERE SHE IS ABOUT TO DROP SOME BULLSHIT IN MY LAP.

OH, AND NO MATTER WHAT YOU SAY, LADY, KNOW THIS...

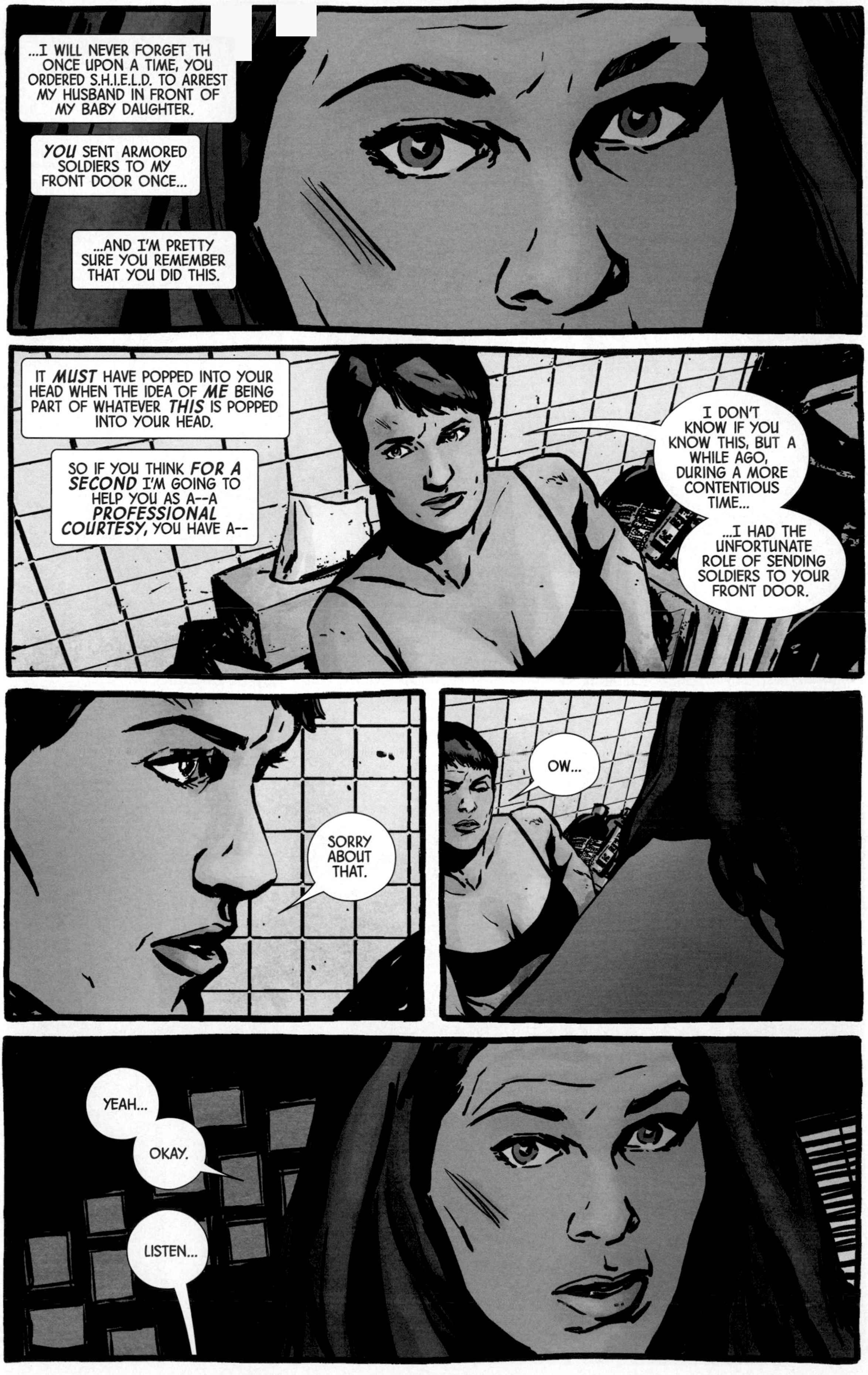
...I WILL NEVER FORGET TH
ONCE UPON A TIME, YOU ORDERED S.H.I.E.L.D. TO ARREST MY HUSBAND IN FRONT OF MY BABY DAUGHTER.
YOU SENT ARMORED SOLDIERS TO MY FRONT DOOR ONCE...
...AND I'M PRETTY SURE YOU REMEMBER THAT YOU DID THIS.
IT MUST HAVE POPPED INTO YOUR HEAD WHEN THE IDEA OF ME BEING PART OF WHATEVER THIS IS POPPED INTO YOUR HEAD.
SO IF YOU THINK FOR A SECOND I'M GOING TO HELP YOU AS A--A PROFESSIONAL COURTESY, YOU HAVE A--
I DON'T KNOW IF YOU KNOW THIS, BUT A WHILE AGO, DURING A MORE CONTENTIOUS TIME...
...I HAD THE UNFORTUNATE ROLE OF SENDING SOLDIERS TO YOUR FRONT DOOR.
SORRY ABOUT THAT.
OW...
YEAH...
OKAY.
LISTEN...

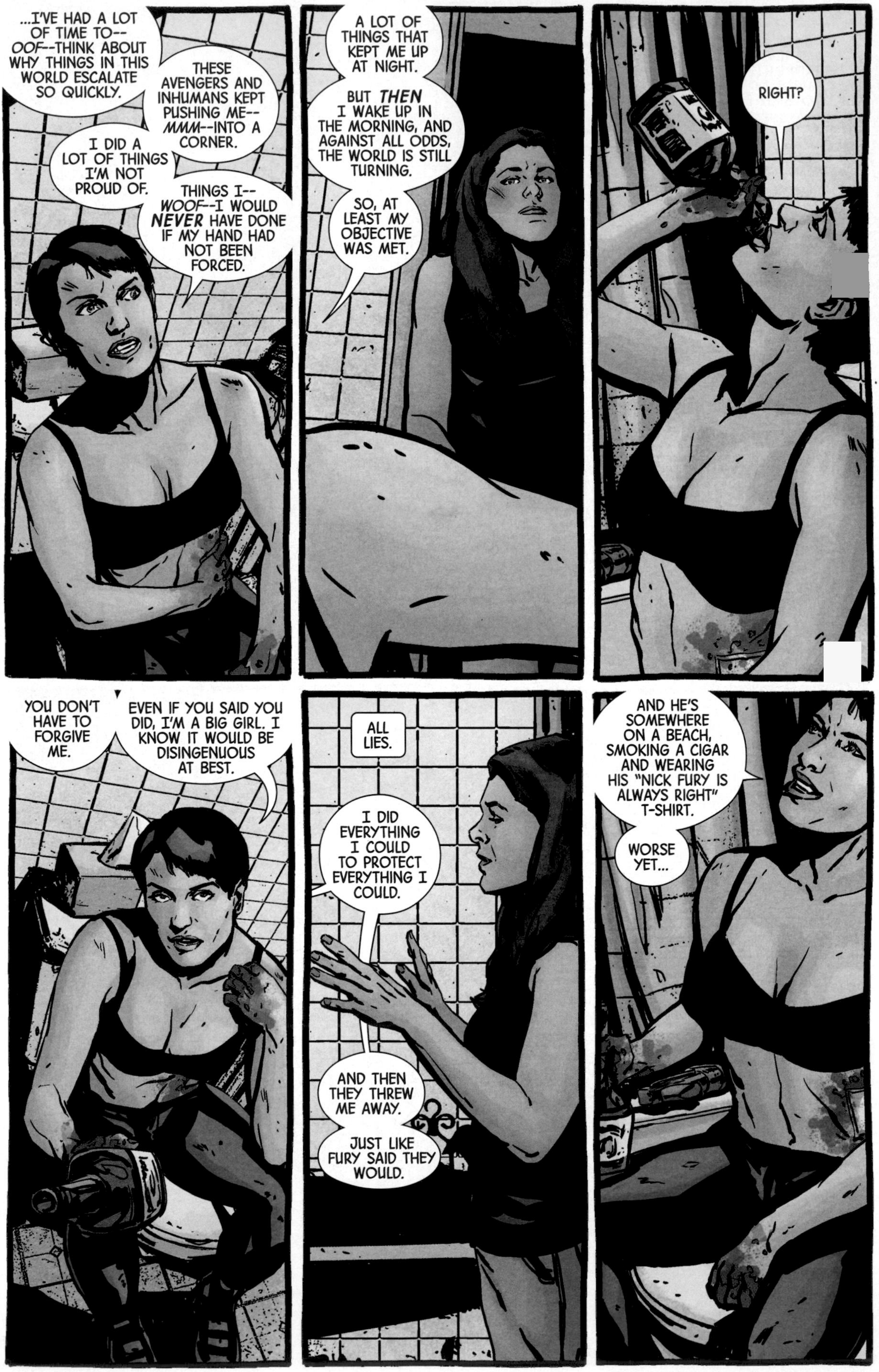
...I'VE HAD A LOT OF TIME TO-- OOF--THINK ABOUT WHY THINGS IN THIS WORLD ESCALATE SO QUICKLY.
THESE AVENGERS AND INHUMANS KEPT PUSHING ME-- MMM--INTO A CORNER.
I DID A LOT OF THINGS I'M NOT PROUD OF.
THINGS I-- WOOF--I WOULD NEVER HAVE DONE IF MY HAND HAD NOT BEEN FORCED.
A LOT OF THINGS THAT KEPT ME UP AT NIGHT.
BUT THEN I WAKE UP IN THE MORNING, AND AGAINST ALL ODDS, THE WORLD IS STILL TURNING.
SO, AT LEAST MY OBJECTIVE WAS MET.
RIGHT?
YOU DON'T HAVE TO FORGIVE ME.
EVEN IF YOU SAID YOU DID, I'M A BIG GIRL. I KNOW IT WOULD BE DISINGENUOUS AT BEST.
ALL LIES.
I DID EVERYTHING I COULD TO PROTECT EVERYTHING I COULD.
AND THEN THEY THREW ME AWAY.
JUST LIKE FURY SAID THEY WOULD.
AND HE'S SOMEWHERE ON A BEACH, SMOKING A CIGAR AND WEARING HIS "NICK FURY IS ALWAYS RIGHT" T-SHIRT.
WORSE YET...

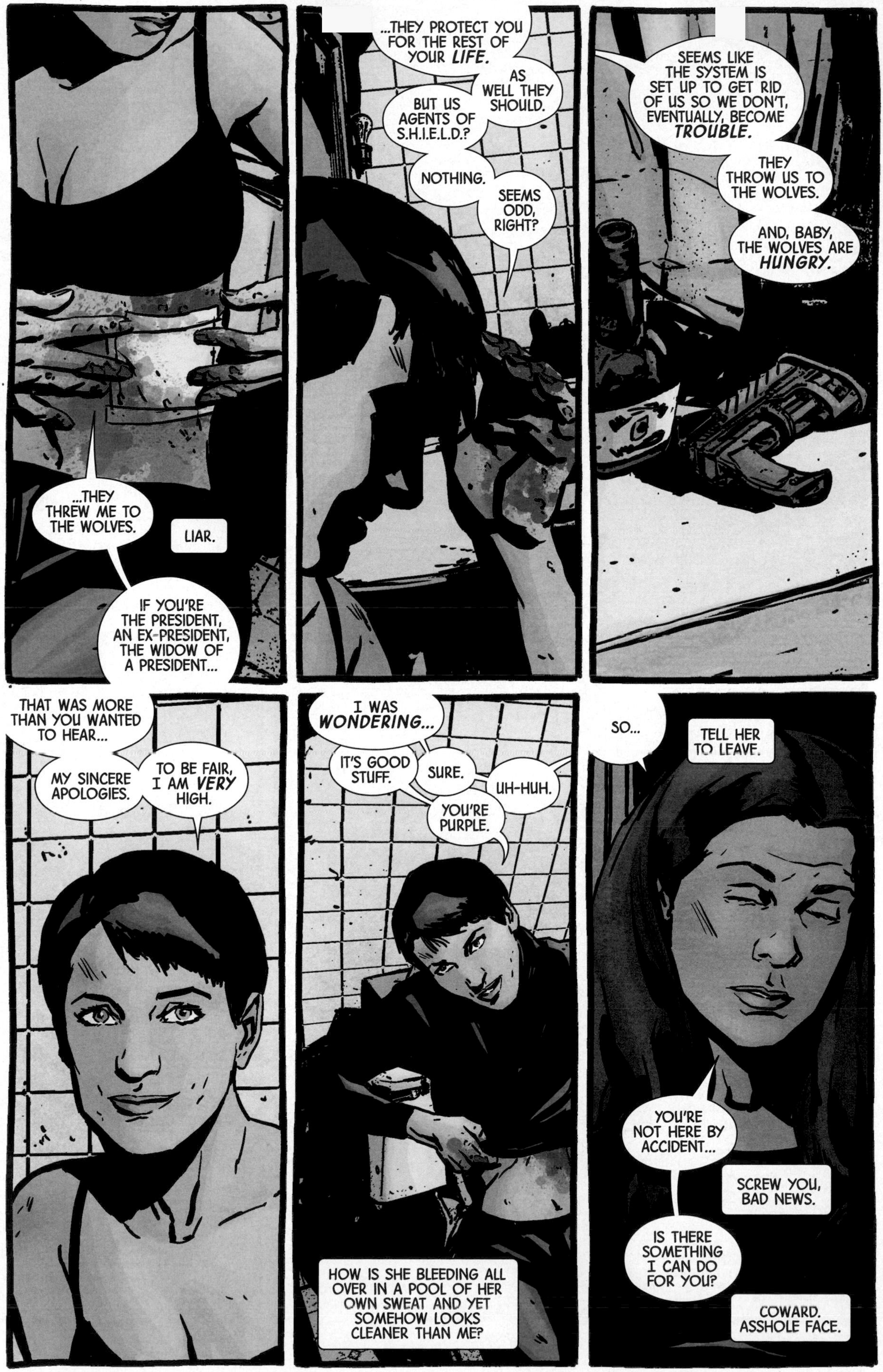

...THEY THREW ME TO THE WOLVES.
LIAR.
IF YOU'RE THE PRESIDENT, AN EX-PRESIDENT, THE WIDOW OF A PRESIDENT...
...THEY PROTECT YOU FOR THE REST OF YOUR *LIFE.*
AS WELL THEY SHOULD.
BUT US AGENTS OF S.H.I.E.L.D.?
NOTHING.
SEEMS ODD, RIGHT?
SEEMS LIKE THE SYSTEM IS SET UP TO GET RID OF US SO WE DON'T, EVENTUALLY, BECOME *TROUBLE.*
THEY THROW US TO THE WOLVES.
AND, BABY, THE WOLVES ARE *HUNGRY.*
THAT WAS MORE THAN YOU WANTED TO HEAR...
MY SINCERE APOLOGIES.
TO BE FAIR, I AM *VERY* HIGH.
I WAS *WONDERING...*
IT'S GOOD STUFF.
SURE.
UH-HUH.
YOU'RE PURPLE.
HOW IS SHE BLEEDING ALL OVER IN A POOL OF HER OWN SWEAT AND YET SOMEHOW LOOKS CLEANER THAN ME?
SO...
TELL HER TO LEAVE.
YOU'RE NOT HERE BY ACCIDENT...
SCREW YOU, BAD NEWS.
IS THERE SOMETHING I CAN DO FOR YOU?
COWARD. ASSHOLE FACE.

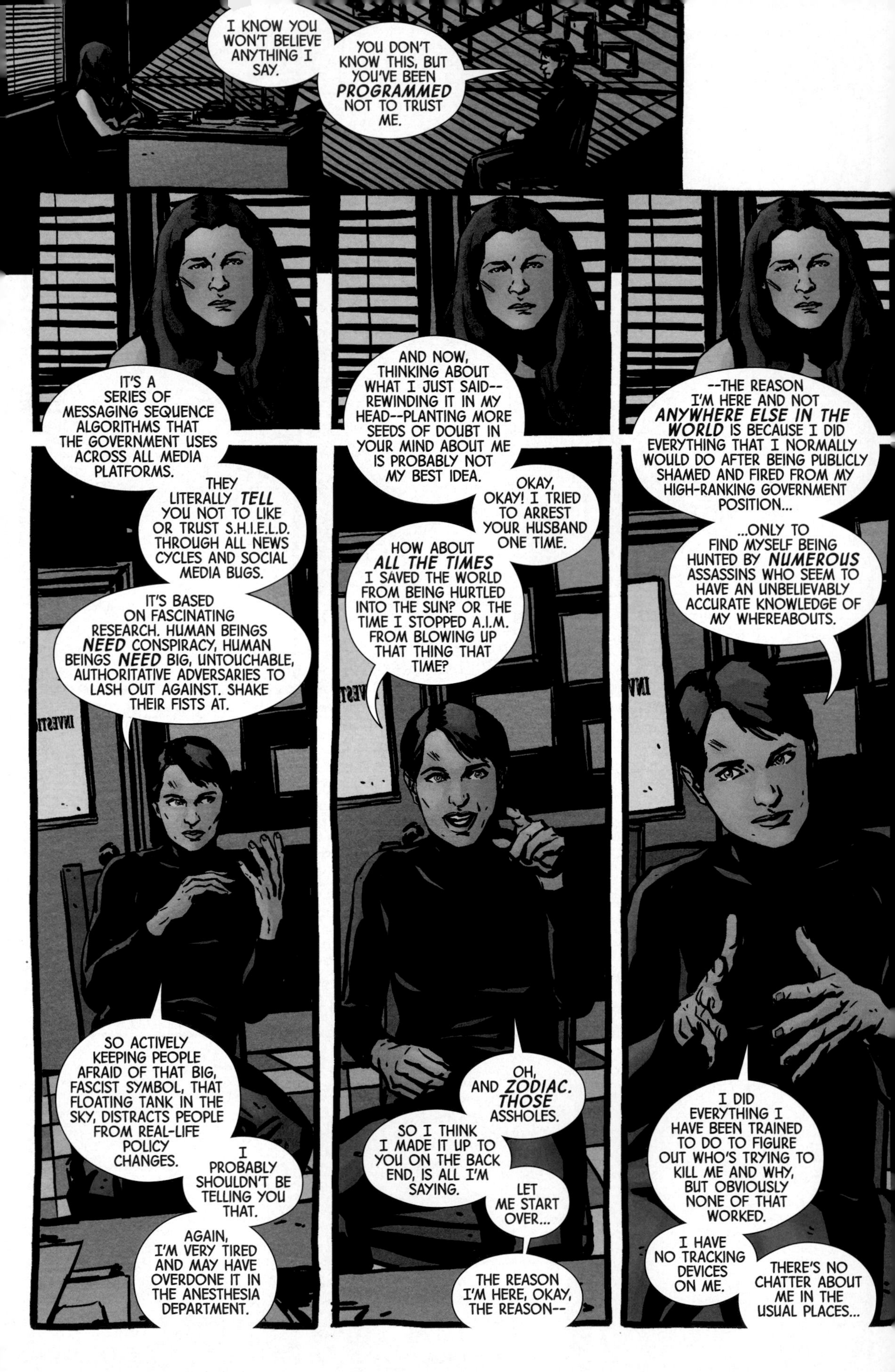
I KNOW YOU WON'T BELIEVE ANYTHING I SAY.
YOU DON'T KNOW THIS, BUT YOU'VE BEEN PROGRAMMED NOT TO TRUST ME.
IT'S A SERIES OF MESSAGING SEQUENCE ALGORITHMS THAT THE GOVERNMENT USES ACROSS ALL MEDIA PLATFORMS.
THEY LITERALLY TELL YOU NOT TO LIKE OR TRUST S.H.I.E.L.D. THROUGH ALL NEWS CYCLES AND SOCIAL MEDIA BUGS.
IT'S BASED ON FASCINATING RESEARCH. HUMAN BEINGS NEED CONSPIRACY, HUMAN BEINGS NEED BIG, UNTOUCHABLE, AUTHORITATIVE ADVERSARIES TO LASH OUT AGAINST. SHAKE THEIR FISTS AT.
SO ACTIVELY KEEPING PEOPLE AFRAID OF THAT BIG, FASCIST SYMBOL, THAT FLOATING TANK IN THE SKY, DISTRACTS PEOPLE FROM REAL-LIFE POLICY CHANGES.
I PROBABLY SHOULDN'T BE TELLING YOU THAT.
AGAIN, I'M VERY TIRED AND MAY HAVE OVERDONE IT IN THE ANESTHESIA DEPARTMENT.
AND NOW, THINKING ABOUT WHAT I JUST SAID--REWINDING IT IN MY HEAD--PLANTING MORE SEEDS OF DOUBT IN YOUR MIND ABOUT ME IS PROBABLY NOT MY BEST IDEA.
OKAY, OKAY! I TRIED TO ARREST YOUR HUSBAND ONE TIME.
HOW ABOUT ALL THE TIMES I SAVED THE WORLD FROM BEING HURTLED INTO THE SUN? OR THE TIME I STOPPED A.I.M. FROM BLOWING UP THAT THING THAT TIME?
OH, AND ZODIAC. THOSE ASSHOLES.
SO I THINK I MADE IT UP TO YOU ON THE BACK END, IS ALL I'M SAYING.
LET ME START OVER...
THE REASON I'M HERE, OKAY, THE REASON--
--THE REASON I'M HERE AND NOT ANYWHERE ELSE IN THE WORLD IS BECAUSE I DID EVERYTHING THAT I NORMALLY WOULD DO AFTER BEING PUBLICLY SHAMED AND FIRED FROM MY HIGH-RANKING GOVERNMENT POSITION...
...ONLY TO FIND MYSELF BEING HUNTED BY NUMEROUS ASSASSINS WHO SEEM TO HAVE AN UNBELIEVABLY ACCURATE KNOWLEDGE OF MY WHEREABOUTS.
I DID EVERYTHING I HAVE BEEN TRAINED TO DO TO FIGURE OUT WHO'S TRYING TO KILL ME AND WHY, BUT OBVIOUSLY NONE OF THAT WORKED.
I HAVE NO TRACKING DEVICES ON ME.
THERE'S NO CHATTER ABOUT ME IN THE USUAL PLACES...

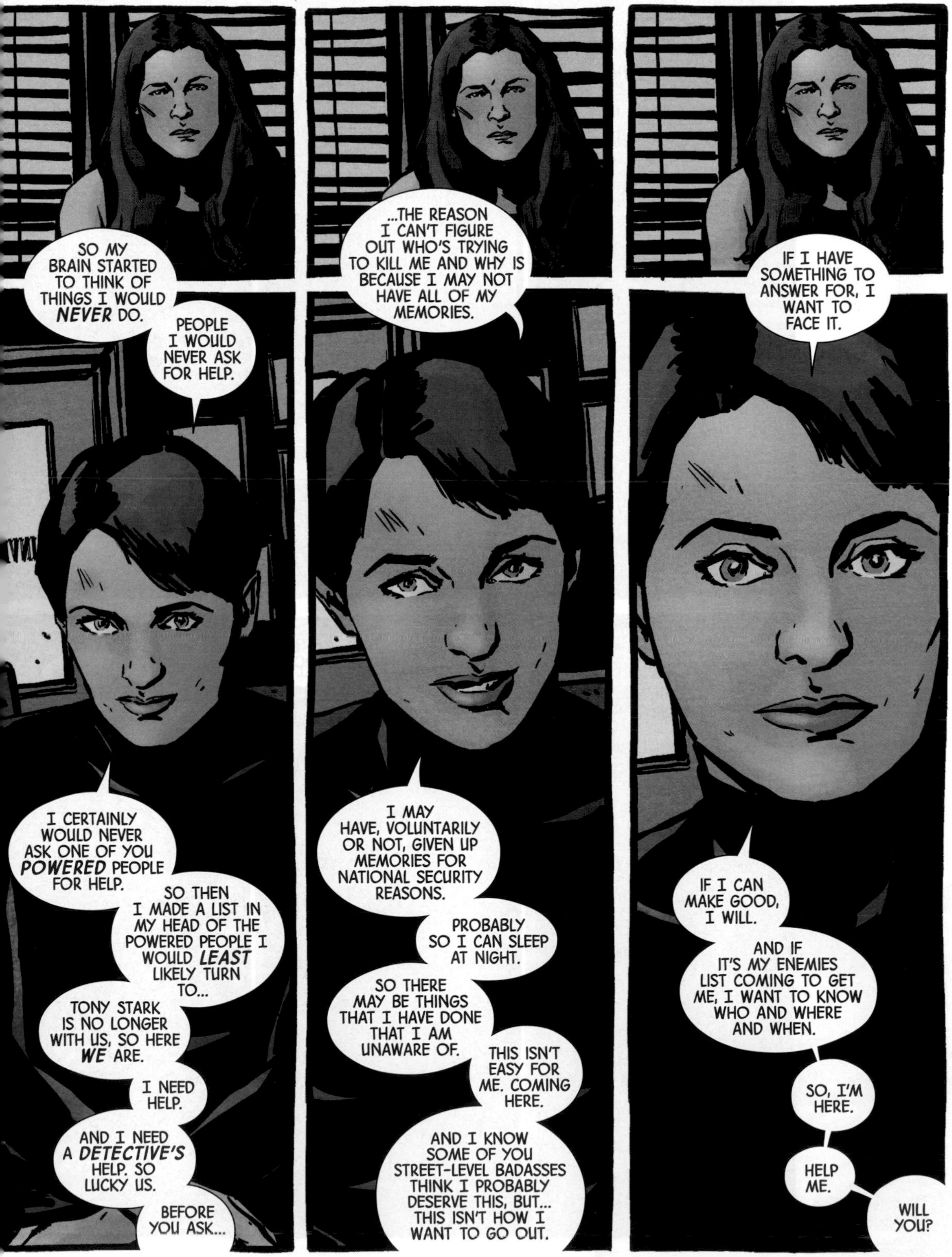

SO MY BRAIN STARTED TO THINK OF THINGS I WOULD NEVER DO.
PEOPLE I WOULD NEVER ASK FOR HELP.
I CERTAINLY WOULD NEVER ASK ONE OF YOU POWERED PEOPLE FOR HELP.
SO THEN I MADE A LIST IN MY HEAD OF THE POWERED PEOPLE I WOULD LEAST LIKELY TURN TO...
TONY STARK IS NO LONGER WITH US, SO HERE WE ARE.
I NEED HELP.
AND I NEED A DETECTIVE'S HELP. SO LUCKY US.
BEFORE YOU ASK...
...THE REASON I CAN'T FIGURE OUT WHO'S TRYING TO KILL ME AND WHY IS BECAUSE I MAY NOT HAVE ALL OF MY MEMORIES.
I MAY HAVE, VOLUNTARILY OR NOT, GIVEN UP MEMORIES FOR NATIONAL SECURITY REASONS.
PROBABLY SO I CAN SLEEP AT NIGHT.
SO THERE MAY BE THINGS THAT I HAVE DONE THAT I AM UNAWARE OF.
THIS ISN'T EASY FOR ME. COMING HERE.
AND I KNOW SOME OF YOU STREET-LEVEL BADASSES THINK I PROBABLY DESERVE THIS, BUT... THIS ISN'T HOW I WANT TO GO OUT.
IF I HAVE SOMETHING TO ANSWER FOR, I WANT TO FACE IT.
IF I CAN MAKE GOOD, I WILL.
AND IF IT'S MY ENEMIES LIST COMING TO GET ME, I WANT TO KNOW WHO AND WHERE AND WHEN.
SO, I'M HERE.
HELP ME.
WILL YOU?

AND I'M CHARGING YOU A "TRYING TO ARREST MY HUSBAND" TAX.

I CAN'T BELIEVE I JUST SAID THAT...

IT WAS ONE TIME...

AND I CAN'T BELIEVE IT JUST WORKED.

NEED TO BE CLOSIN' ME EYES FOR A SECOND.

(PIRATE BOOTY.)

HELLO?

OH, THIS IS ALL I NEED.

BUT I GOT YOUR MONEY, BITCH, AND YOU CAN--WAIT, IS SHE--?

PHEW.

OKAY, GOOD. STILL ALIVE.

DON'T NEED *THAT* NONSENSE.

PROBABLY ISN'T EVEN REAL MONEY.

BUT IF IT IS... MAMAS GOIN' TO KATE SPADE.

OR I PUT IT AWAY FOR DANI'S COLLEGE.

I'LL DECIDE AFTER I TRY ON THE BOOTS.

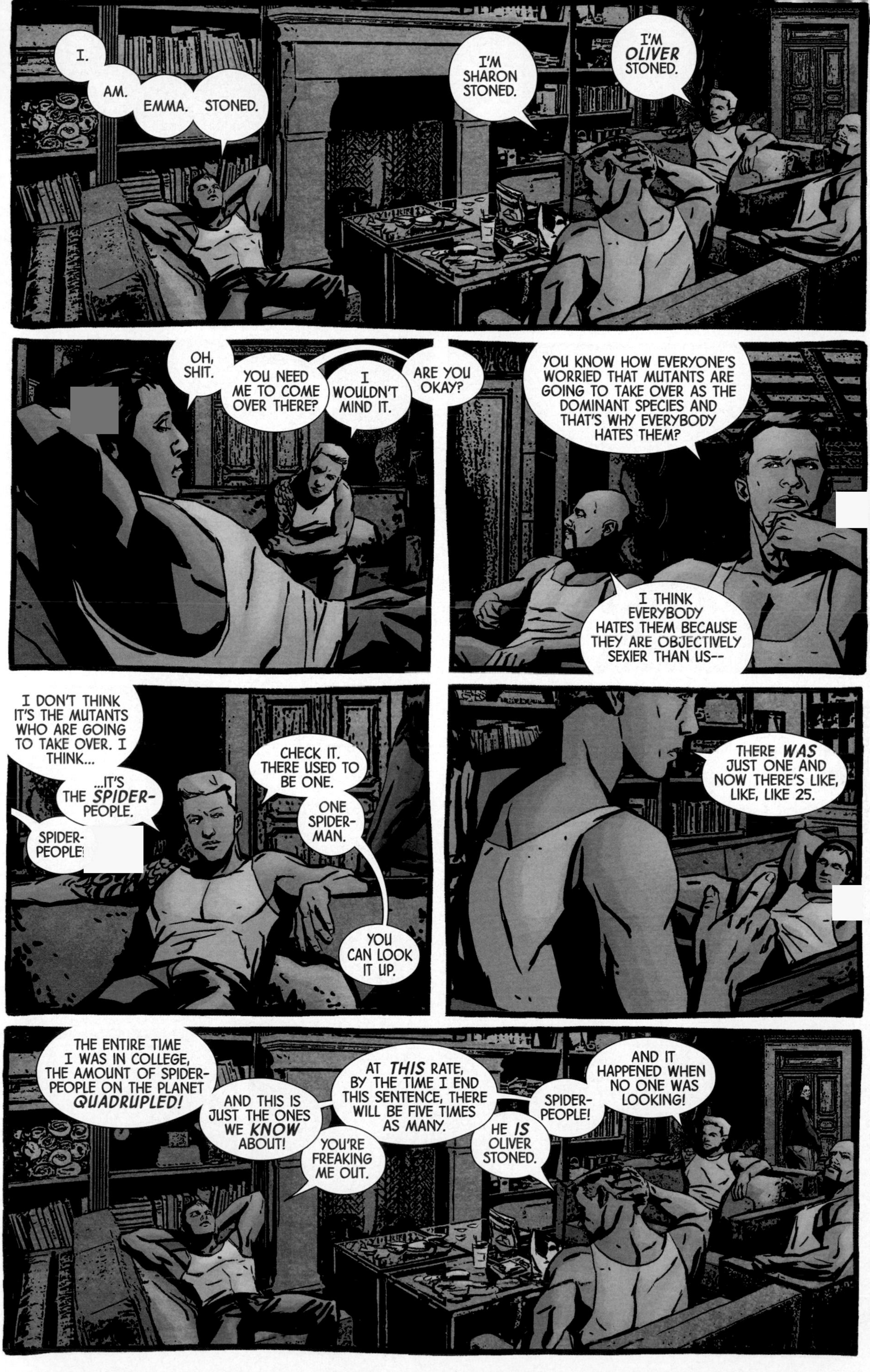
I.
AM.
EMMA.
STONED.
I'M SHARON STONED.
I'M *OLIVER* STONED.
OH, SHIT.
YOU NEED ME TO COME OVER THERE?
I WOULDN'T MIND IT.
ARE YOU OKAY?
YOU KNOW HOW EVERYONE'S WORRIED THAT MUTANTS ARE GOING TO TAKE OVER AS THE DOMINANT SPECIES AND THAT'S WHY EVERYBODY HATES THEM?
I THINK EVERYBODY HATES THEM BECAUSE THEY ARE OBJECTIVELY SEXIER THAN US--
I DON'T THINK IT'S THE MUTANTS WHO ARE GOING TO TAKE OVER. I THINK...
...IT'S THE *SPIDER*-PEOPLE.
SPIDER-PEOPLE!
CHECK IT. THERE USED TO BE ONE.
ONE SPIDER-MAN.
YOU CAN LOOK IT UP.
THERE *WAS* JUST ONE AND NOW THERE'S LIKE, LIKE, LIKE 25.
THE ENTIRE TIME I WAS IN COLLEGE, THE AMOUNT OF SPIDER-PEOPLE ON THE PLANET *QUADRUPLED!*
AND THIS IS JUST THE ONES WE *KNOW* ABOUT!
AT *THIS* RATE, BY THE TIME I END THIS SENTENCE, THERE WILL BE FIVE TIMES AS MANY.
YOU'RE FREAKING ME OUT.
HE *IS* OLIVER STONED.
SPIDER-PEOPLE!
AND IT HAPPENED WHEN NO ONE WAS LOOKING!

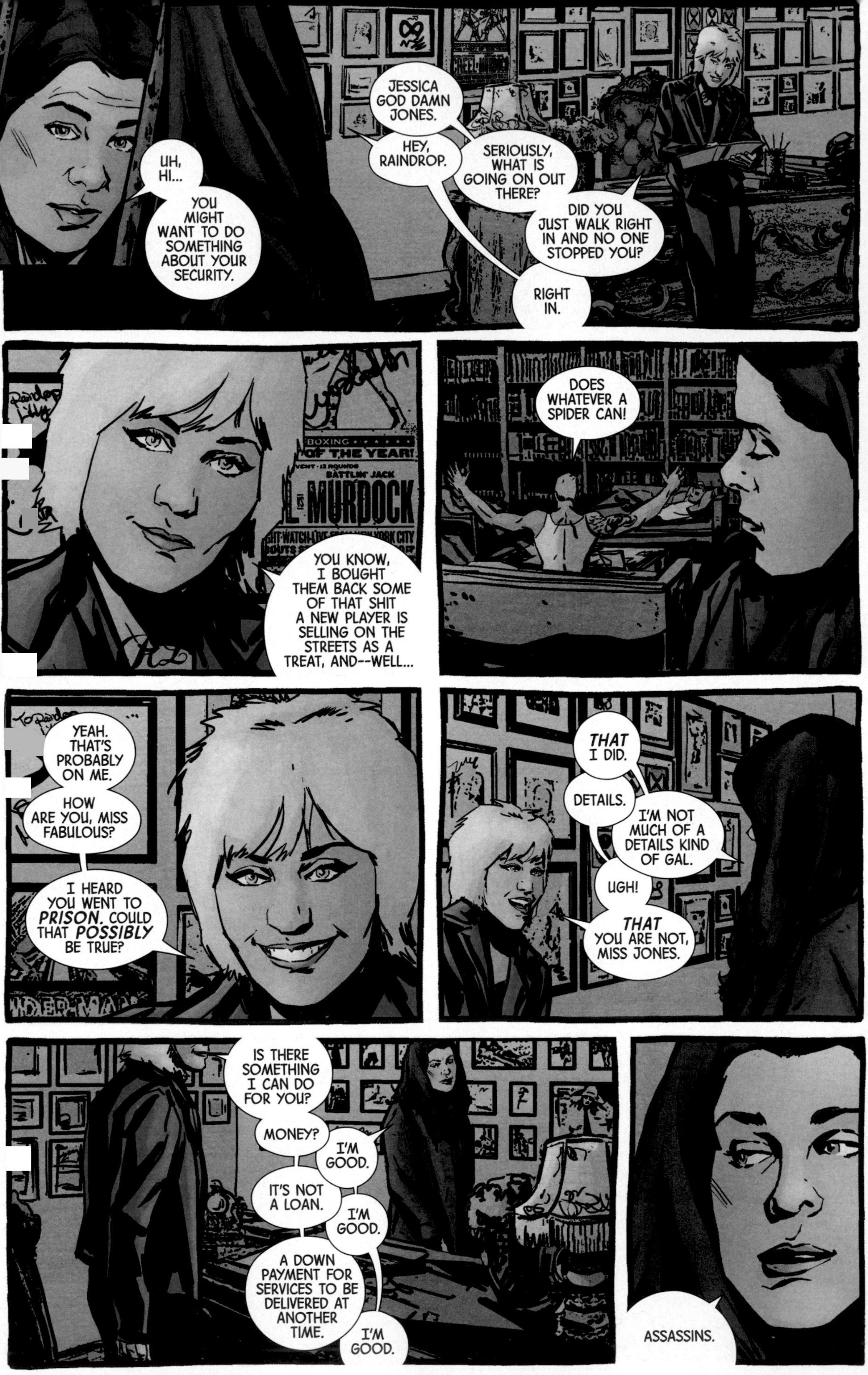
UH, HI...
YOU MIGHT WANT TO DO SOMETHING ABOUT YOUR SECURITY.
JESSICA GOD DAMN JONES.
HEY, RAINDROP.
SERIOUSLY, WHAT IS GOING ON OUT THERE?
DID YOU JUST WALK RIGHT IN AND NO ONE STOPPED YOU?
RIGHT IN.
BOXING
OF THE YEAR!
BATTLIN' JACK
MURDOCK
YOU KNOW, I BOUGHT THEM BACK SOME OF THAT SHIT A NEW PLAYER IS SELLING ON THE STREETS AS A TREAT, AND--WELL...
DOES WHATEVER A SPIDER CAN!
YEAH. THAT'S PROBABLY ON ME.
HOW ARE YOU, MISS FABULOUS?
I HEARD YOU WENT TO *PRISON.* COULD THAT *POSSIBLY* BE TRUE?
THAT I DID.
DETAILS.
I'M NOT MUCH OF A DETAILS KIND OF GAL.
UGH!
THAT YOU ARE NOT, MISS JONES.
IS THERE SOMETHING I CAN DO FOR YOU?
MONEY?
I'M GOOD.
IT'S NOT A LOAN.
I'M GOOD.
A DOWN PAYMENT FOR SERVICES TO BE DELIVERED AT ANOTHER TIME.
I'M GOOD.
ASSASSINS.

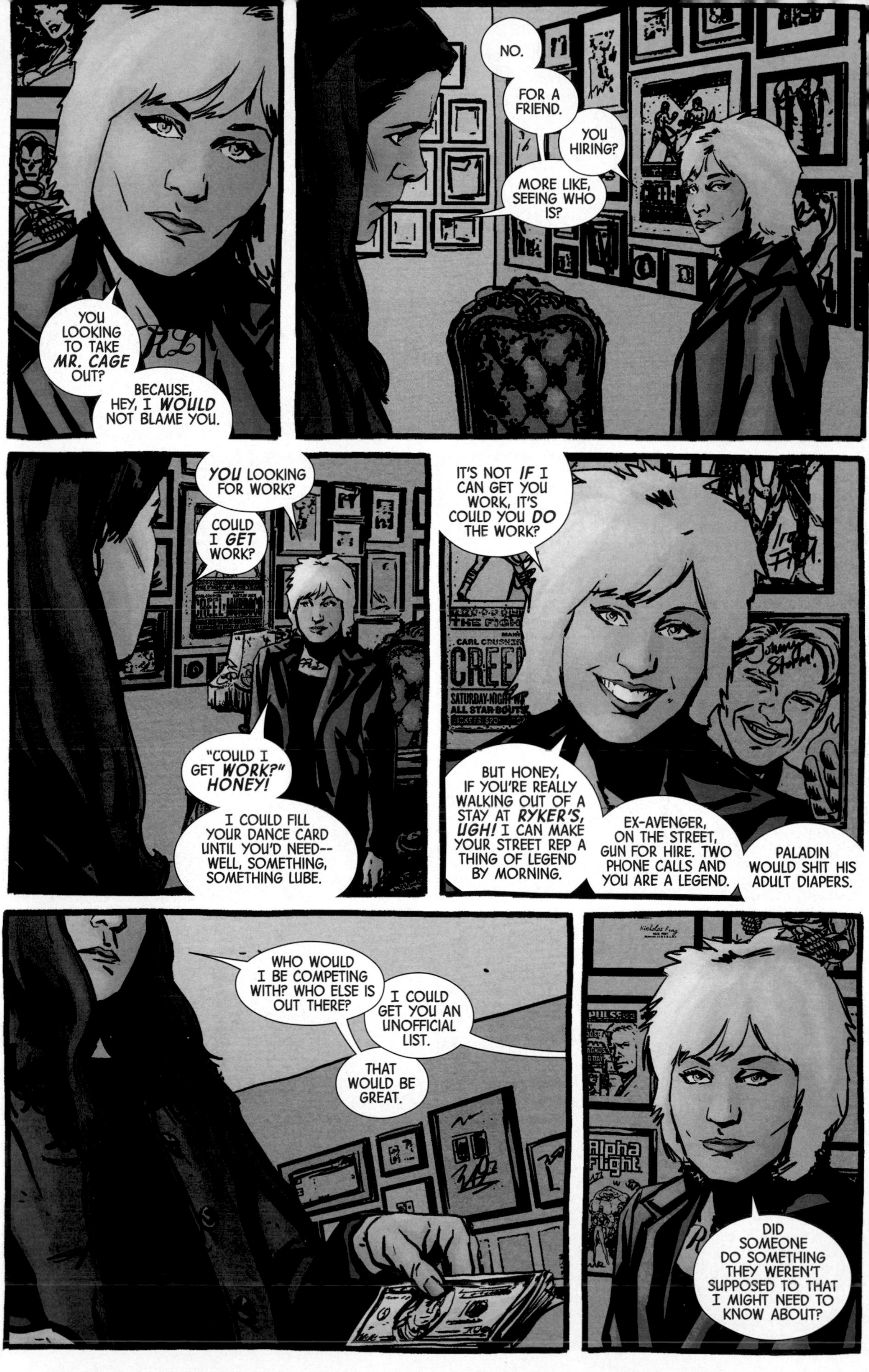
YOU LOOKING TO TAKE MR. CAGE OUT?
BECAUSE, HEY, I WOULD NOT BLAME YOU.
NO.
FOR A FRIEND.
YOU HIRING?
MORE LIKE, SEEING WHO IS?
YOU LOOKING FOR WORK?
COULD I GET WORK?
"COULD I GET WORK?" HONEY!
I COULD FILL YOUR DANCE CARD UNTIL YOU'D NEED-- WELL, SOMETHING, SOMETHING LUBE.
IT'S NOT IF I CAN GET YOU WORK, IT'S COULD YOU DO THE WORK?
BUT HONEY, IF YOU'RE REALLY WALKING OUT OF A STAY AT RYKER'S, UGH! I CAN MAKE YOUR STREET REP A THING OF LEGEND BY MORNING.
EX-AVENGER, ON THE STREET, GUN FOR HIRE. TWO PHONE CALLS AND YOU ARE A LEGEND.
PALADIN WOULD SHIT HIS ADULT DIAPERS.
WHO WOULD I BE COMPETING WITH? WHO ELSE IS OUT THERE?
I COULD GET YOU AN UNOFFICIAL LIST.
THAT WOULD BE GREAT.
DID SOMEONE DO SOMETHING THEY WEREN'T SUPPOSED TO THAT I MIGHT NEED TO KNOW ABOUT?

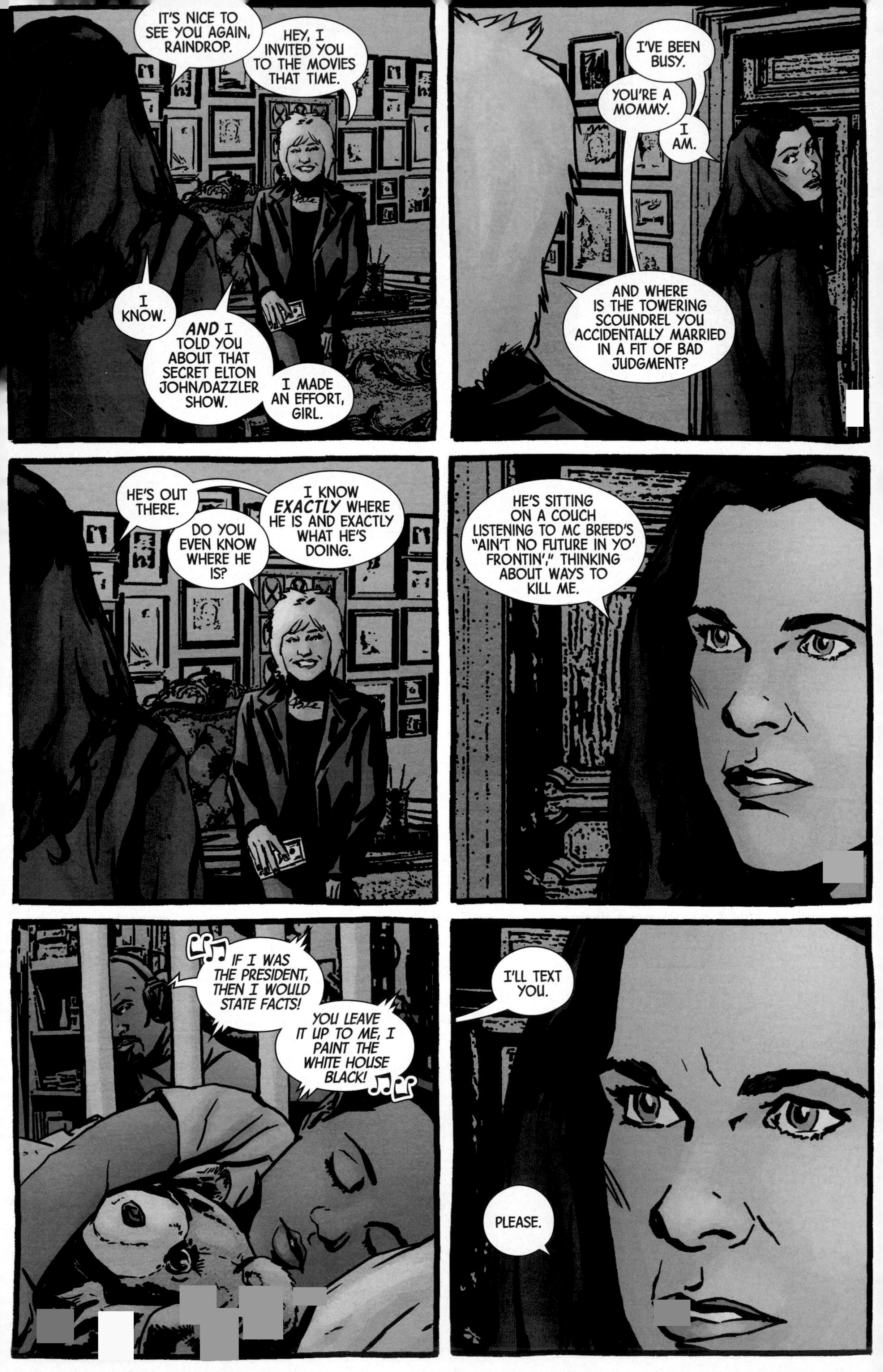
IT'S NICE TO SEE YOU AGAIN, RAINDROP.
HEY, I INVITED YOU TO THE MOVIES THAT TIME.
I KNOW.
AND I TOLD YOU ABOUT THAT SECRET ELTON JOHN/DAZZLER SHOW.
I MADE AN EFFORT, GIRL.
I'VE BEEN BUSY.
YOU'RE A MOMMY.
I AM.
AND WHERE IS THE TOWERING SCOUNDREL YOU ACCIDENTALLY MARRIED IN A FIT OF BAD JUDGMENT?
HE'S OUT THERE.
DO YOU EVEN KNOW WHERE HE IS?
I KNOW EXACTLY WHERE HE IS AND EXACTLY WHAT HE'S DOING.
HE'S SITTING ON A COUCH LISTENING TO MC BREED'S "AIN'T NO FUTURE IN YO' FRONTIN'," THINKING ABOUT WAYS TO KILL ME.
IF I WAS THE PRESIDENT, THEN I WOULD STATE FACTS!
YOU LEAVE IT UP TO ME, I PAINT THE WHITE HOUSE BLACK!
I'LL TEXT YOU.
PLEASE.

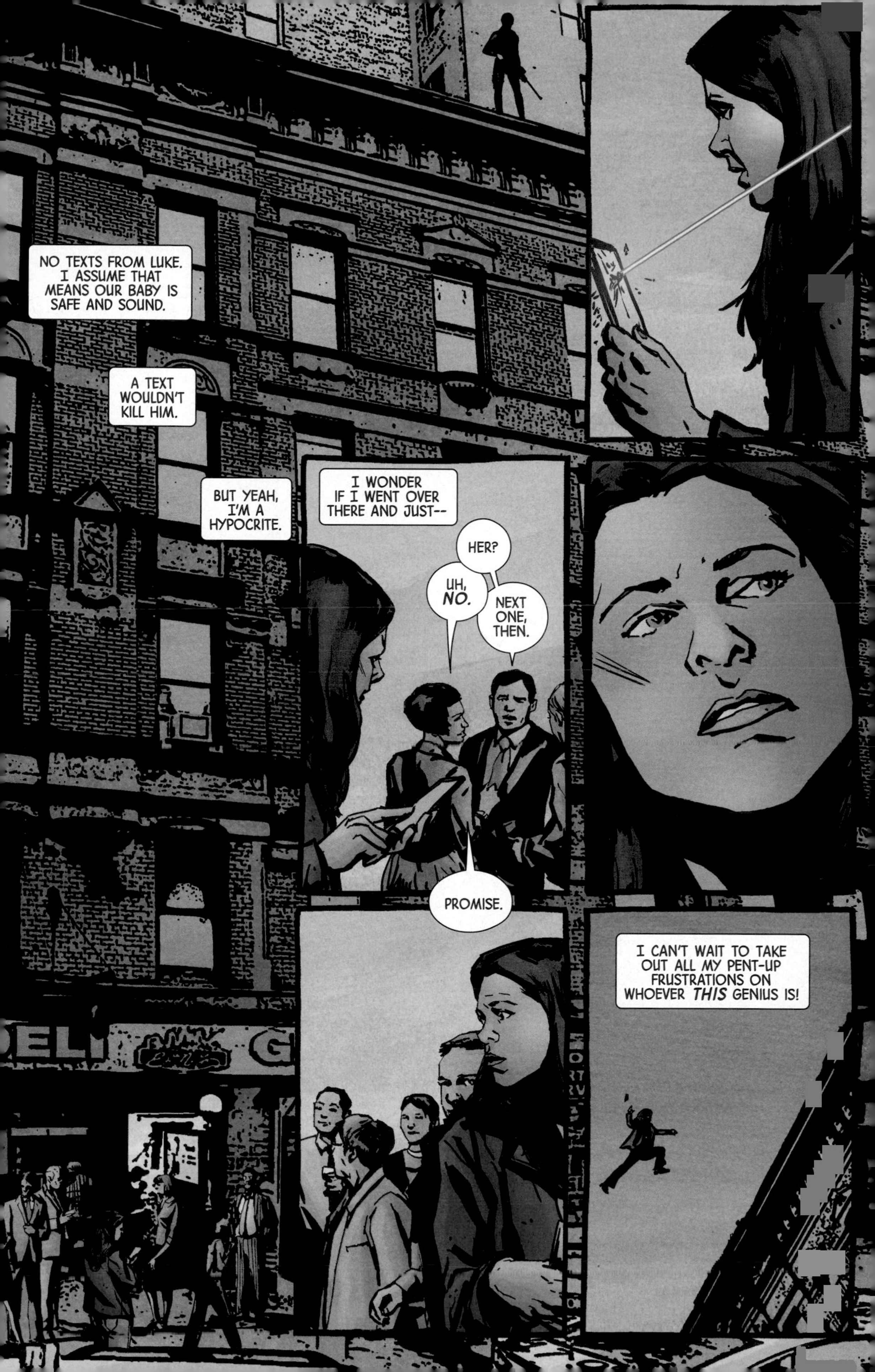
NO TEXTS FROM LUKE. I ASSUME THAT MEANS OUR BABY IS SAFE AND SOUND.
A TEXT WOULDN'T KILL HIM.
BUT YEAH, I'M A HYPOCRITE.
I WONDER IF I WENT OVER THERE AND JUST--
HER?
UH, NO.
NEXT ONE, THEN.
PROMISE.
I CAN'T WAIT TO TAKE OUT ALL MY PENT-UP FRUSTRATIONS ON WHOEVER THIS GENIUS IS!
DELI

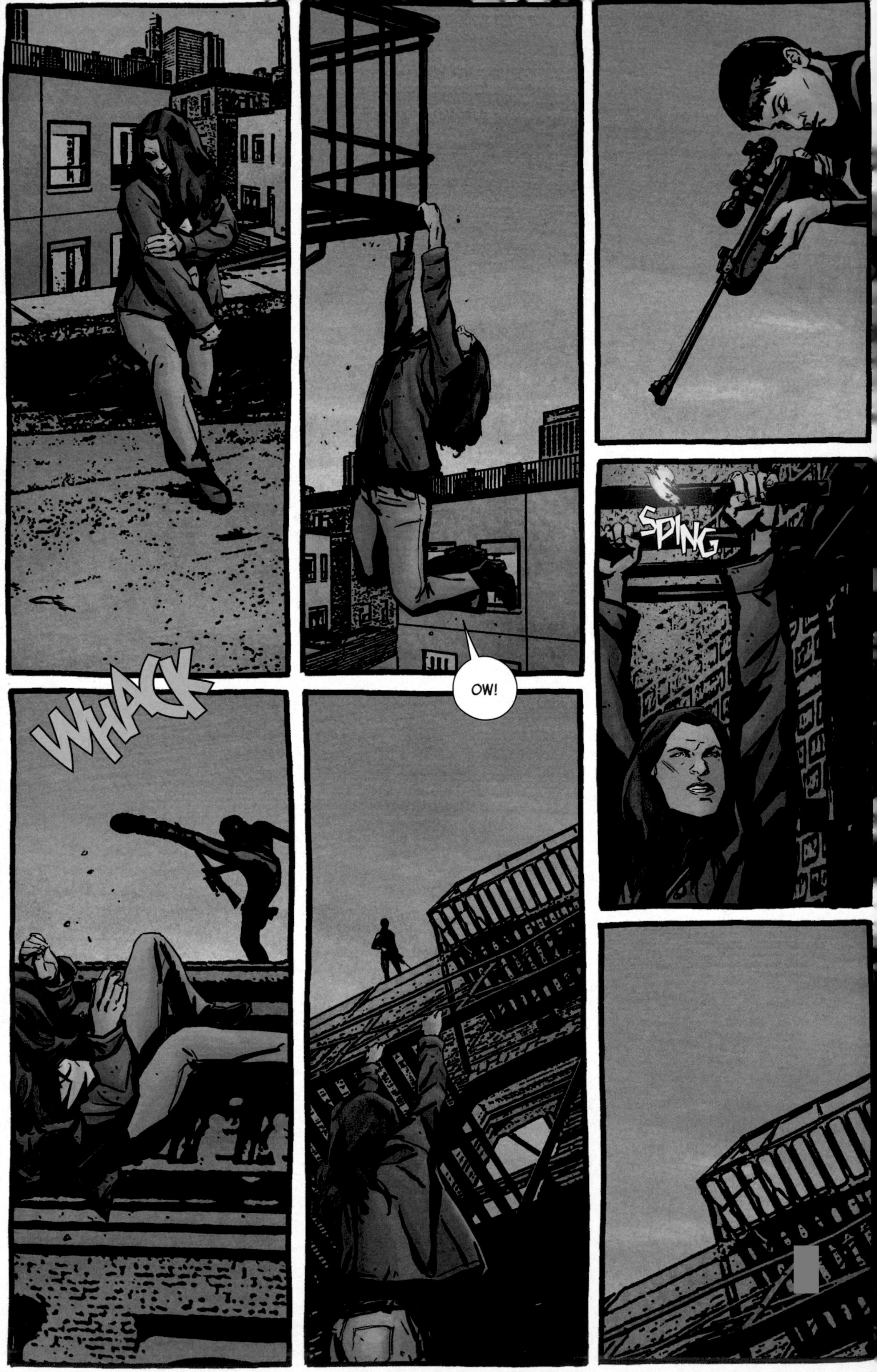
OW!
SPING
WHACK

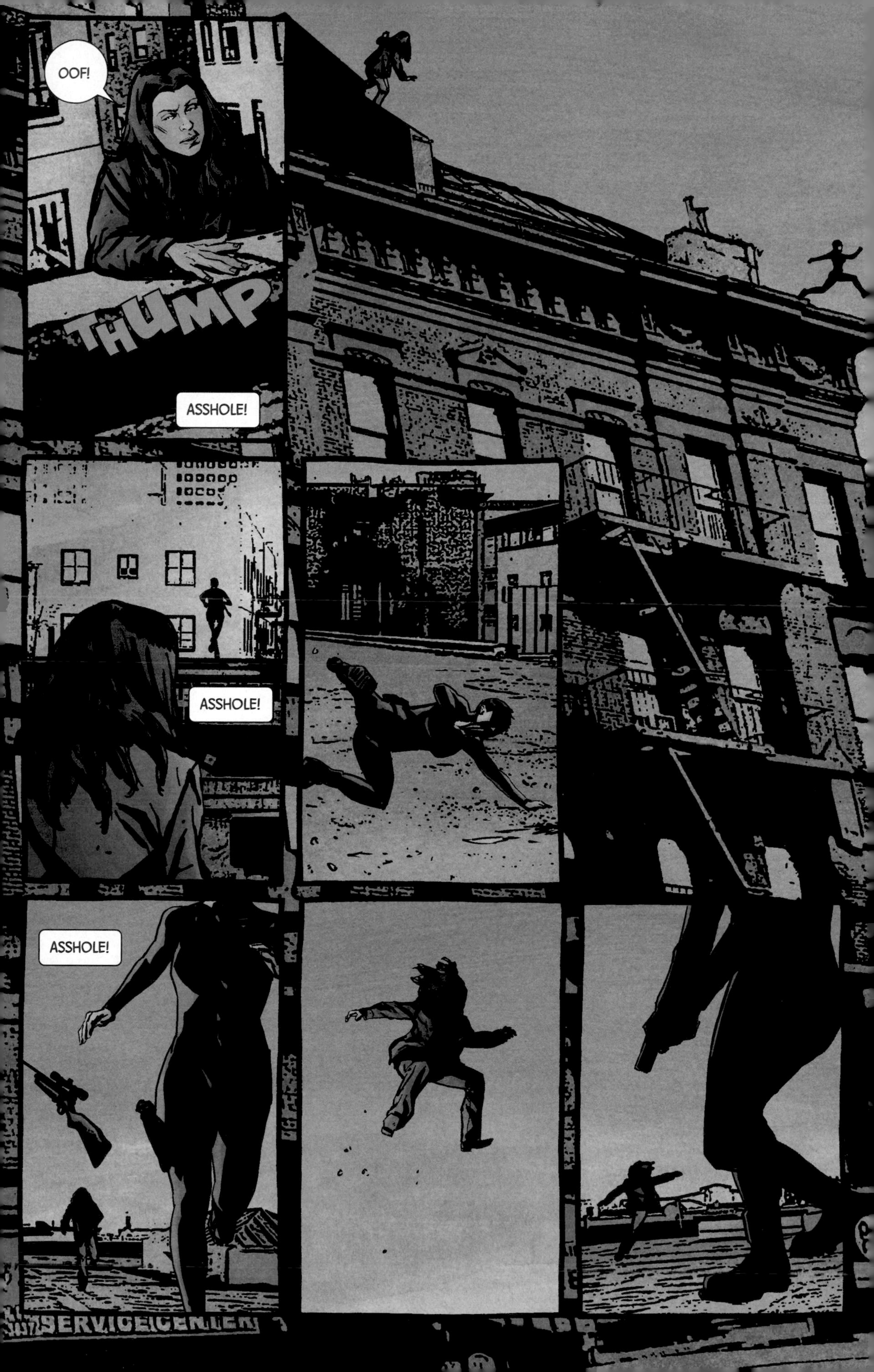
OOF!
THUMP
ASSHOLE!
ASSHOLE!
ASSHOLE!
SERVICE CENTER

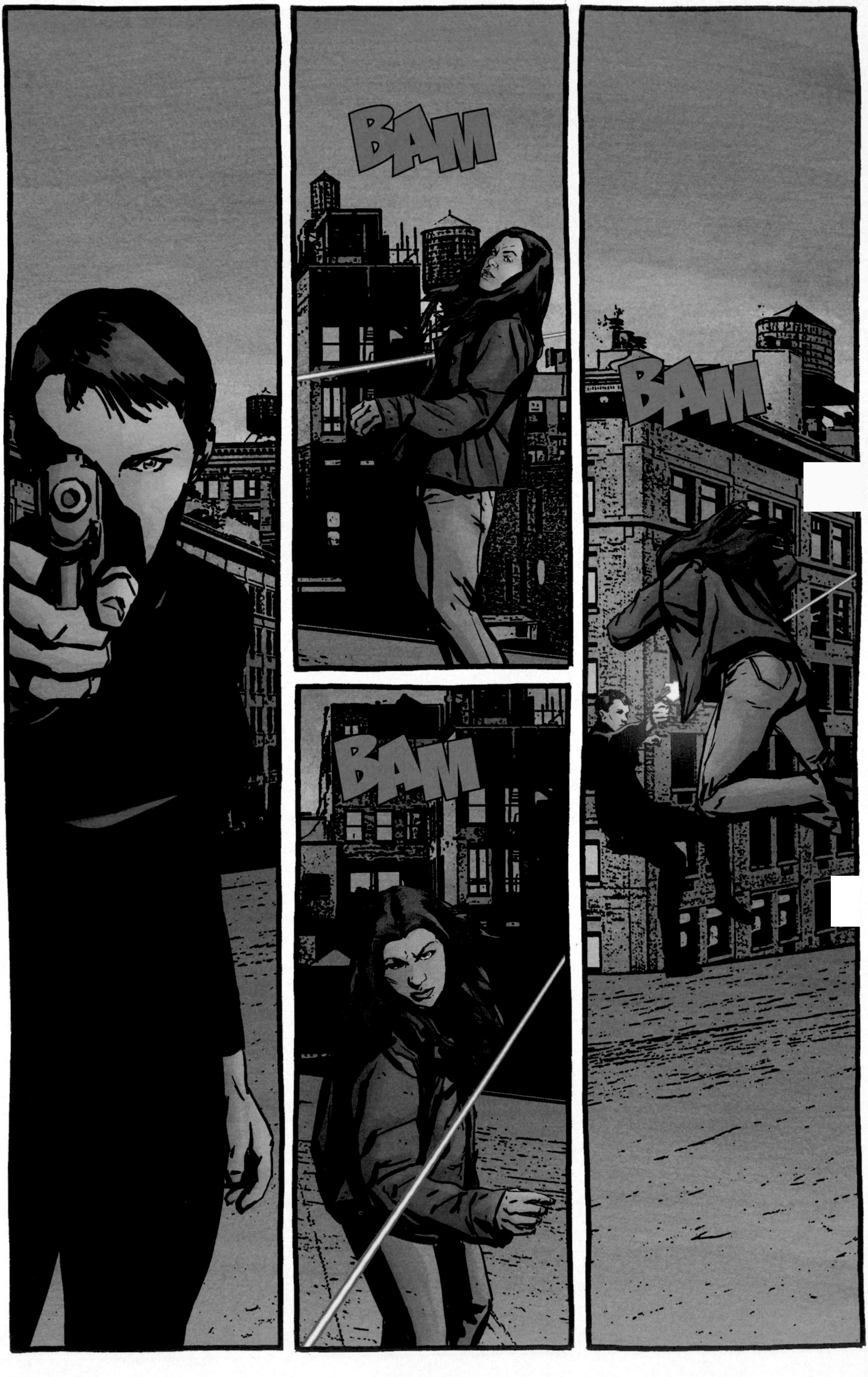
BAM
BAM
BAM

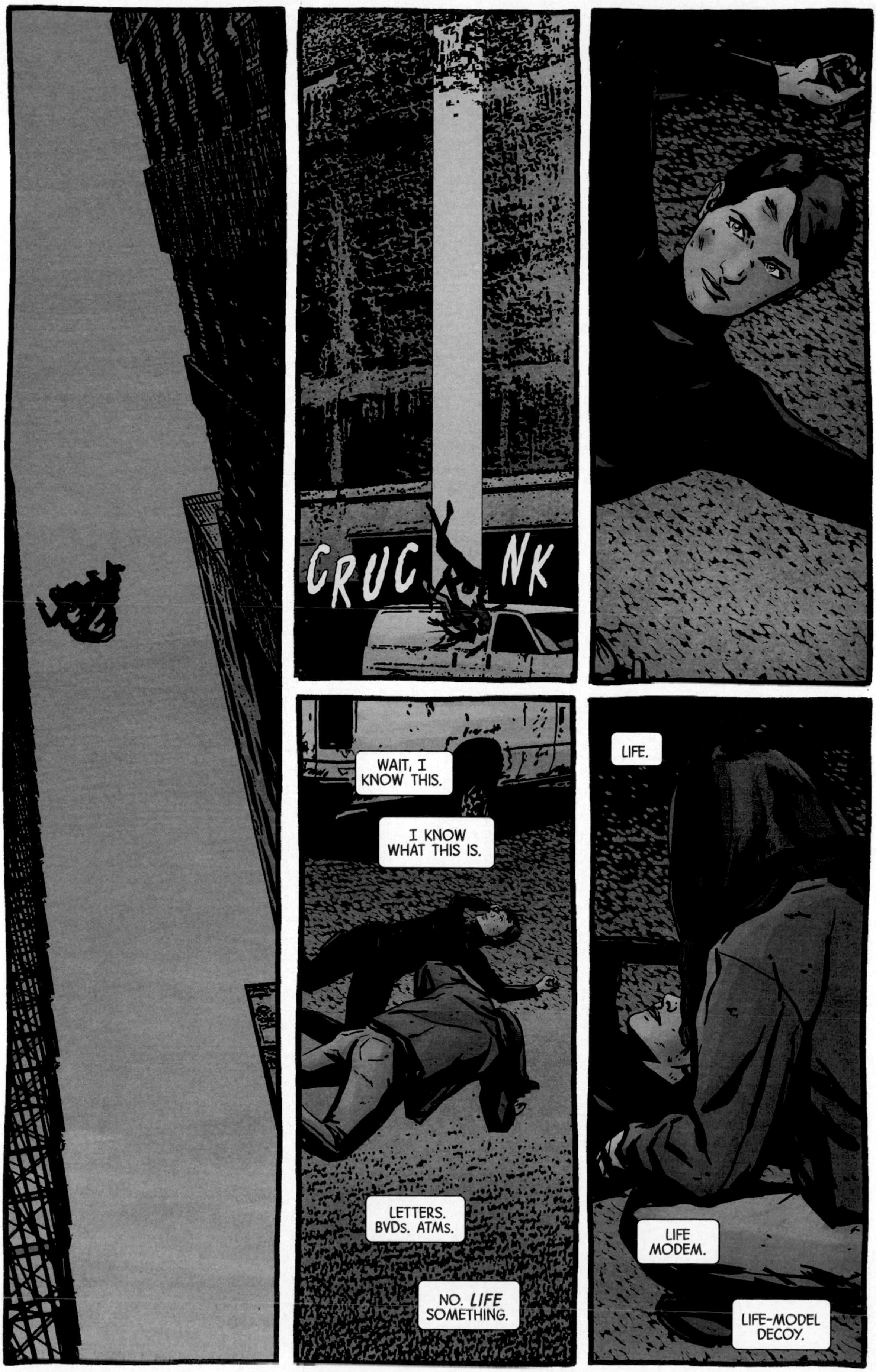
CRUCHNK
WAIT, I KNOW THIS.
I KNOW WHAT THIS IS.
LETTERS. BVDs. ATMs.
NO. *LIFE* SOMETHING.
LIFE.
LIFE MODEM.
LIFE-MODEL DECOY.

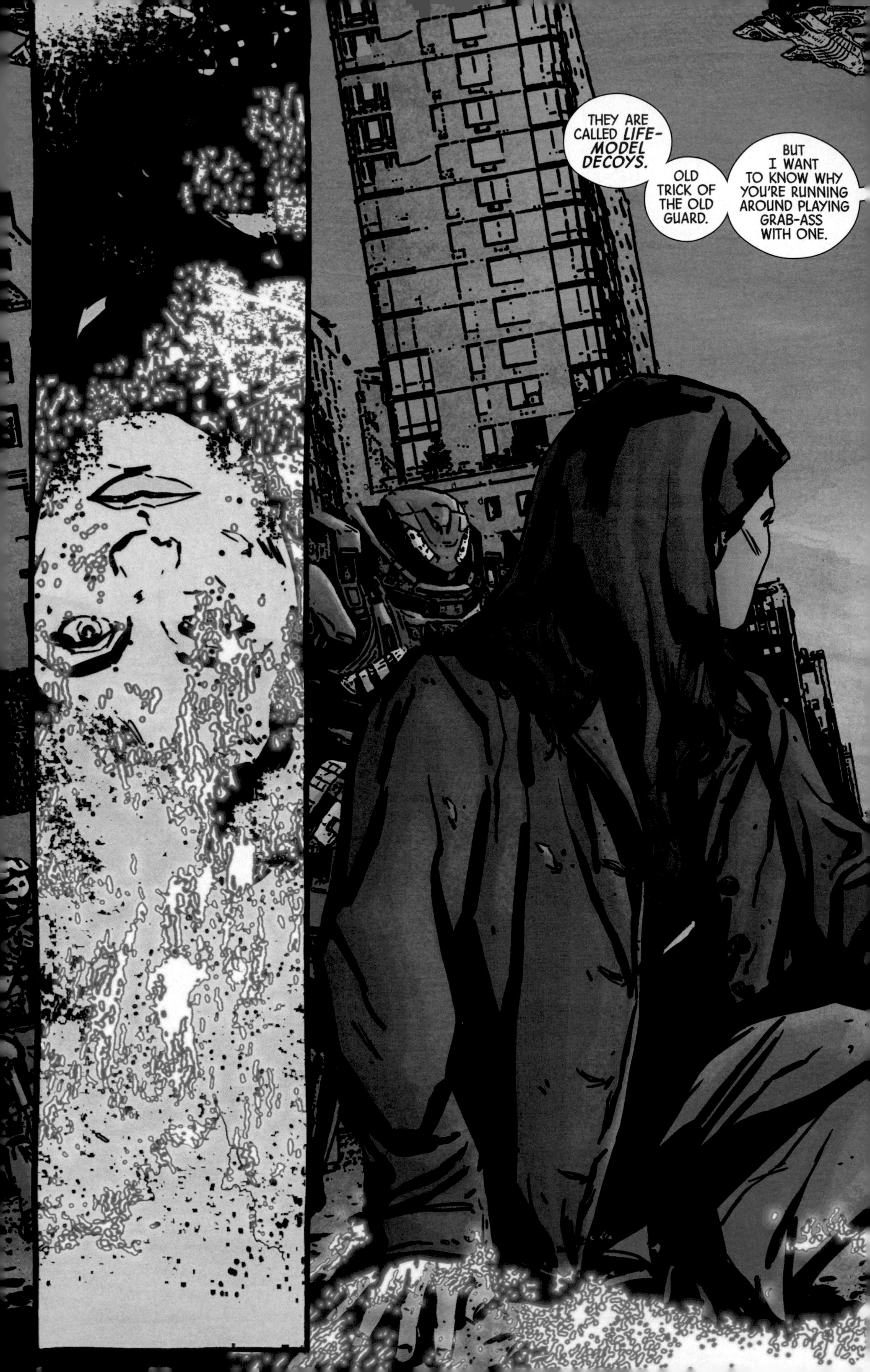
THEY ARE CALLED LIFE-MODEL DECOYS.
OLD TRICK OF THE OLD GUARD.
BUT I WANT TO KNOW WHY YOU'RE RUNNING AROUND PLAYING GRAB-ASS WITH ONE.

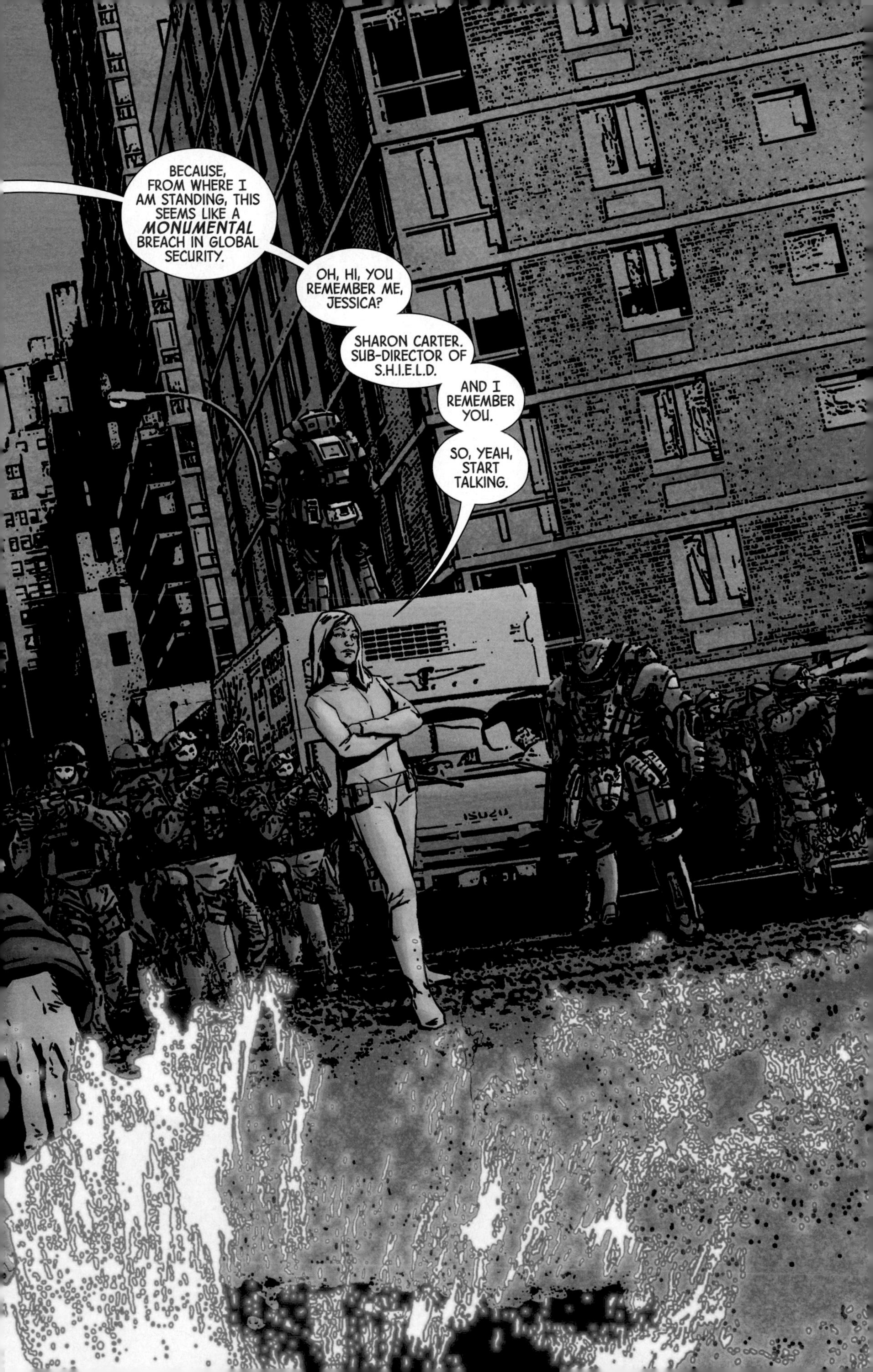
BECAUSE, FROM WHERE I AM STANDING, THIS SEEMS LIKE A *MONUMENTAL* BREACH IN GLOBAL SECURITY.
OH, HI, YOU REMEMBER ME, JESSICA?
SHARON CARTER. SUB-DIRECTOR OF S.H.I.E.L.D.
AND I REMEMBER YOU.
SO, YEAH, START TALKING.
ISUZU

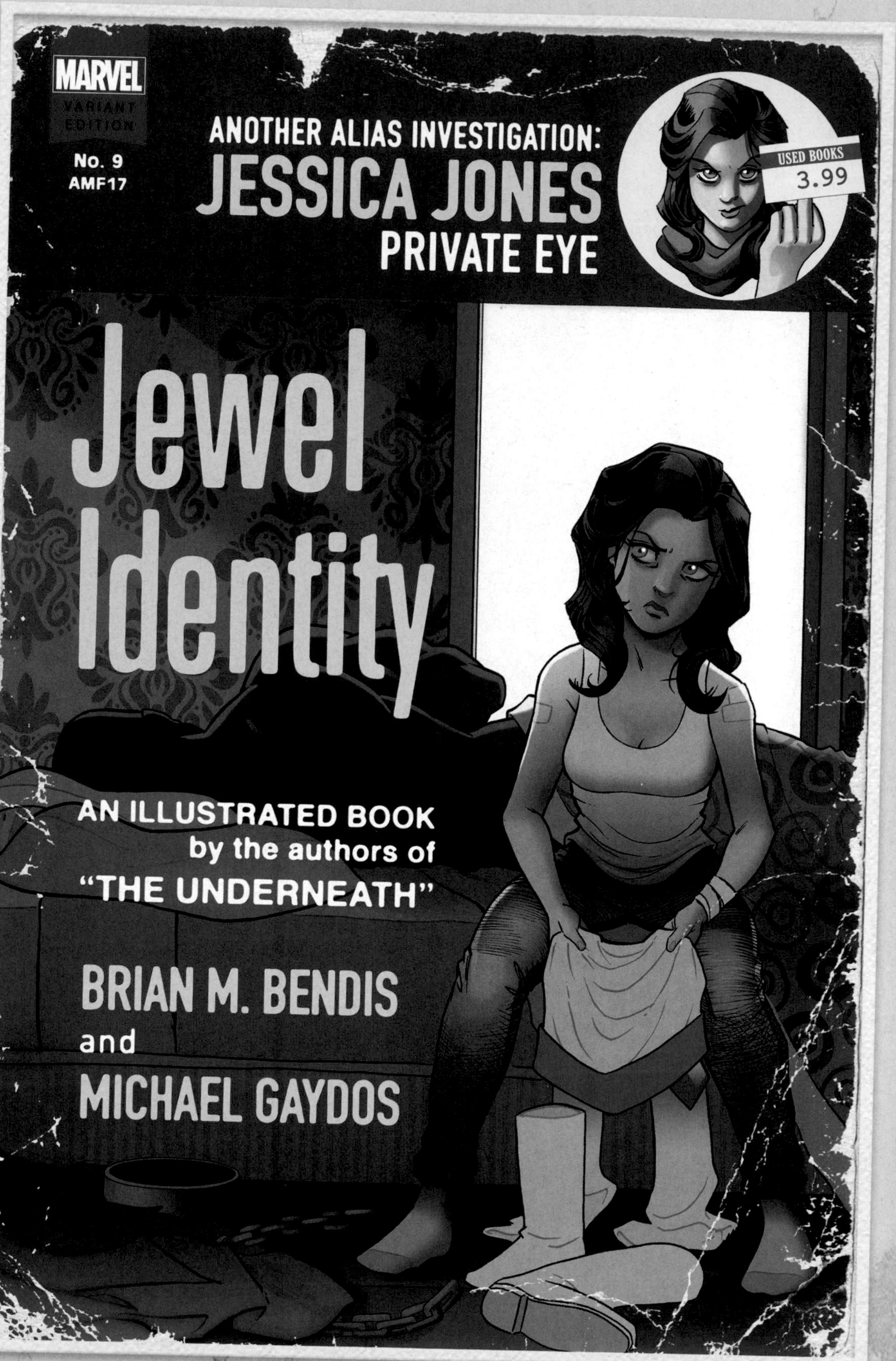
MARVEL
VARIANT EDITION
No. 9
AMF17
ANOTHER ALIAS INVESTIGATION:
JESSICA JONES
PRIVATE EYE
USED BOOKS
3.99
Jewel Identity
AN ILLUSTRATED BOOK
by the authors of
"THE UNDERNEATH"
BRIAN M. BENDIS
and
MICHAEL GAYDOS

#9 variant by **Tony Fleecs**

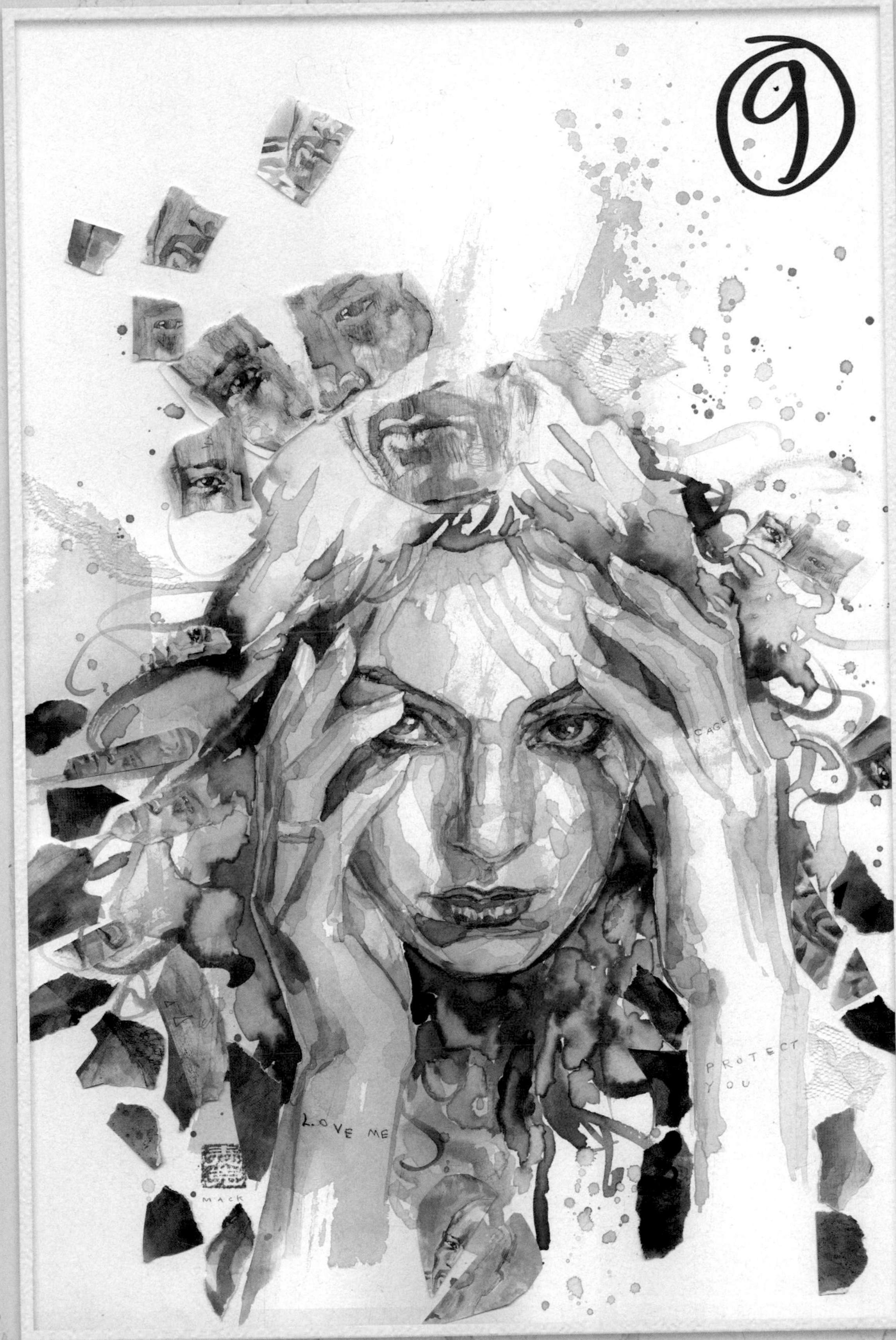
9
CAGE
PROTECT YOU
LOVE ME
MACK

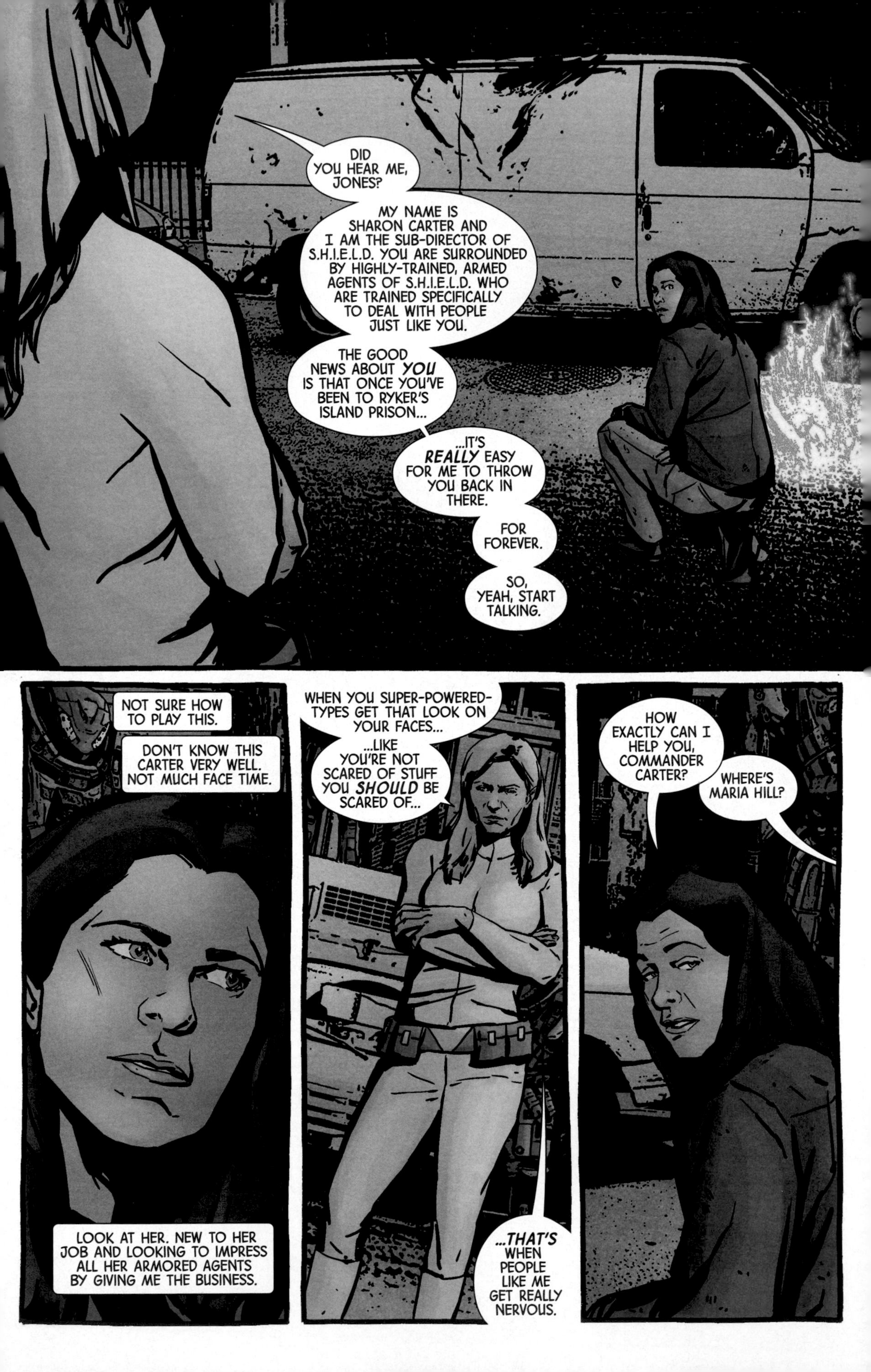
DID YOU HEAR ME, JONES?
MY NAME IS SHARON CARTER AND I AM THE SUB-DIRECTOR OF S.H.I.E.L.D. YOU ARE SURROUNDED BY HIGHLY-TRAINED, ARMED AGENTS OF S.H.I.E.L.D. WHO ARE TRAINED SPECIFICALLY TO DEAL WITH PEOPLE JUST LIKE YOU.
THE GOOD NEWS ABOUT *YOU* IS THAT ONCE YOU'VE BEEN TO RYKER'S ISLAND PRISON...
...IT'S *REALLY* EASY FOR ME TO THROW YOU BACK IN THERE.
FOR FOREVER.
SO, YEAH, START TALKING.
NOT SURE HOW TO PLAY THIS.
DON'T KNOW THIS CARTER VERY WELL. NOT MUCH FACE TIME.
LOOK AT HER. NEW TO HER JOB AND LOOKING TO IMPRESS ALL HER ARMORED AGENTS BY GIVING ME THE BUSINESS.
WHEN YOU SUPER-POWERED-TYPES GET THAT LOOK ON YOUR FACES...
...LIKE YOU'RE NOT SCARED OF STUFF YOU *SHOULD* BE SCARED OF...
...THAT'S WHEN PEOPLE LIKE ME GET REALLY NERVOUS.
HOW EXACTLY CAN I HELP YOU, COMMANDER CARTER?
WHERE'S MARIA HILL?

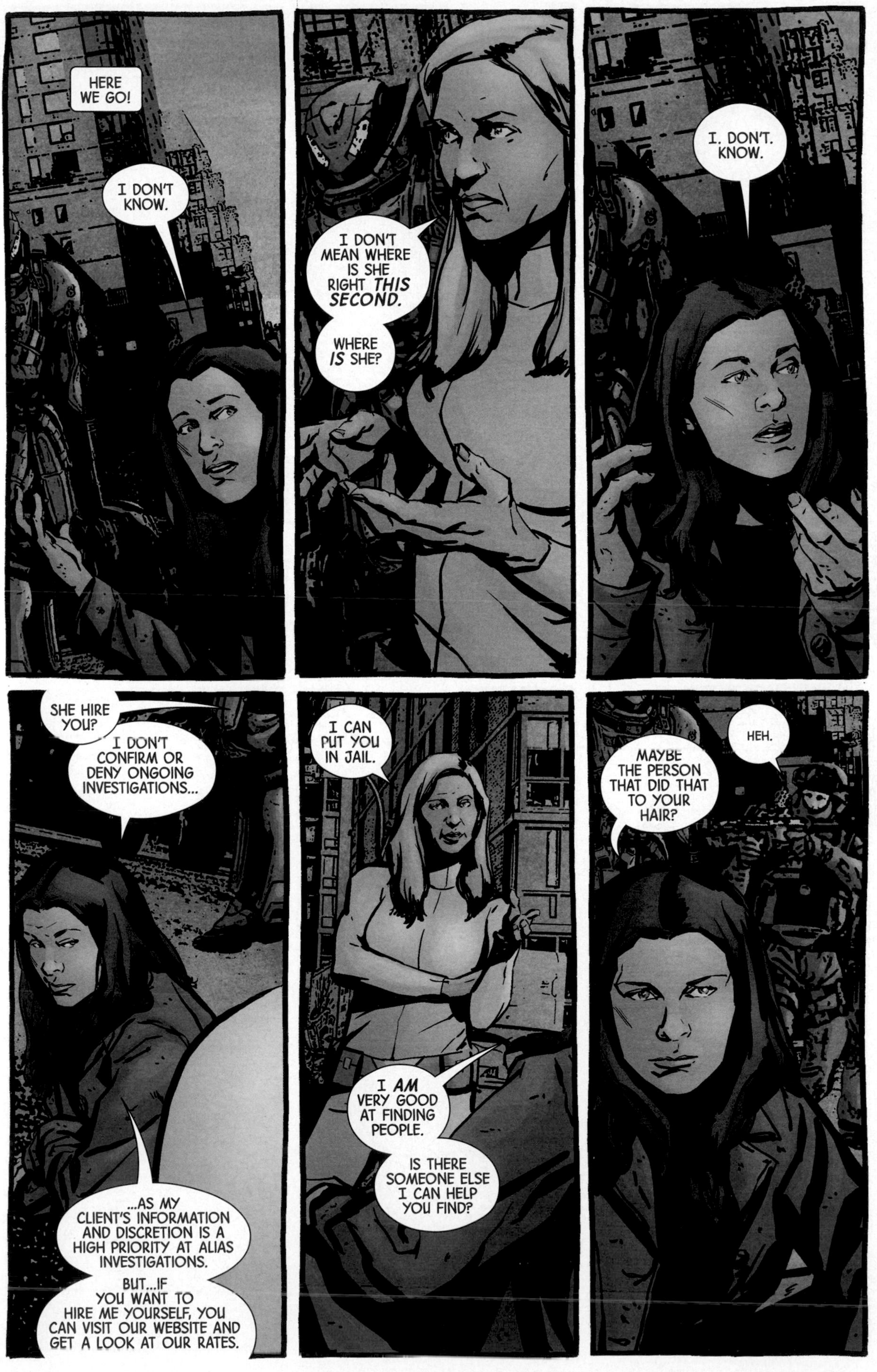
HERE WE GO!
I DON'T KNOW.
I DON'T MEAN WHERE IS SHE RIGHT *THIS SECOND.*
WHERE *IS* SHE?
I. DON'T. KNOW.
SHE HIRE YOU?
I DON'T CONFIRM OR DENY ONGOING INVESTIGATIONS...
...AS MY CLIENT'S INFORMATION AND DISCRETION IS A HIGH PRIORITY AT ALIAS INVESTIGATIONS.
BUT...IF YOU WANT TO HIRE ME YOURSELF, YOU CAN VISIT OUR WEBSITE AND GET A LOOK AT OUR RATES.
I CAN PUT YOU IN JAIL.
I *AM* VERY GOOD AT FINDING PEOPLE.
IS THERE SOMEONE ELSE I CAN HELP YOU FIND?
MAYBE THE PERSON THAT DID THAT TO YOUR HAIR?
HEH.

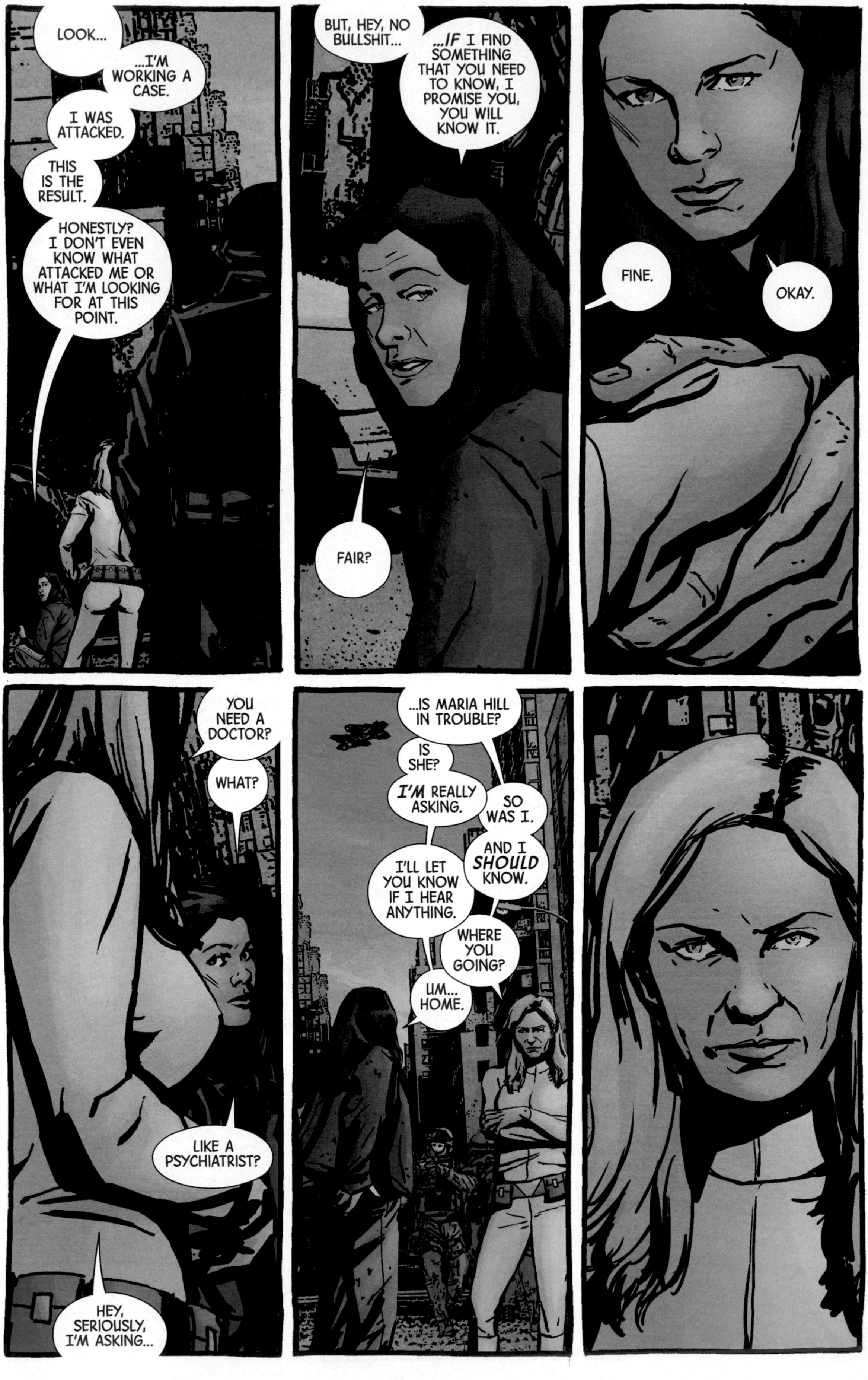

LOOK...
...I'M WORKING A CASE.
I WAS ATTACKED.
THIS IS THE RESULT.
HONESTLY? I DON'T EVEN KNOW WHAT ATTACKED ME OR WHAT I'M LOOKING FOR AT THIS POINT.
BUT, HEY, NO BULLSHIT...
...IF I FIND SOMETHING THAT YOU NEED TO KNOW, I PROMISE YOU, YOU WILL KNOW IT.
FAIR?
FINE.
OKAY.
YOU NEED A DOCTOR?
WHAT?
LIKE A PSYCHIATRIST?
HEY, SERIOUSLY, I'M ASKING...
...IS MARIA HILL IN TROUBLE?
IS SHE?
I'M REALLY ASKING.
SO WAS I.
AND I SHOULD KNOW.
I'LL LET YOU KNOW IF I HEAR ANYTHING.
WHERE YOU GOING?
UM... HOME.

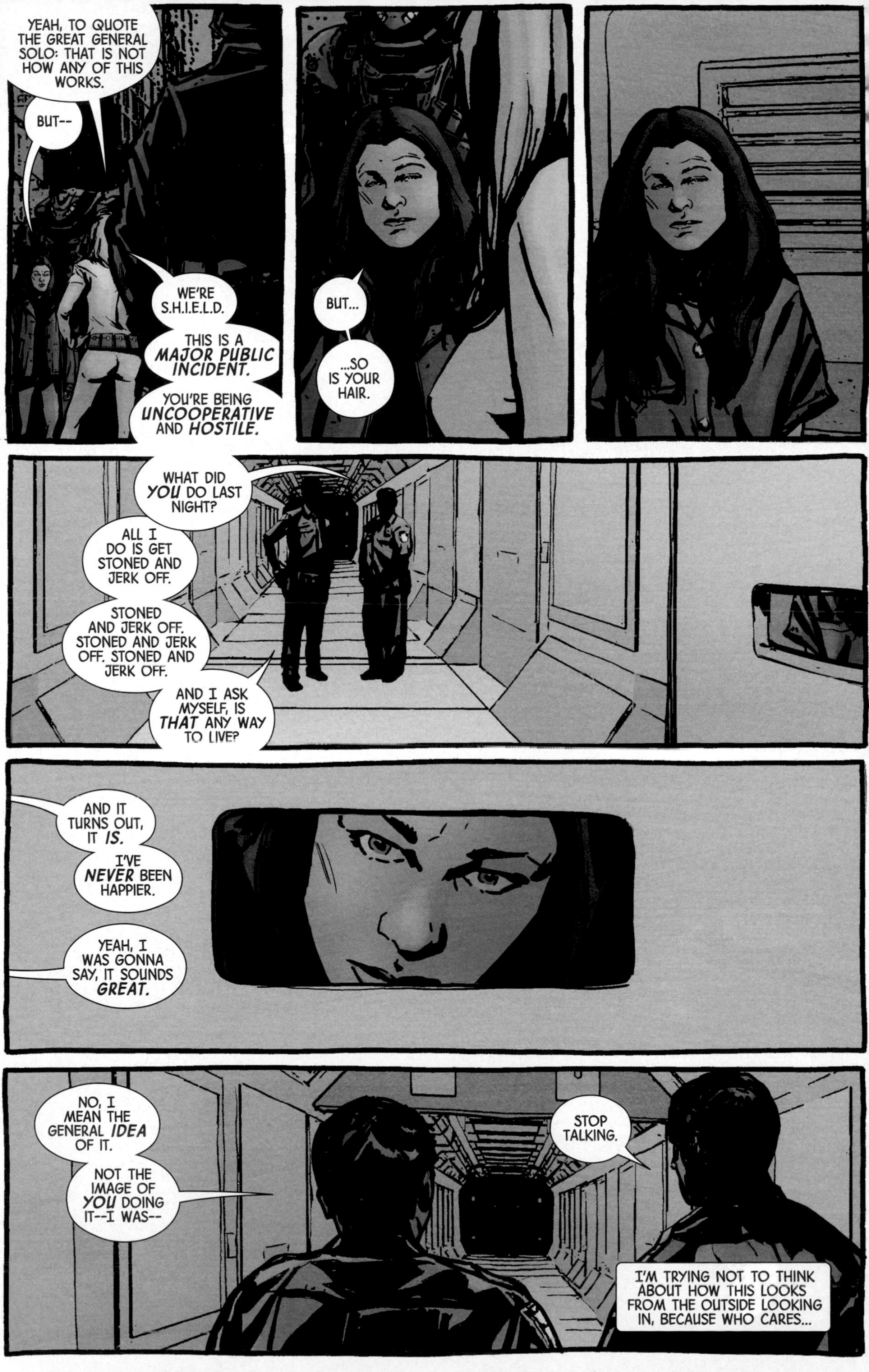
YEAH, TO QUOTE THE GREAT GENERAL SOLO: THAT IS NOT HOW ANY OF THIS WORKS.
BUT--
WE'RE S.H.I.E.L.D.
THIS IS A MAJOR PUBLIC INCIDENT.
YOU'RE BEING UNCOOPERATIVE AND HOSTILE.
BUT...
...SO IS YOUR HAIR.
WHAT DID YOU DO LAST NIGHT?
ALL I DO IS GET STONED AND JERK OFF.
STONED AND JERK OFF. STONED AND JERK OFF. STONED AND JERK OFF.
AND I ASK MYSELF, IS THAT ANY WAY TO LIVE?
AND IT TURNS OUT, IT IS.
I'VE NEVER BEEN HAPPIER.
YEAH, I WAS GONNA SAY, IT SOUNDS GREAT.
NO, I MEAN THE GENERAL IDEA OF IT.
NOT THE IMAGE OF YOU DOING IT--I WAS--
STOP TALKING.
I'M TRYING NOT TO THINK ABOUT HOW THIS LOOKS FROM THE OUTSIDE LOOKING IN, BECAUSE WHO CARES...

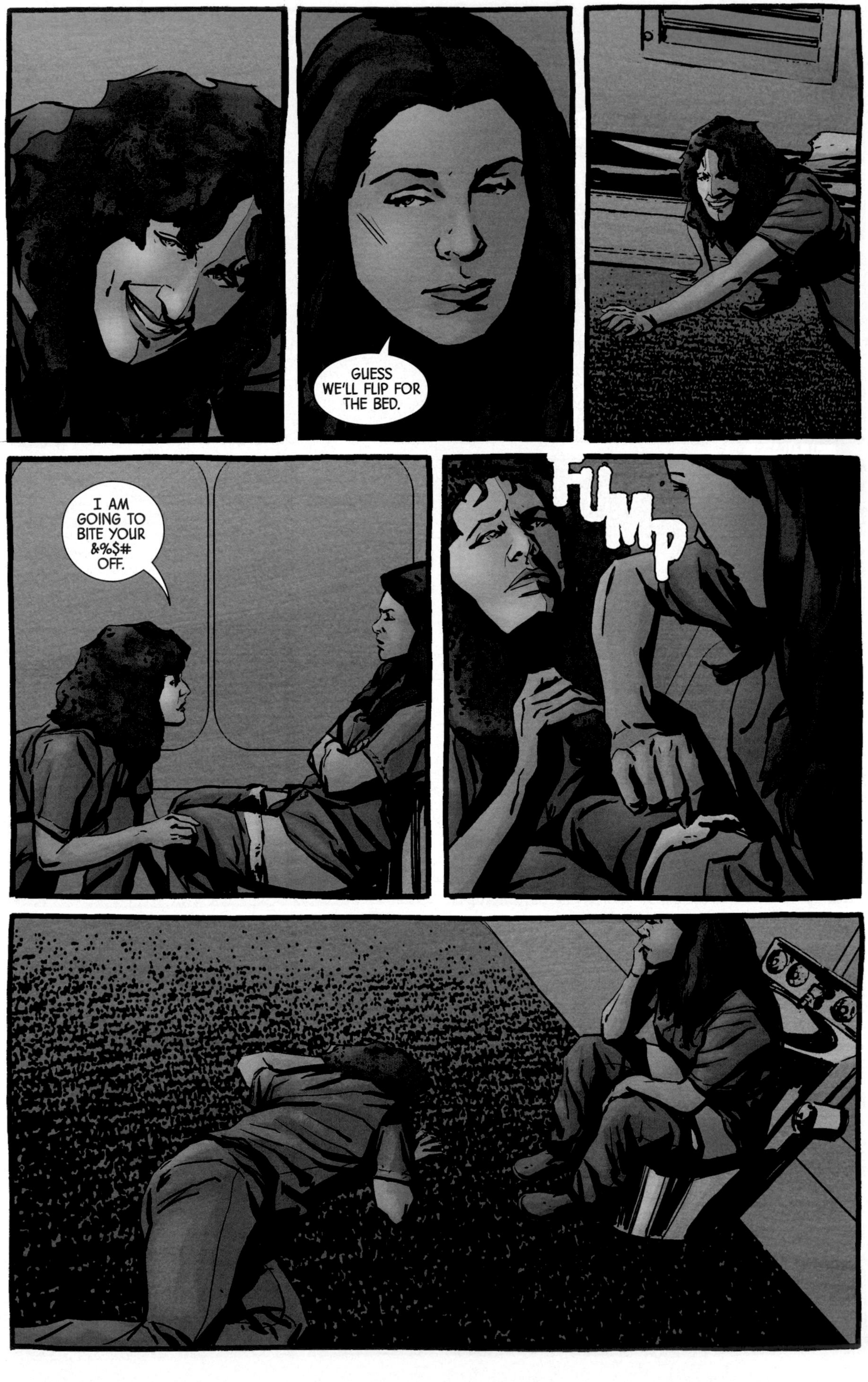
GUESS WE'LL FLIP FOR THE BED.
I AM GOING TO BITE YOUR &%$# OFF.
FUMP

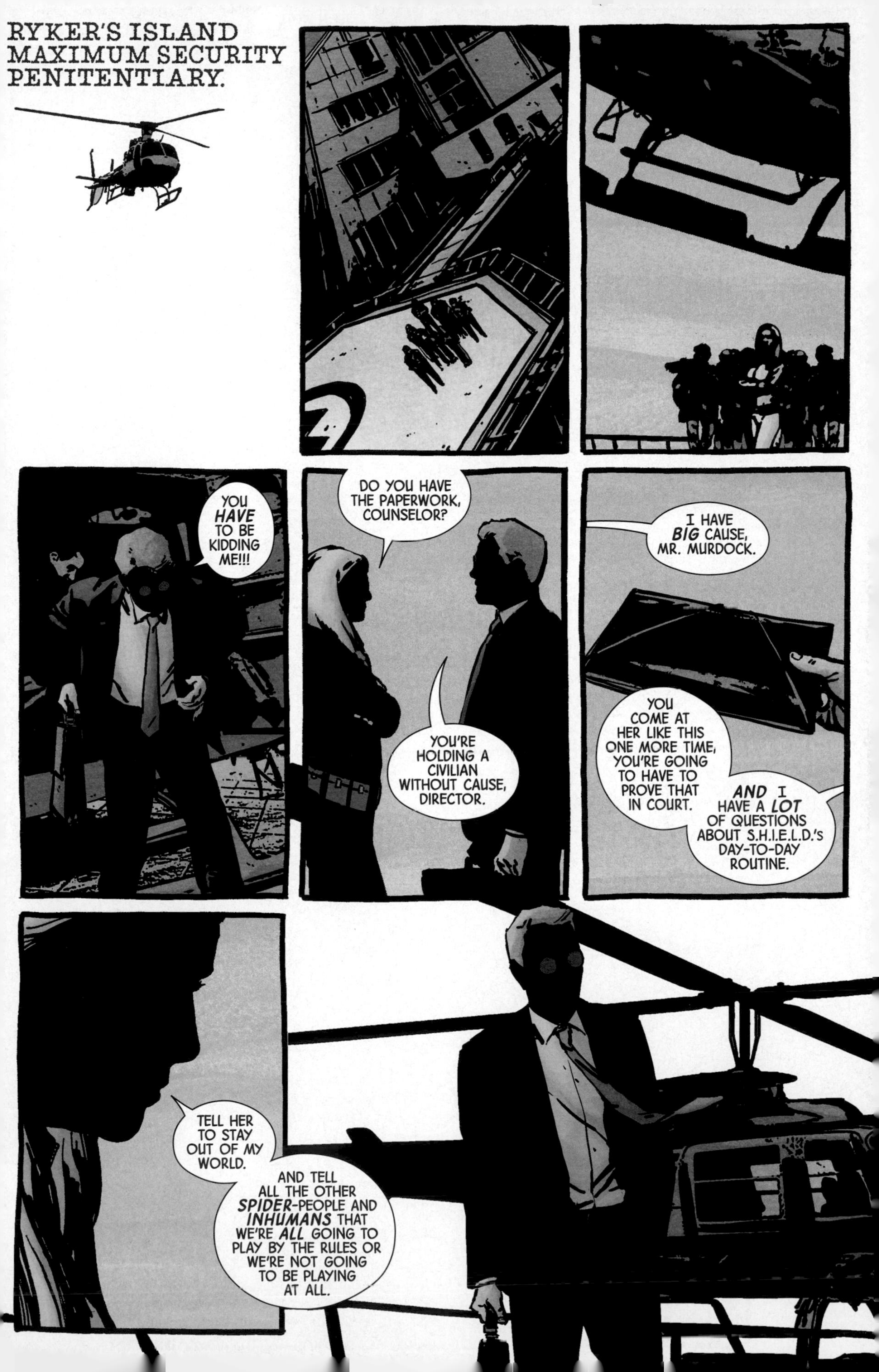

RYKER'S ISLAND MAXIMUM SECURITY PENITENTIARY.
YOU HAVE TO BE KIDDING ME!!!
DO YOU HAVE THE PAPERWORK, COUNSELOR?
YOU'RE HOLDING A CIVILIAN WITHOUT CAUSE, DIRECTOR.
I HAVE BIG CAUSE, MR. MURDOCK.
YOU COME AT HER LIKE THIS ONE MORE TIME, YOU'RE GOING TO HAVE TO PROVE THAT IN COURT.
AND I HAVE A LOT OF QUESTIONS ABOUT S.H.I.E.L.D.'s DAY-TO-DAY ROUTINE.
TELL HER TO STAY OUT OF MY WORLD.
AND TELL ALL THE OTHER SPIDER-PEOPLE AND INHUMANS THAT WE'RE ALL GOING TO PLAY BY THE RULES OR WE'RE NOT GOING TO BE PLAYING AT ALL.

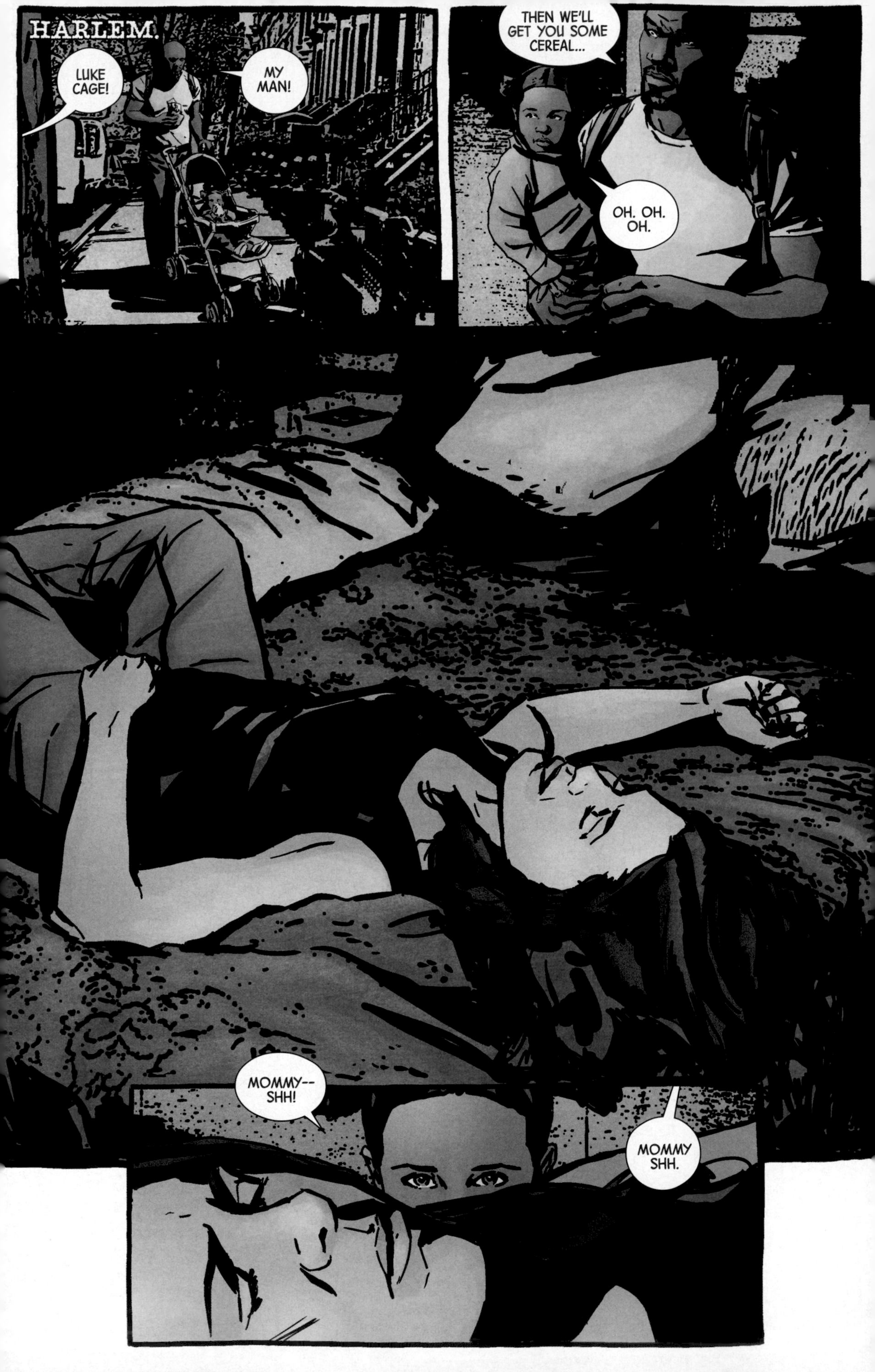
HARLEM.
LUKE CAGE!
MY MAN!
THEN WE'LL GET YOU SOME CEREAL...
OH. OH. OH.
MOMMY-- SHH!
MOMMY SHH.

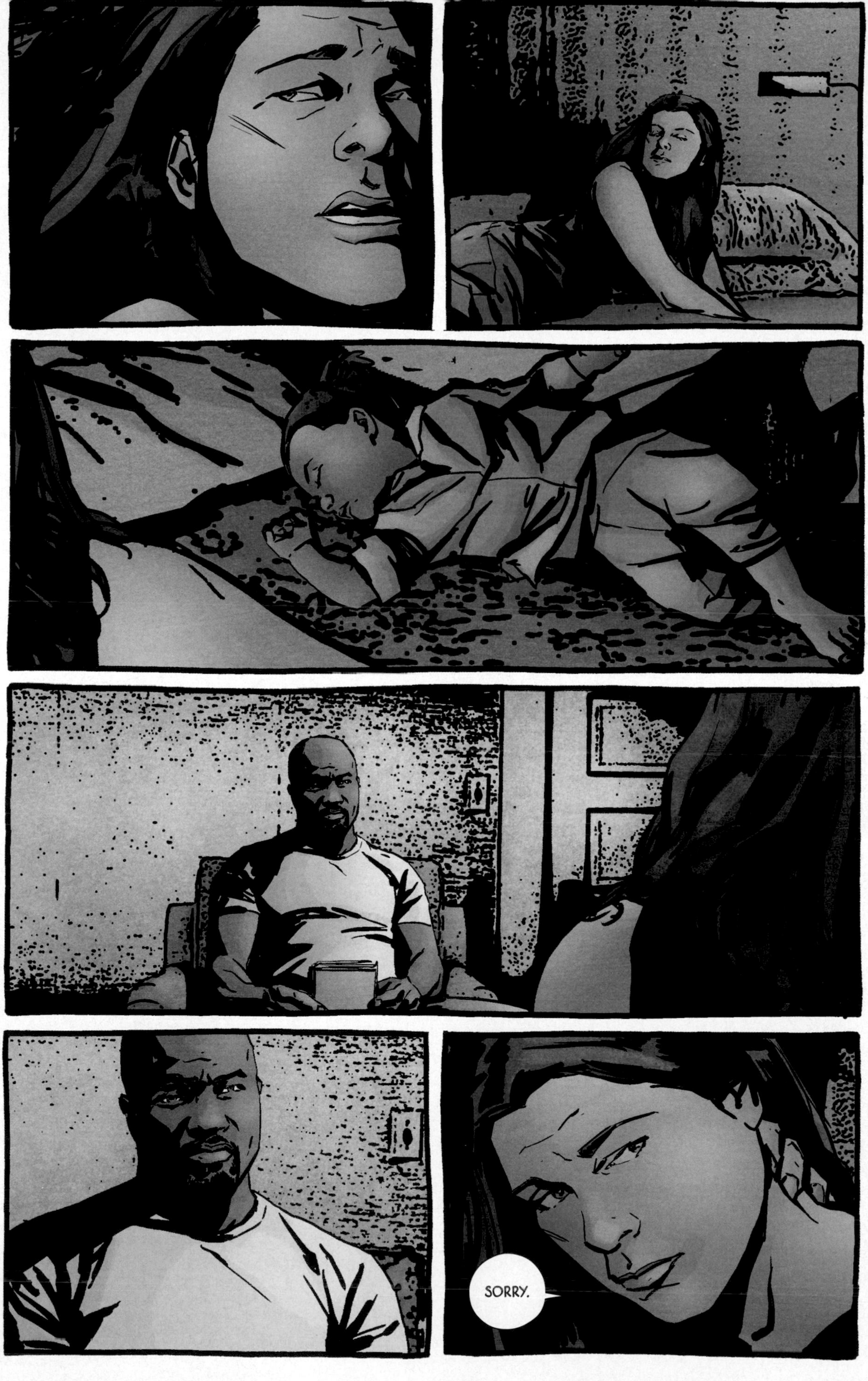
SORRY.

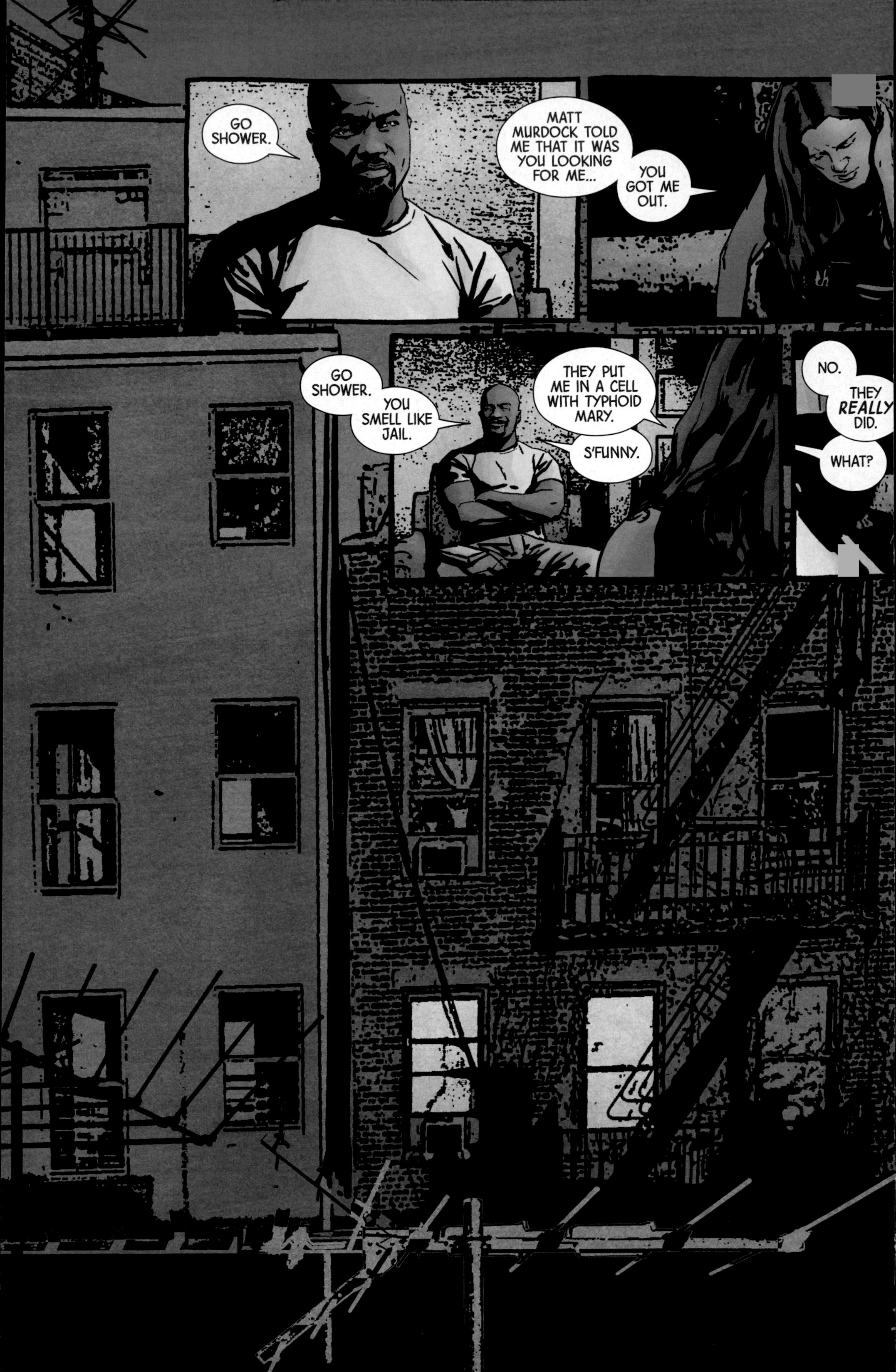
GO SHOWER.
MATT MURDOCK TOLD ME THAT IT WAS YOU LOOKING FOR ME...
YOU GOT ME OUT.
GO SHOWER.
YOU SMELL LIKE JAIL.
THEY PUT ME IN A CELL WITH TYPHOID MARY.
S'FUNNY.
NO.
THEY REALLY DID.
WHAT?

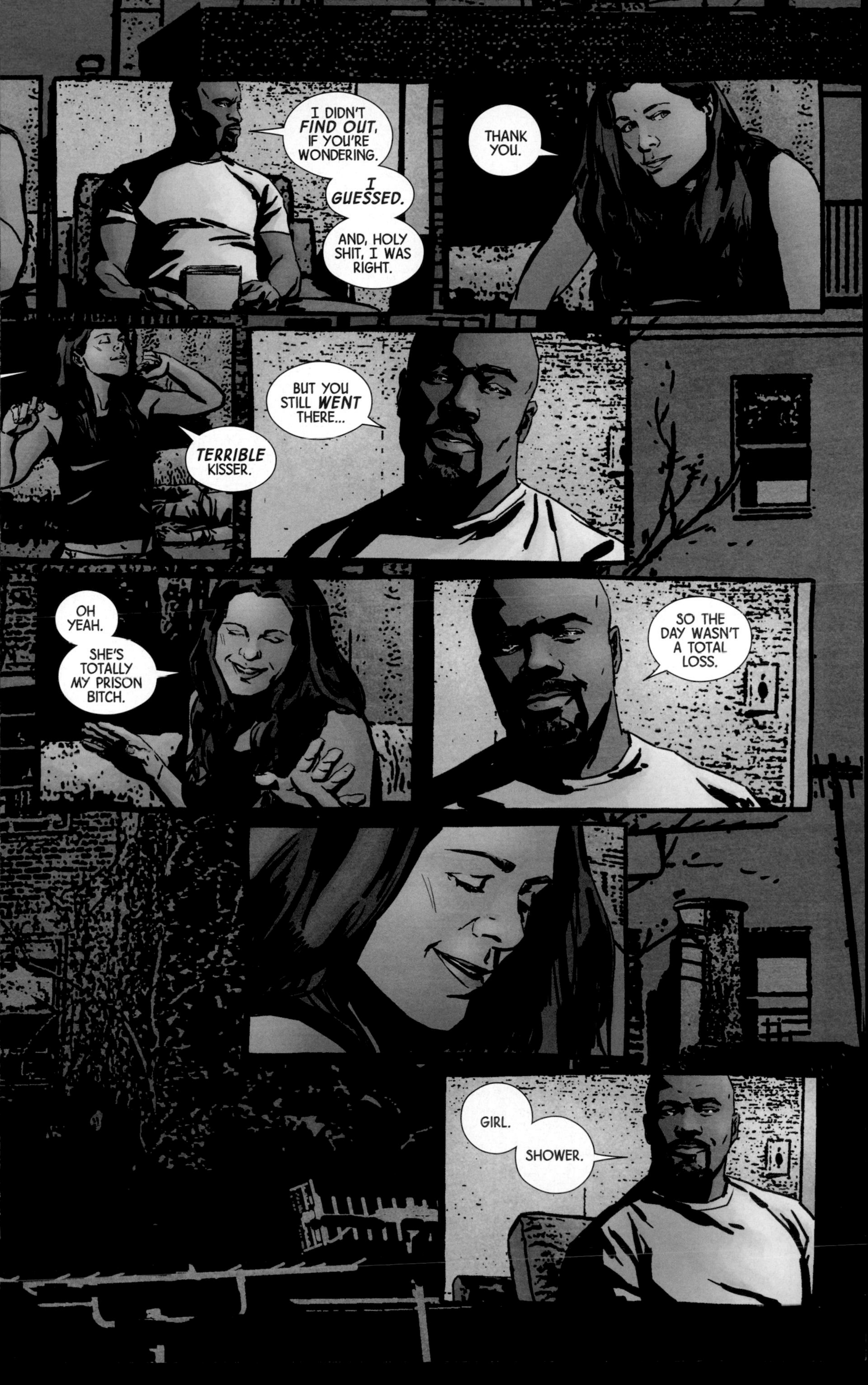
I DIDN'T FIND OUT, IF YOU'RE WONDERING.
I GUESSED.
AND, HOLY SHIT, I WAS RIGHT.
THANK YOU.
TERRIBLE KISSER.
BUT YOU STILL WENT THERE...
OH YEAH.
SHE'S TOTALLY MY PRISON BITCH.
SO THE DAY WASN'T A TOTAL LOSS.
GIRL.
SHOWER.

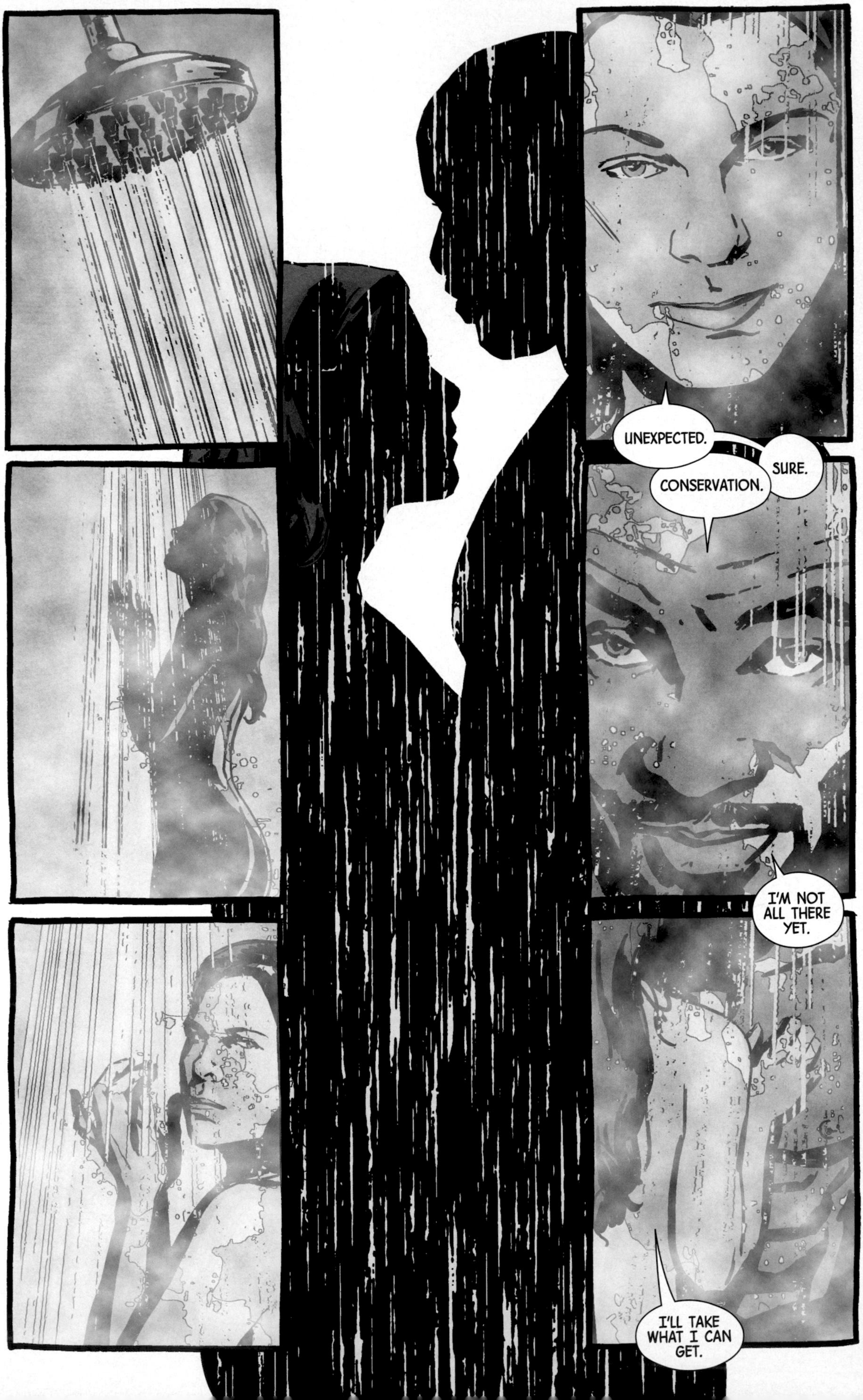
UNEXPECTED.
SURE.
CONSERVATION.
I'M NOT ALL THERE YET.
I'LL TAKE WHAT I CAN GET.

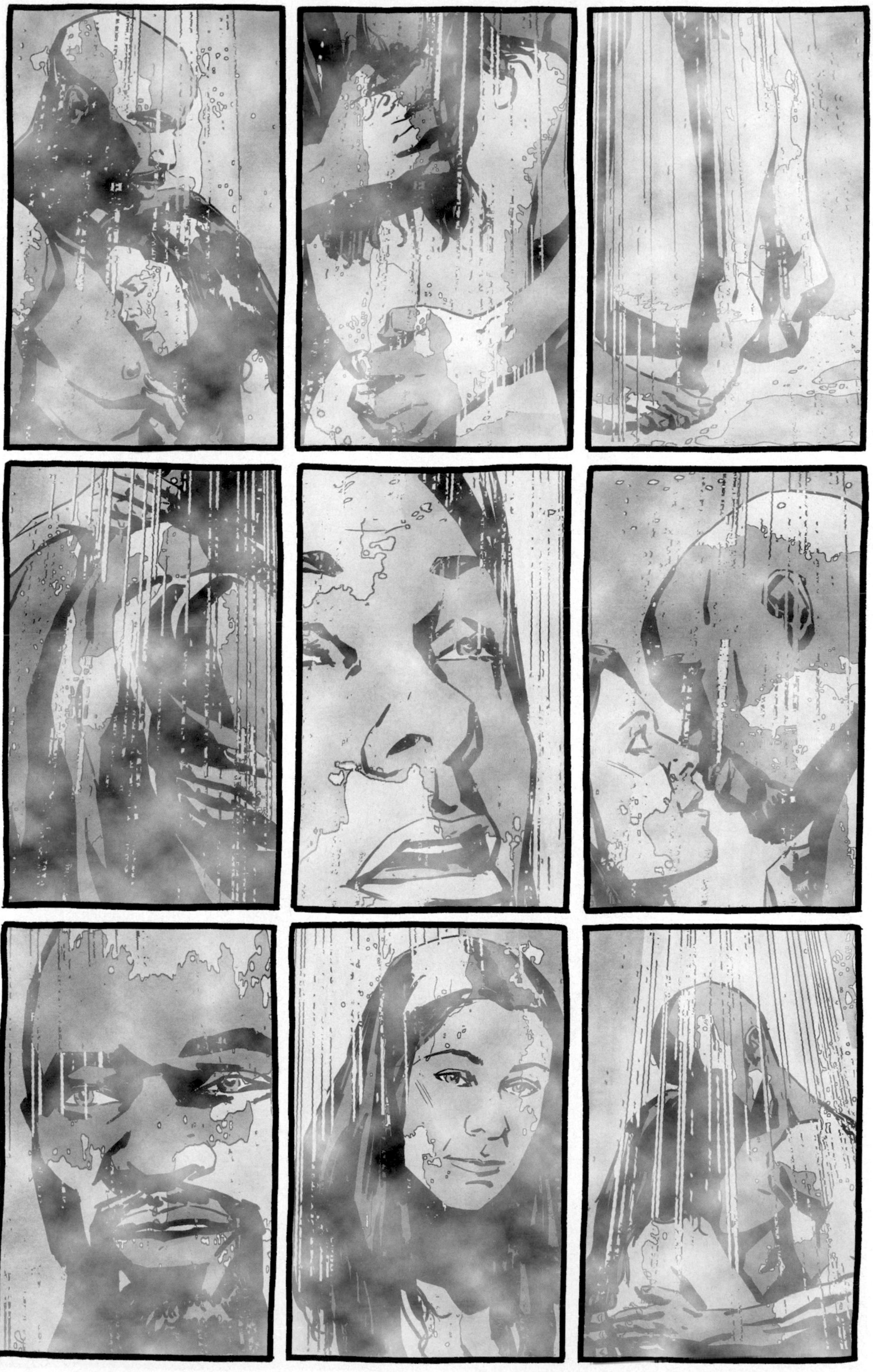

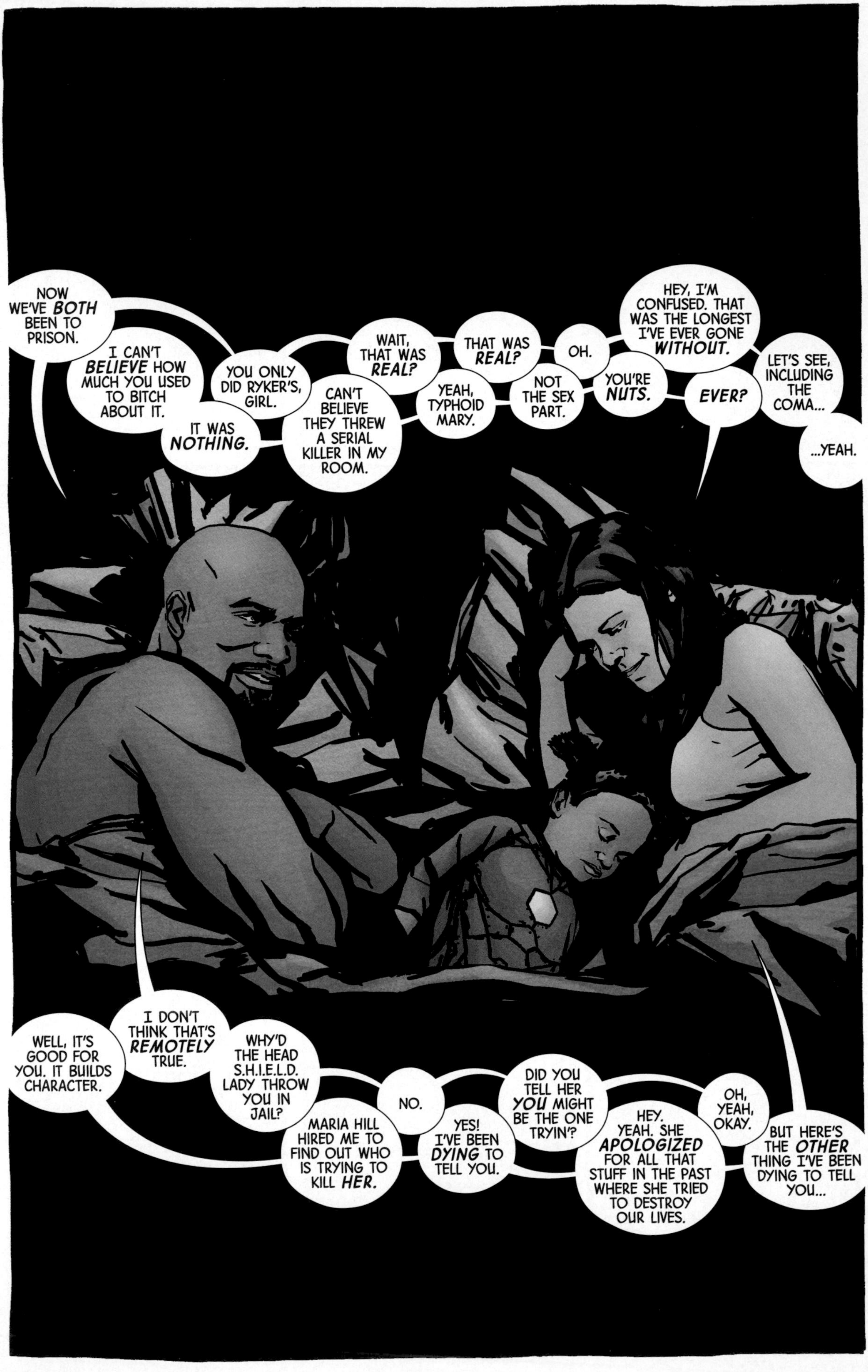
NOW WE'VE **BOTH** BEEN TO PRISON.
I CAN'T **BELIEVE** HOW MUCH YOU USED TO BITCH ABOUT IT.
IT WAS **NOTHING.**
YOU ONLY DID RYKER'S, GIRL.
CAN'T BELIEVE THEY THREW A SERIAL KILLER IN MY ROOM.
WAIT, THAT WAS **REAL?**
YEAH, TYPHOID MARY.
THAT WAS **REAL?**
NOT THE SEX PART.
OH.
YOU'RE **NUTS.**
HEY, I'M CONFUSED. THAT WAS THE LONGEST I'VE EVER GONE **WITHOUT.**
EVER?
LET'S SEE, INCLUDING THE COMA...
...YEAH.
WELL, IT'S GOOD FOR YOU. IT BUILDS CHARACTER.
I DON'T THINK THAT'S **REMOTELY** TRUE.
WHY'D THE HEAD S.H.I.E.L.D. LADY THROW YOU IN JAIL?
MARIA HILL HIRED ME TO FIND OUT WHO IS TRYING TO KILL **HER.**
NO.
YES! I'VE BEEN **DYING** TO TELL YOU.
DID YOU TELL HER **YOU** MIGHT BE THE ONE TRYIN'?
HEY. YEAH. SHE **APOLOGIZED** FOR ALL THAT STUFF IN THE PAST WHERE SHE TRIED TO DESTROY OUR LIVES.
OH, YEAH, OKAY.
BUT HERE'S THE **OTHER** THING I'VE BEEN DYING TO TELL YOU...

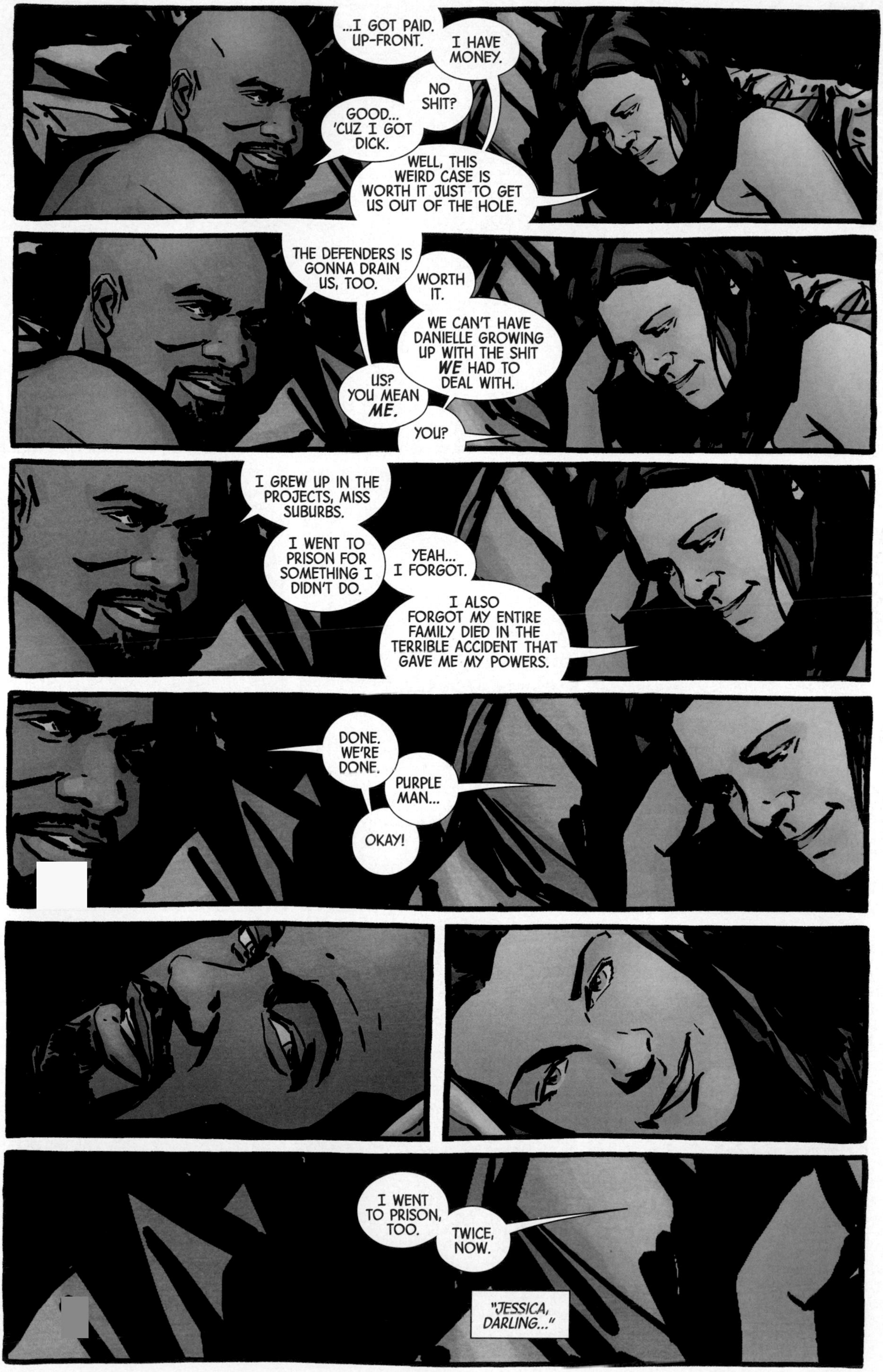
...I GOT PAID. UP-FRONT.
I HAVE MONEY.
NO SHIT?
GOOD... 'CUZ I GOT DICK.
WELL, THIS WEIRD CASE IS WORTH IT JUST TO GET US OUT OF THE HOLE.
THE DEFENDERS IS GONNA DRAIN US, TOO.
WORTH IT.
WE CAN'T HAVE DANIELLE GROWING UP WITH THE SHIT WE HAD TO DEAL WITH.
US? YOU MEAN ME.
YOU?
I GREW UP IN THE PROJECTS, MISS SUBURBS.
I WENT TO PRISON FOR SOMETHING I DIDN'T DO.
YEAH... I FORGOT.
I ALSO FORGOT MY ENTIRE FAMILY DIED IN THE TERRIBLE ACCIDENT THAT GAVE ME MY POWERS.
DONE. WE'RE DONE.
PURPLE MAN...
OKAY!
I WENT TO PRISON, TOO.
TWICE, NOW.
"JESSICA, DARLING..."

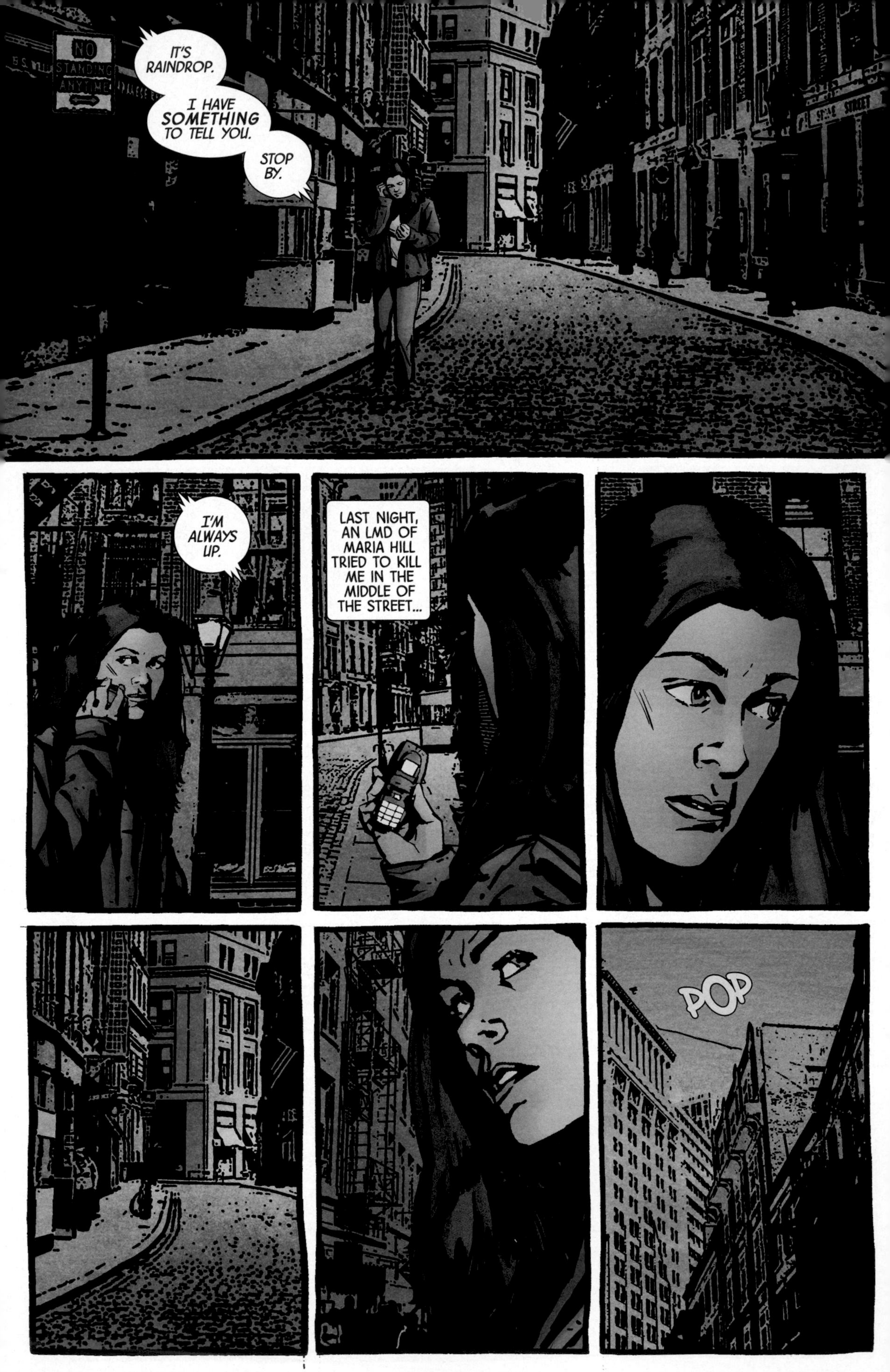
IT'S RAINDROP.
I HAVE SOMETHING TO TELL YOU.
STOP BY.
I'M ALWAYS UP.
LAST NIGHT, AN LMD OF MARIA HILL TRIED TO KILL ME IN THE MIDDLE OF THE STREET...
POP

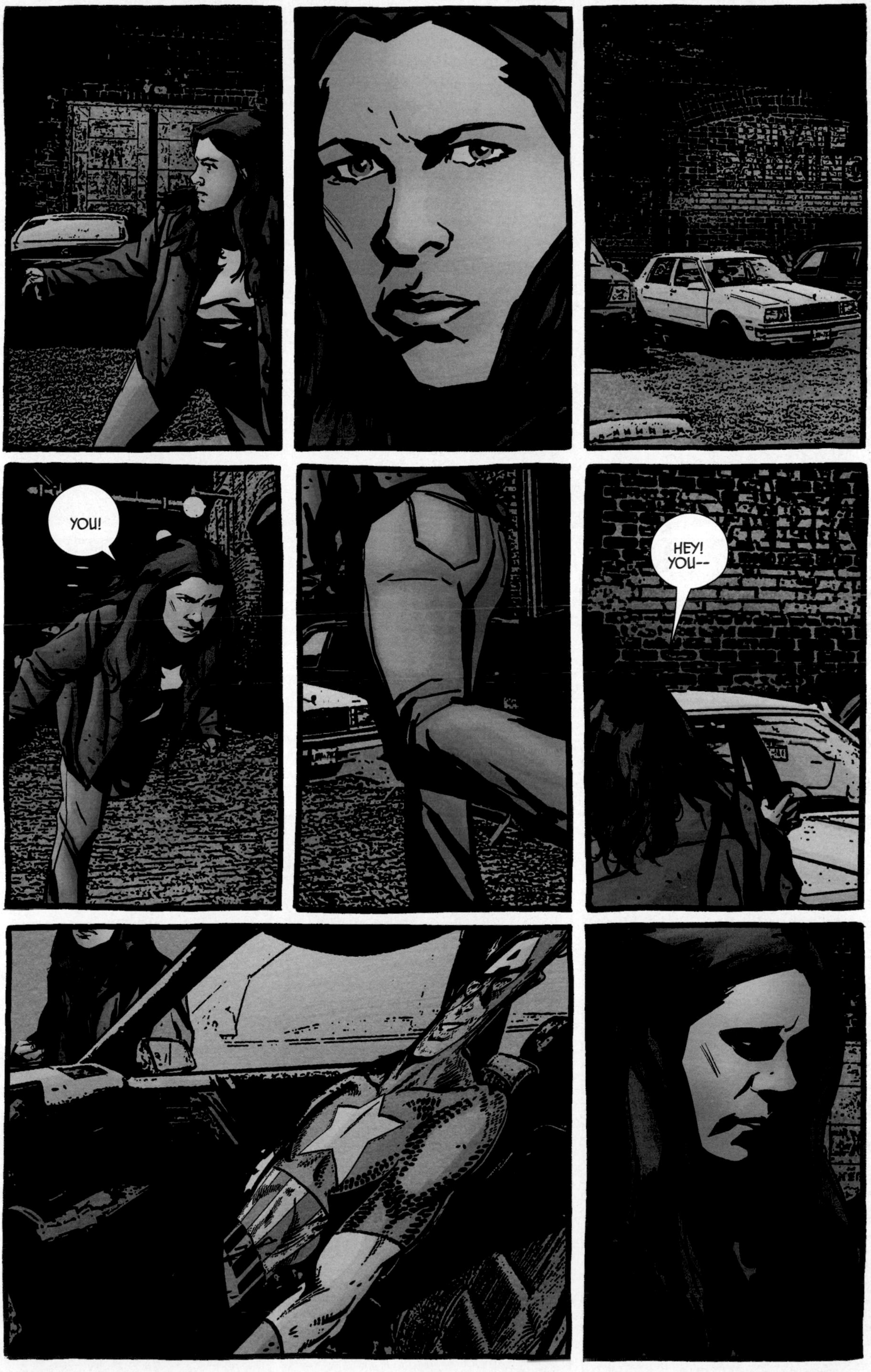
YOU!
HEY! YOU--

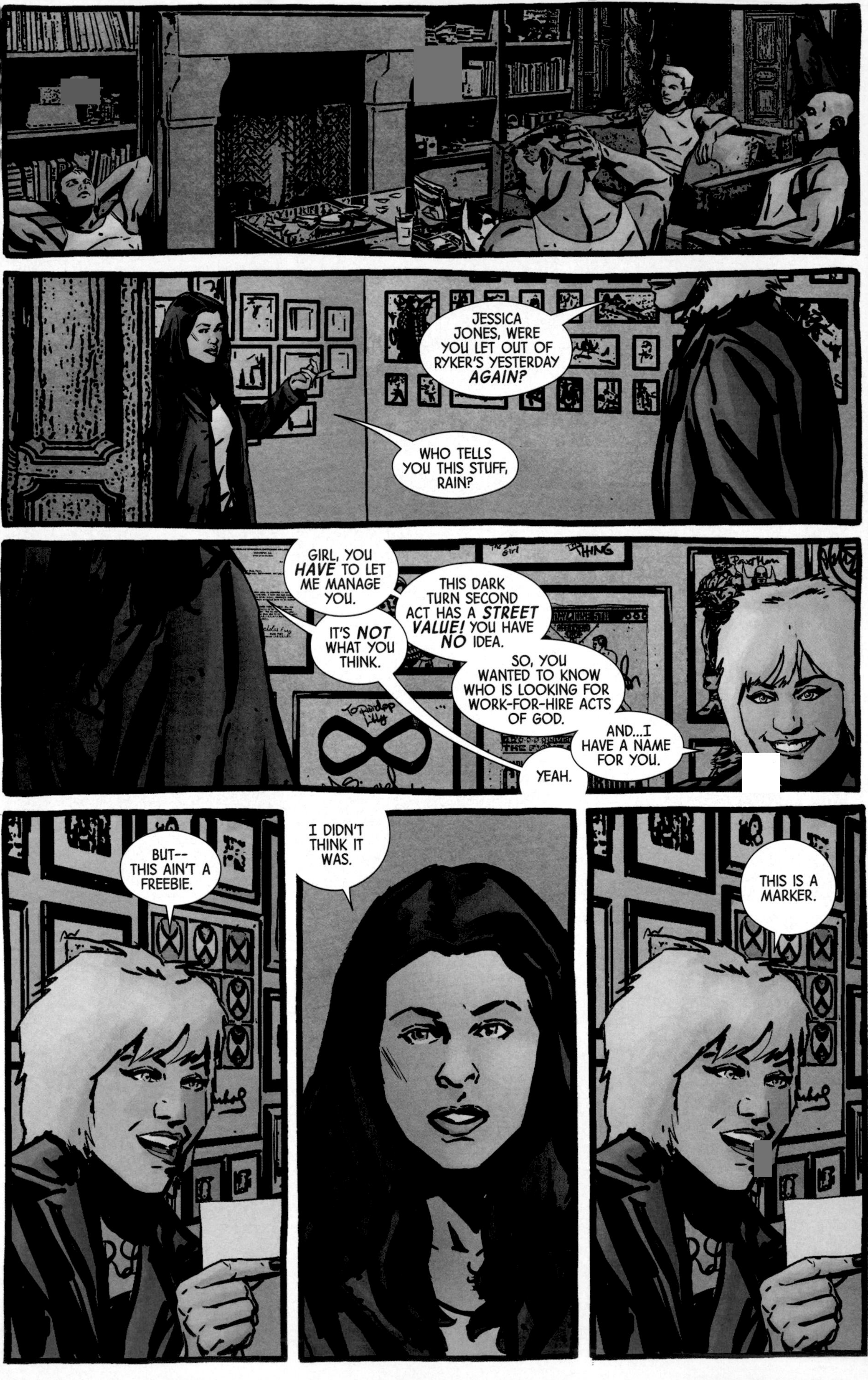
JESSICA JONES, WERE YOU LET OUT OF RYKER'S YESTERDAY AGAIN?
WHO TELLS YOU THIS STUFF, RAIN?
GIRL, YOU HAVE TO LET ME MANAGE YOU.
IT'S NOT WHAT YOU THINK.
THIS DARK TURN SECOND ACT HAS A STREET VALUE! YOU HAVE NO IDEA.
SO, YOU WANTED TO KNOW WHO IS LOOKING FOR WORK-FOR-HIRE ACTS OF GOD.
YEAH.
AND...I HAVE A NAME FOR YOU.
BUT-- THIS AIN'T A FREEBIE.
I DIDN'T THINK IT WAS.
THIS IS A MARKER.

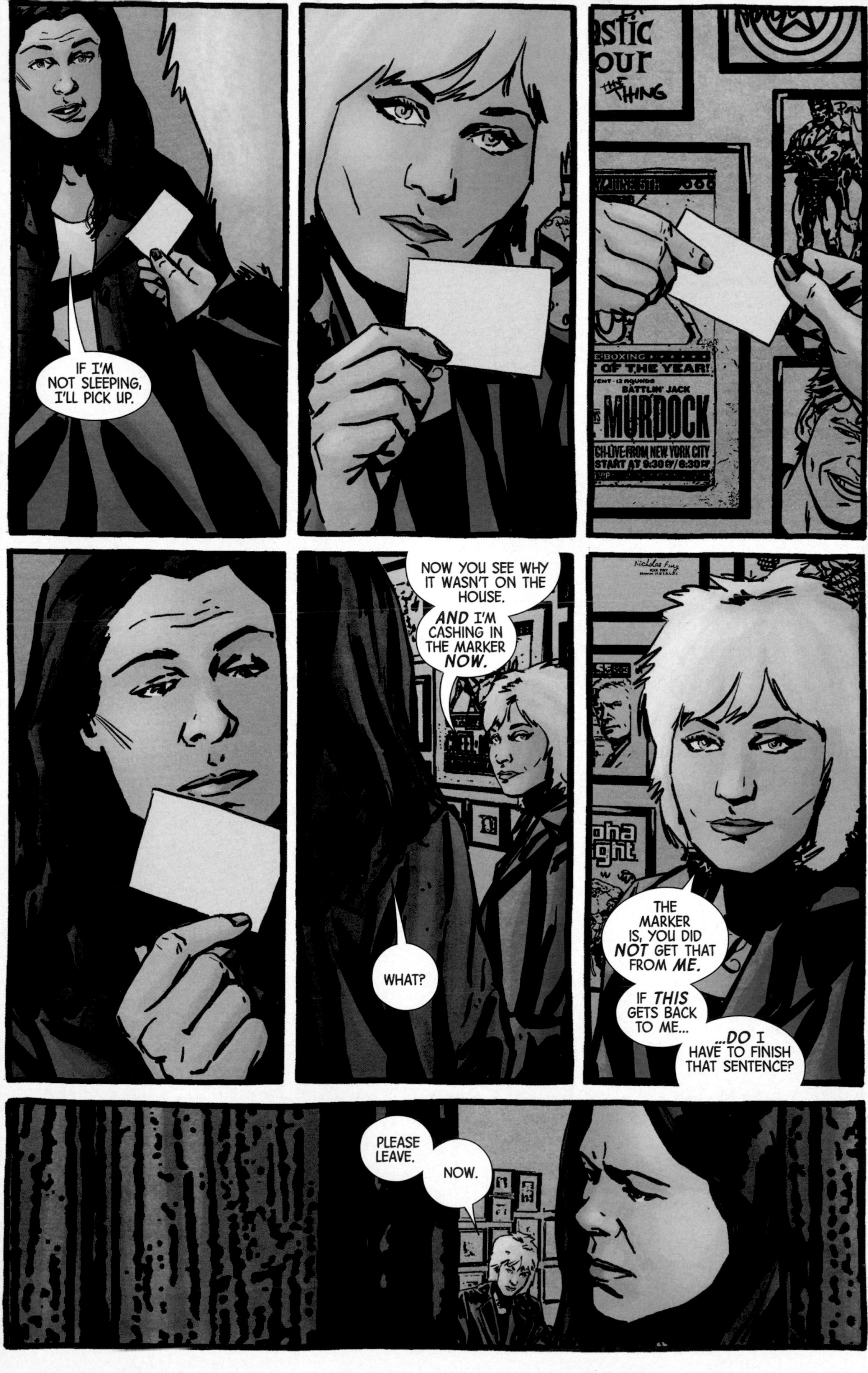
IF I'M NOT SLEEPING, I'LL PICK UP.
BATTLIN' JACK
MURDOCK
LIVE FROM NEW YORK CITY
NOW YOU SEE WHY IT WASN'T ON THE HOUSE.
AND I'M CASHING IN THE MARKER NOW.
WHAT?
THE MARKER IS, YOU DID NOT GET THAT FROM ME.
IF THIS GETS BACK TO ME...
...DO I HAVE TO FINISH THAT SENTENCE?
PLEASE LEAVE.
NOW.

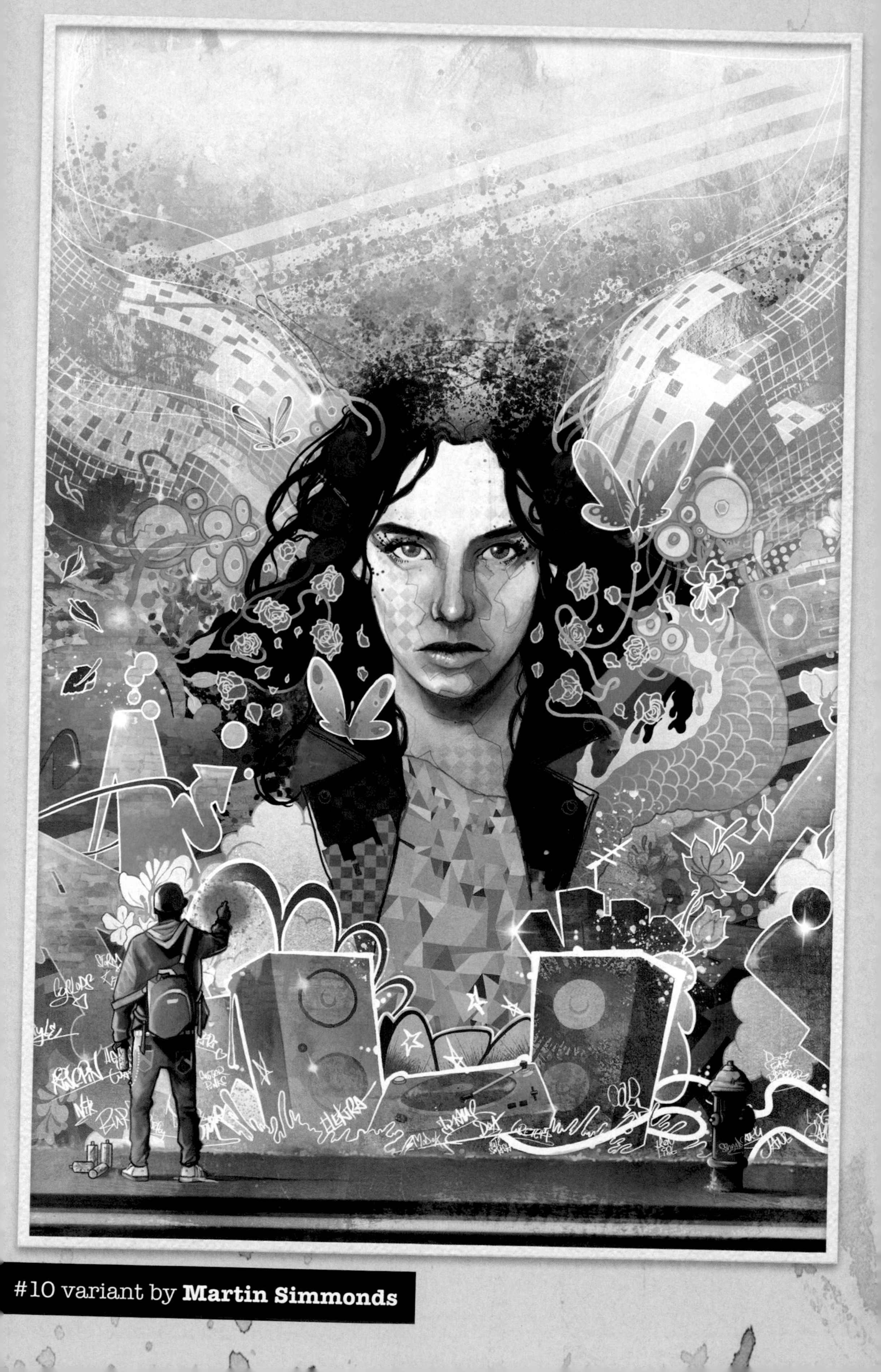

#10 variant by **Martin Simmonds**

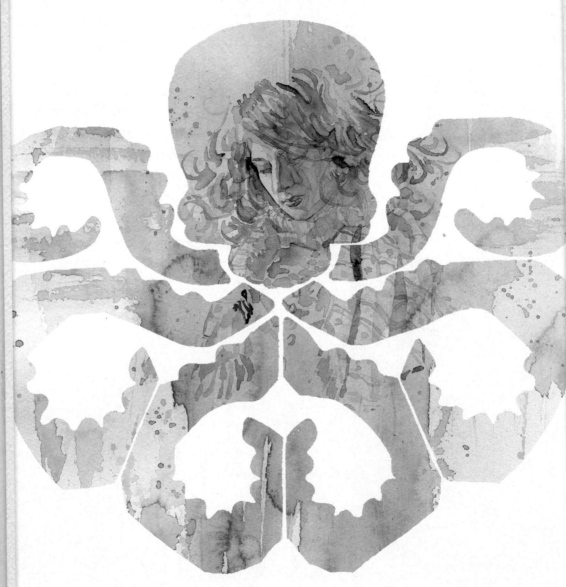

MACK

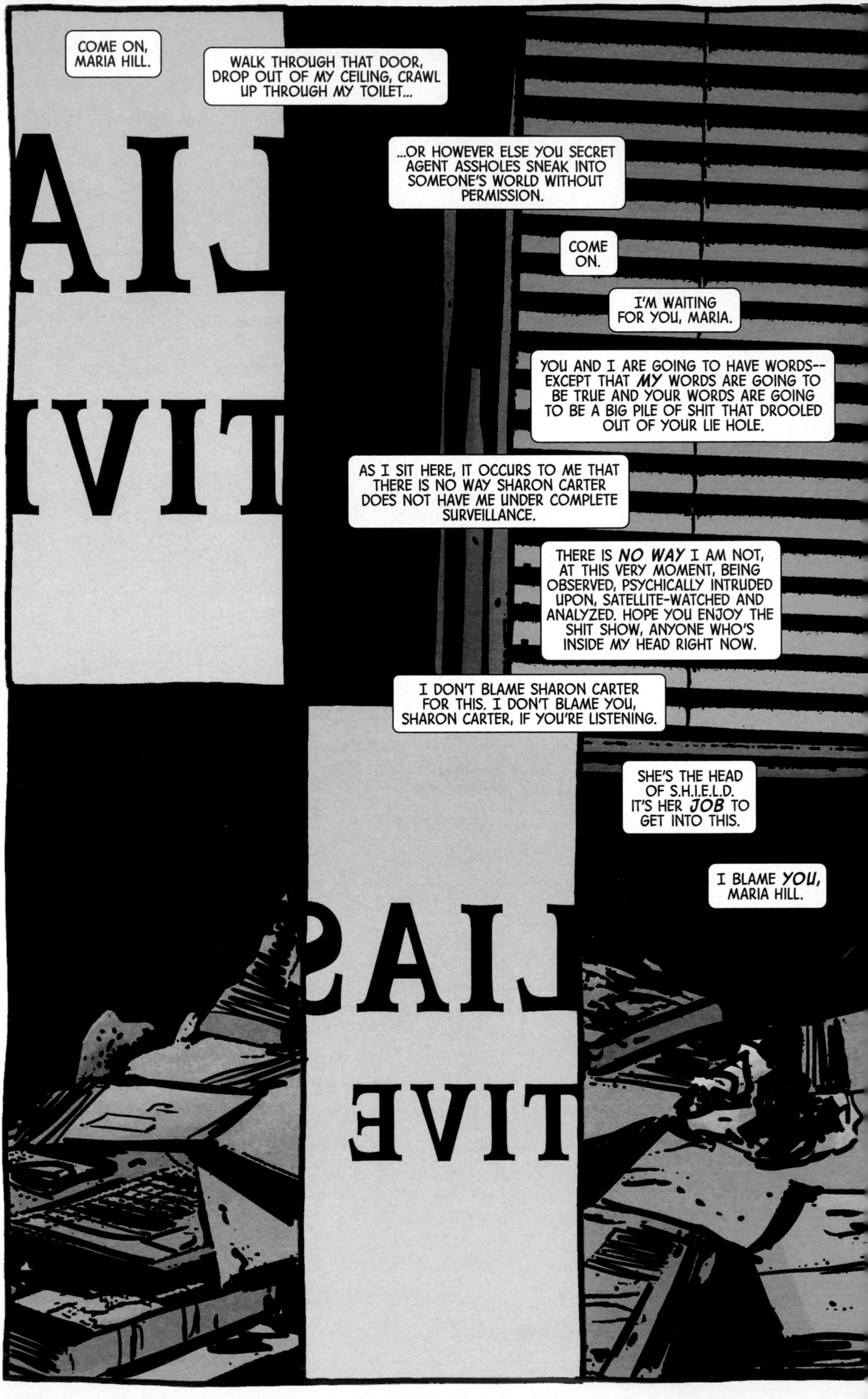
COME ON, MARIA HILL.
WALK THROUGH THAT DOOR, DROP OUT OF MY CEILING, CRAWL UP THROUGH MY TOILET...
...OR HOWEVER ELSE YOU SECRET AGENT ASSHOLES SNEAK INTO SOMEONE'S WORLD WITHOUT PERMISSION.
COME ON.
I'M WAITING FOR YOU, MARIA.
YOU AND I ARE GOING TO HAVE WORDS-- EXCEPT THAT *MY* WORDS ARE GOING TO BE TRUE AND YOUR WORDS ARE GOING TO BE A BIG PILE OF SHIT THAT DROOLED OUT OF YOUR LIE HOLE.
AS I SIT HERE, IT OCCURS TO ME THAT THERE IS NO WAY SHARON CARTER DOES NOT HAVE ME UNDER COMPLETE SURVEILLANCE.
THERE IS *NO WAY* I AM NOT, AT THIS VERY MOMENT, BEING OBSERVED, PSYCHICALLY INTRUDED UPON, SATELLITE-WATCHED AND ANALYZED. HOPE YOU ENJOY THE SHIT SHOW, ANYONE WHO'S INSIDE MY HEAD RIGHT NOW.
I DON'T BLAME SHARON CARTER FOR THIS. I DON'T BLAME YOU, SHARON CARTER, IF YOU'RE LISTENING.
SHE'S THE HEAD OF S.H.I.E.L.D. IT'S HER *JOB* TO GET INTO THIS.
I BLAME *YOU,* MARIA HILL.

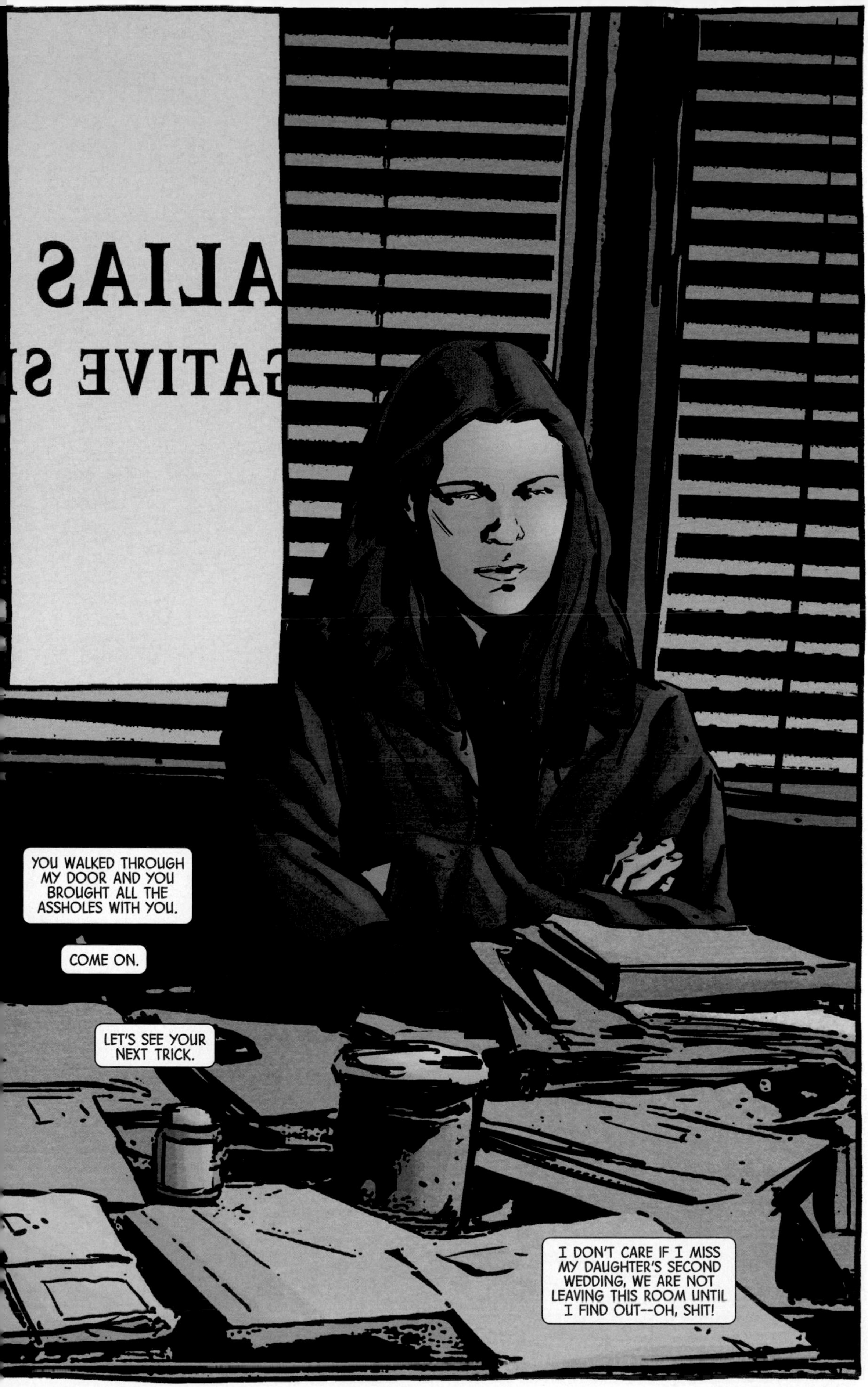
YOU WALKED THROUGH MY DOOR AND YOU BROUGHT ALL THE ASSHOLES WITH YOU.
COME ON.
LET'S SEE YOUR NEXT TRICK.
I DON'T CARE IF I MISS MY DAUGHTER'S SECOND WEDDING, WE ARE NOT LEAVING THIS ROOM UNTIL I FIND OUT--OH, SHIT!

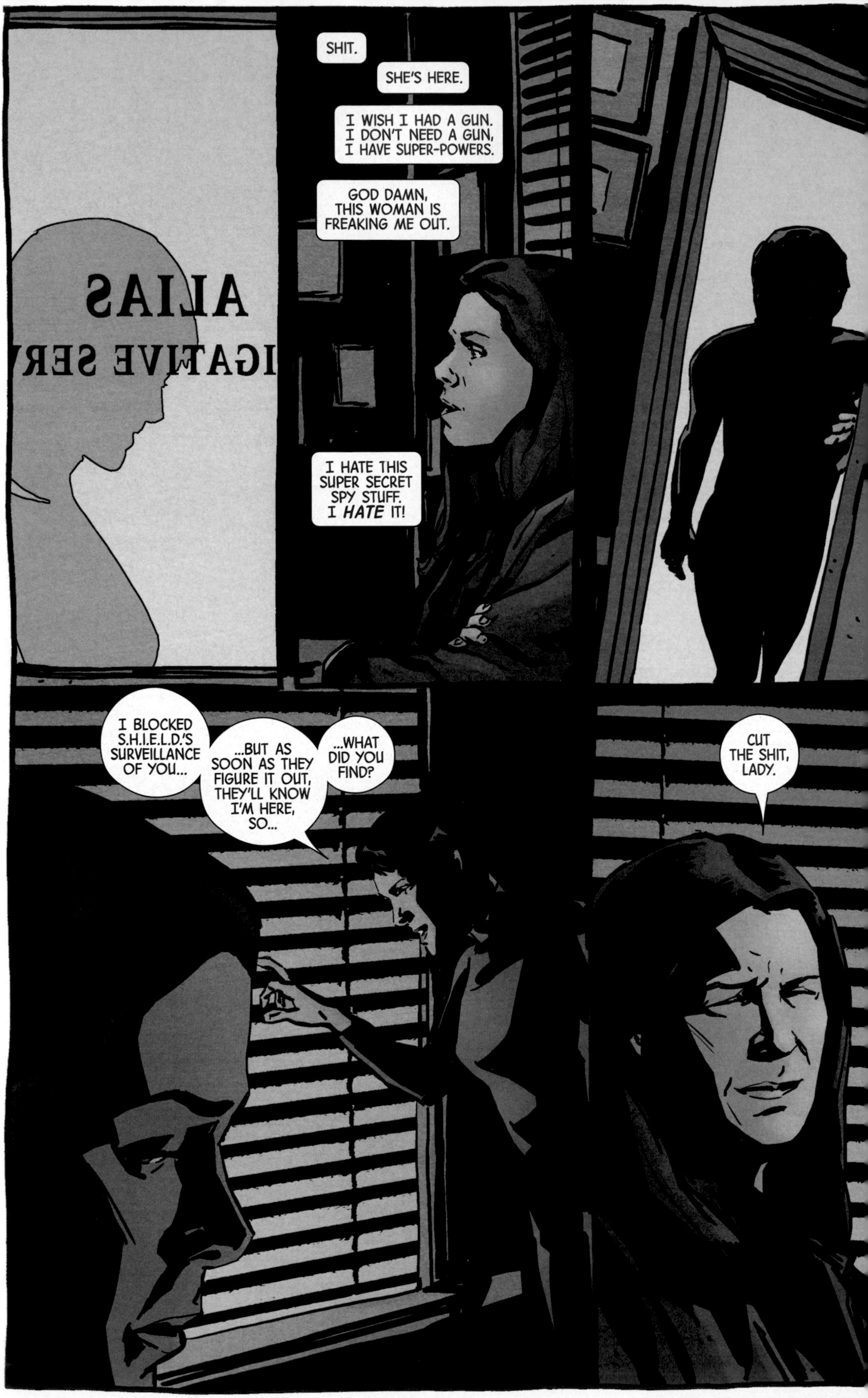

SHIT.
SHE'S HERE.
I WISH I HAD A GUN. I DON'T NEED A GUN, I HAVE SUPER-POWERS.
GOD DAMN, THIS WOMAN IS FREAKING ME OUT.
I HATE THIS SUPER SECRET SPY STUFF. I *HATE* IT!
I BLOCKED S.H.I.E.L.D.'S SURVEILLANCE OF YOU...
...BUT AS SOON AS THEY FIGURE IT OUT, THEY'LL KNOW I'M HERE, SO...
...WHAT DID YOU FIND?
CUT THE SHIT, LADY.

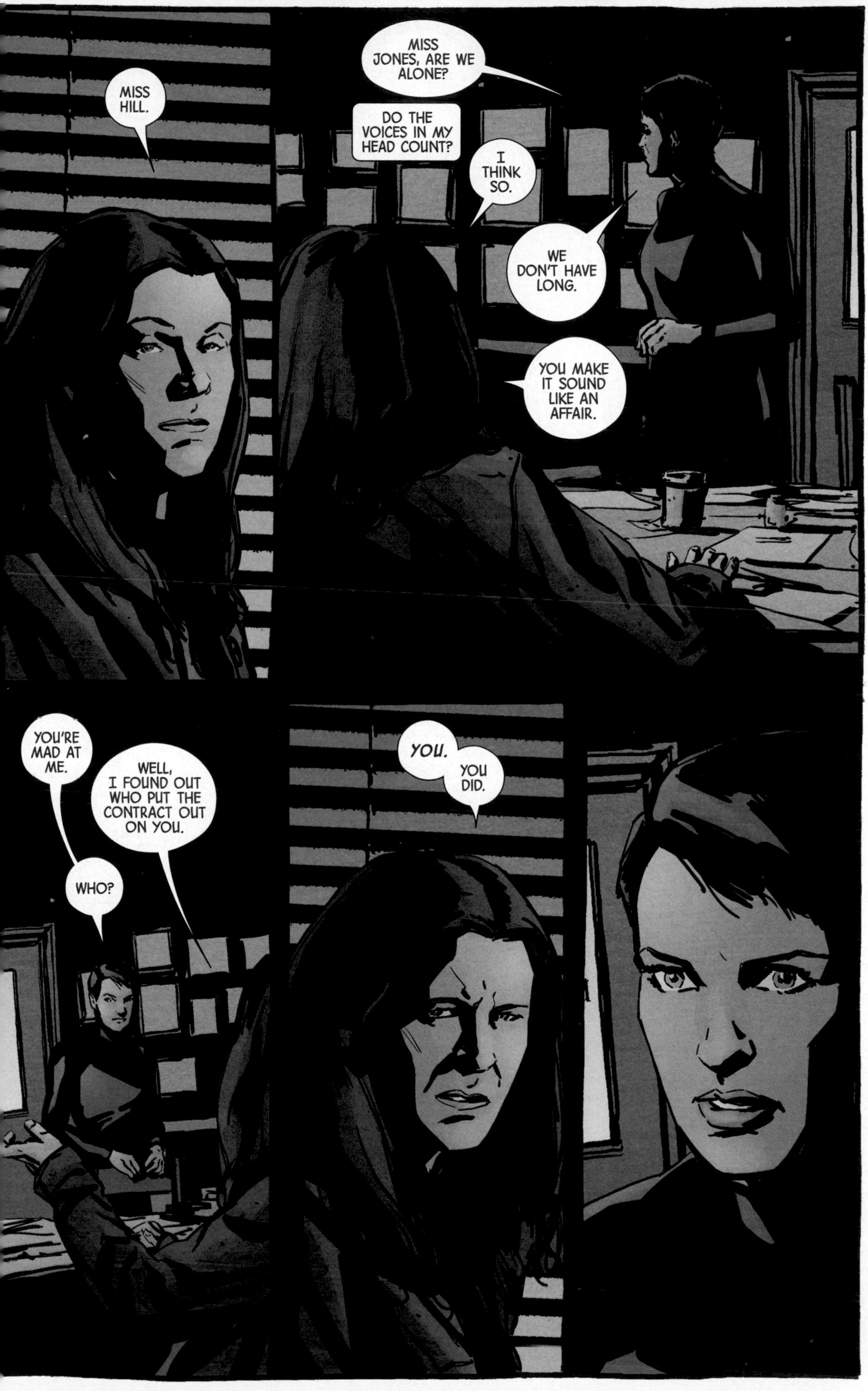

MISS HILL.
MISS JONES, ARE WE ALONE?
DO THE VOICES IN MY HEAD COUNT?
I THINK SO.
WE DON'T HAVE LONG.
YOU MAKE IT SOUND LIKE AN AFFAIR.
YOU'RE MAD AT ME.
WELL, I FOUND OUT WHO PUT THE CONTRACT OUT ON YOU.
WHO?
YOU.
YOU DID.

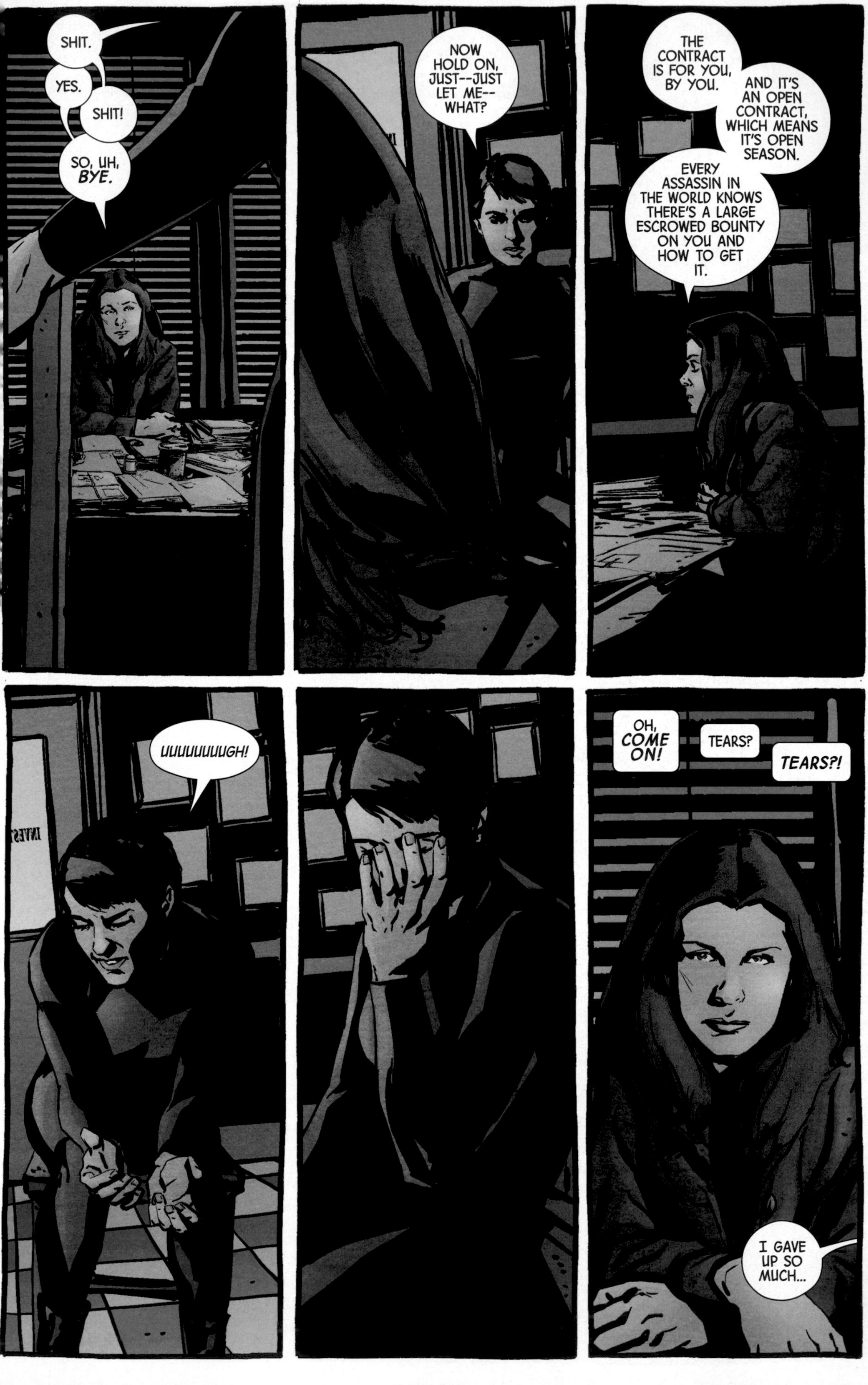

SHIT.
YES.
SHIT!
SO, UH, *BYE.*
NOW HOLD ON, JUST--JUST LET ME-- WHAT?
THE CONTRACT IS FOR YOU, BY YOU.
AND IT'S AN OPEN CONTRACT, WHICH MEANS IT'S OPEN SEASON.
EVERY ASSASSIN IN THE WORLD KNOWS THERE'S A LARGE ESCROWED BOUNTY ON YOU AND HOW TO GET IT.
UUUUUUUUGH!
OH, *COME ON!*
TEARS?
TEARS?!
I GAVE UP SO MUCH...

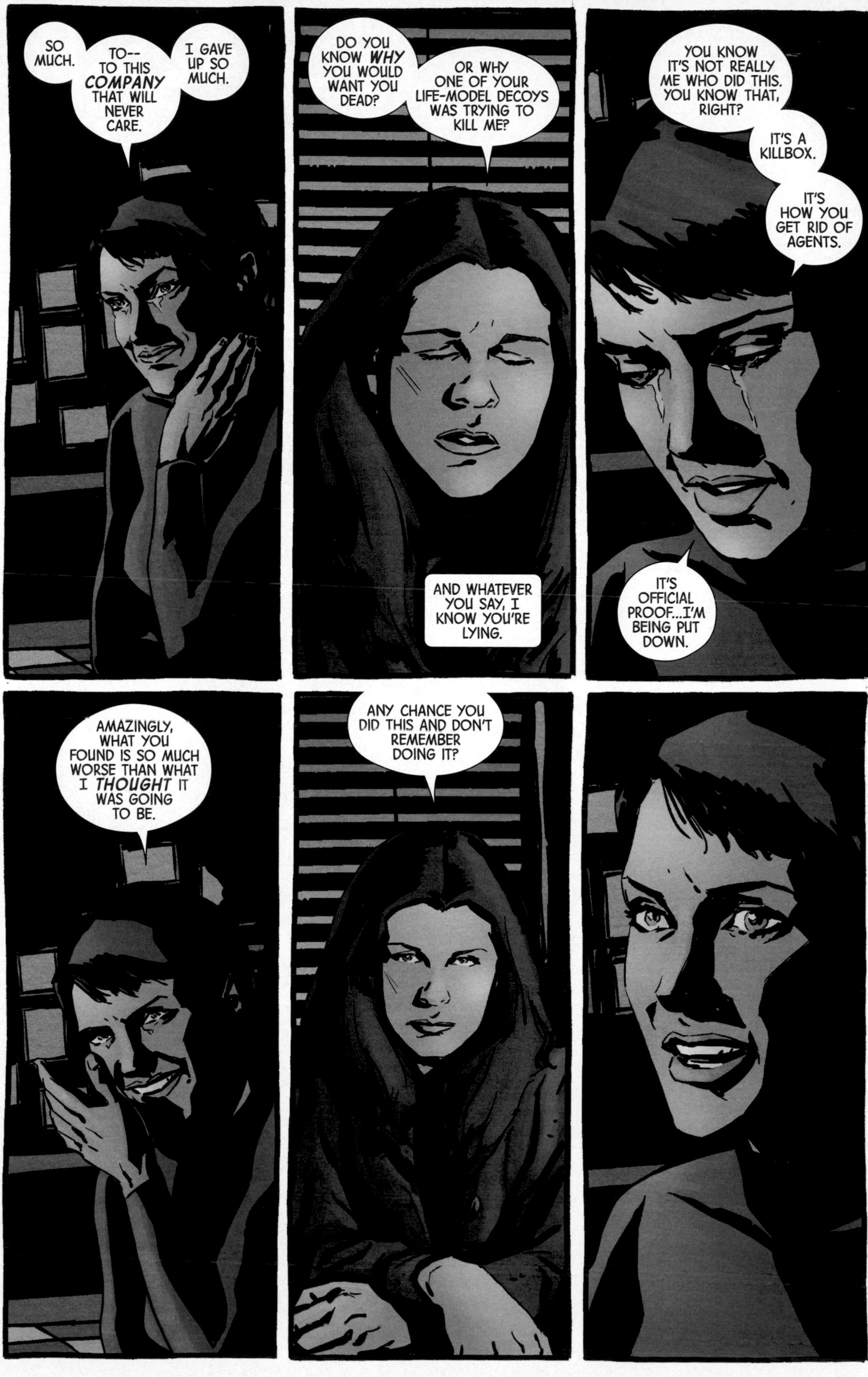
SO MUCH.
TO-- TO THIS *COMPANY* THAT WILL NEVER CARE.
I GAVE UP SO MUCH.
DO YOU KNOW *WHY* YOU WOULD WANT YOU DEAD?
OR WHY ONE OF YOUR LIFE-MODEL DECOYS WAS TRYING TO KILL ME?
AND WHATEVER YOU SAY, I KNOW YOU'RE LYING.
YOU KNOW IT'S NOT REALLY ME WHO DID THIS. YOU KNOW THAT, RIGHT?
IT'S A KILLBOX.
IT'S HOW YOU GET RID OF AGENTS.
IT'S OFFICIAL PROOF...I'M BEING PUT DOWN.
AMAZINGLY, WHAT YOU FOUND IS SO MUCH WORSE THAN WHAT I *THOUGHT* IT WAS GOING TO BE.
ANY CHANCE YOU DID THIS AND DON'T REMEMBER DOING IT?

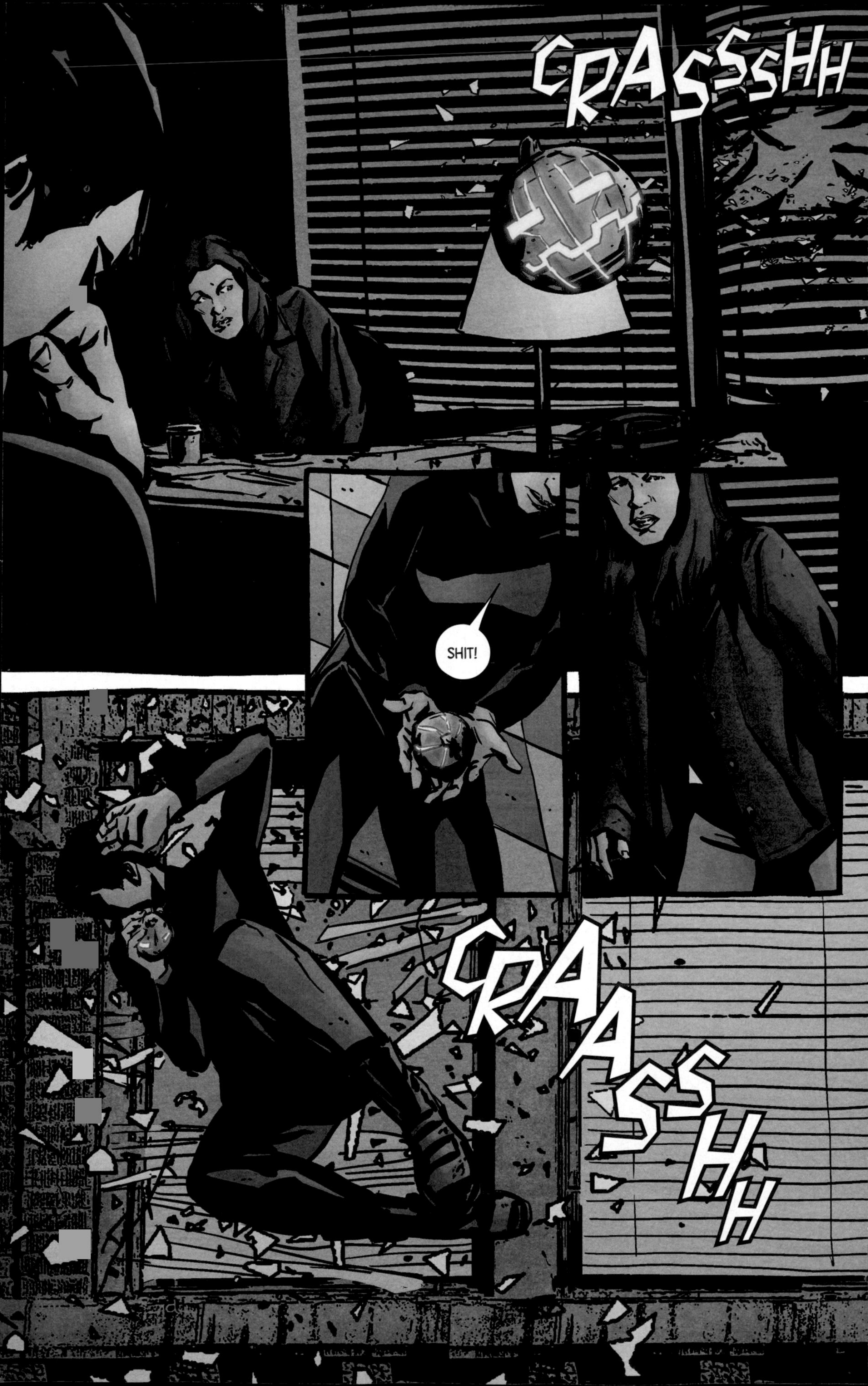
CRASSSHH
SHIT!
CRAASSHH

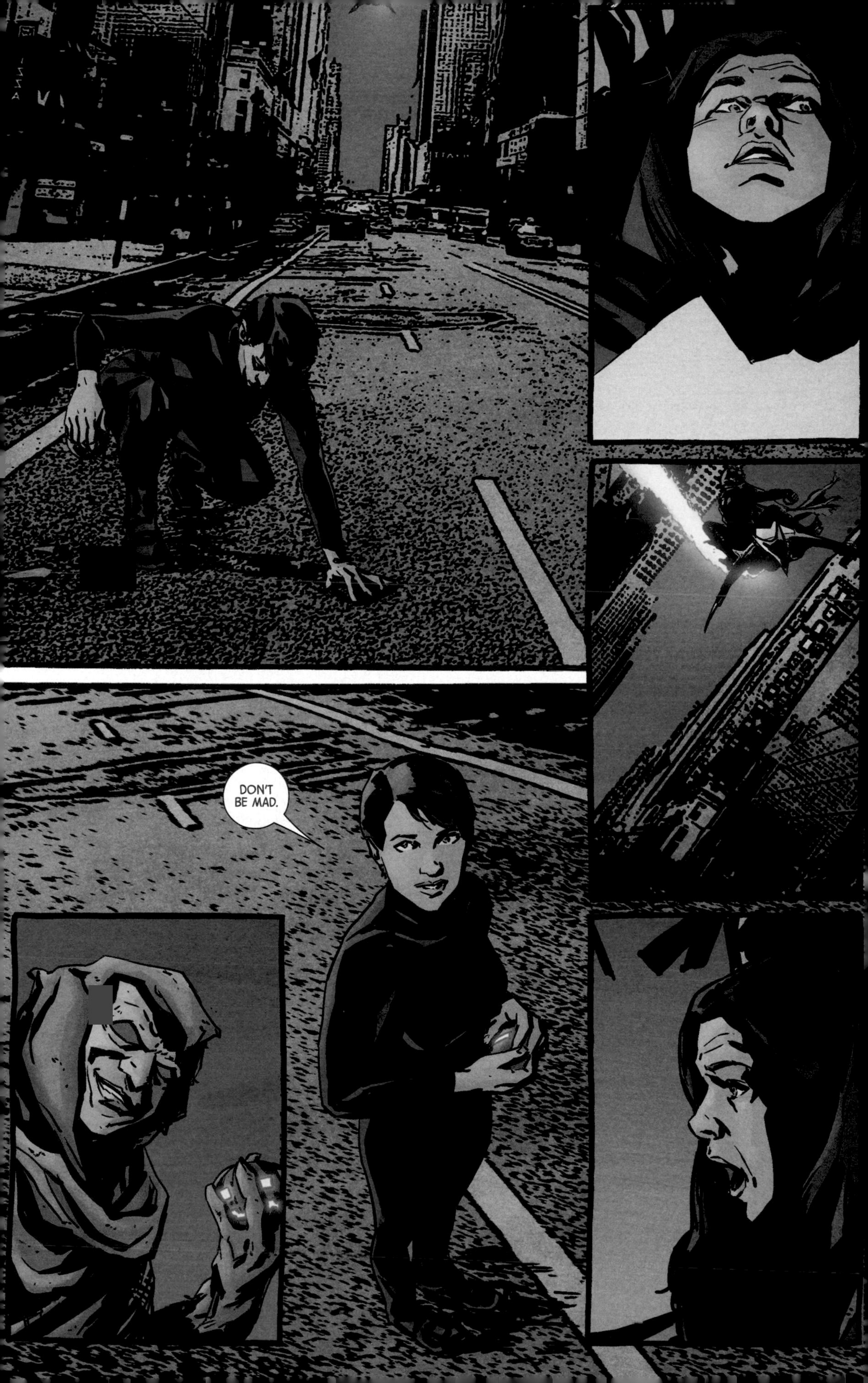
DON'T BE MAD.

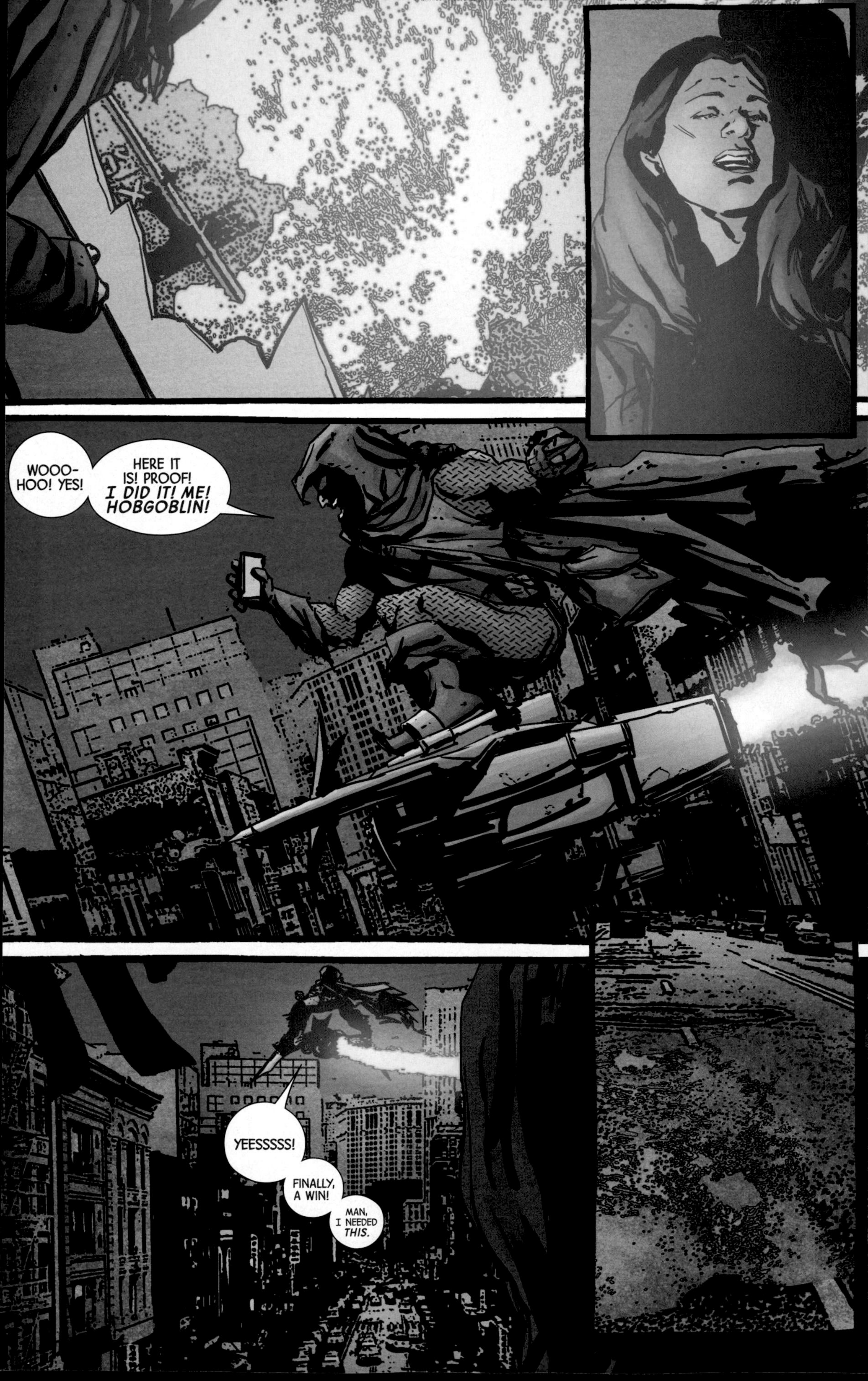
WOOO-HOO! YES!
HERE IT IS! PROOF! I DID IT! ME! HOBGOBLIN!
YEESSSSS!
FINALLY, A WIN!
MAN, I NEEDED THIS.

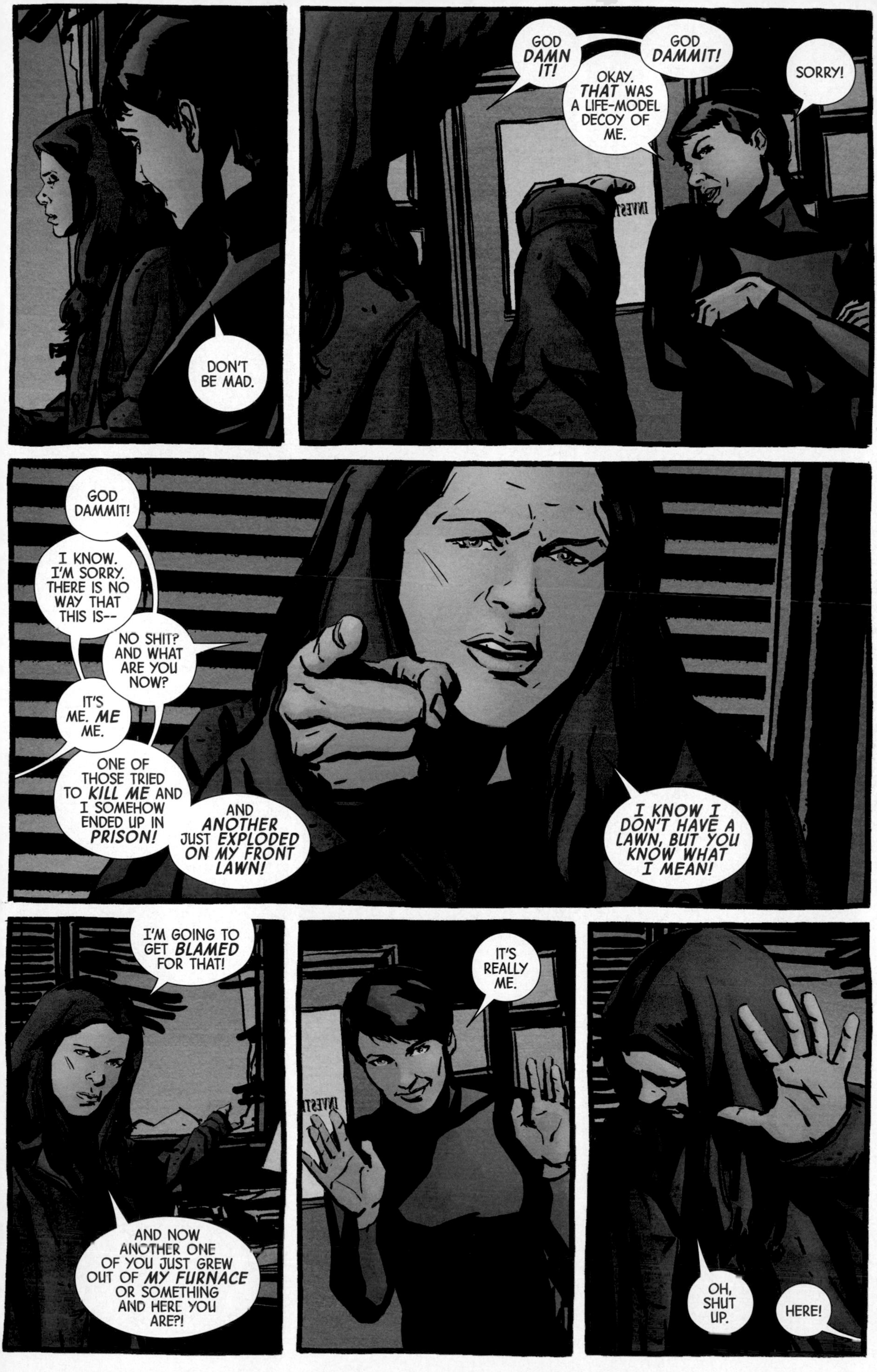
DON'T BE MAD.
GOD DAMN IT!
GOD DAMMIT!
OKAY. THAT WAS A LIFE-MODEL DECOY OF ME.
SORRY!
GOD DAMMIT!
I KNOW. I'M SORRY. THERE IS NO WAY THAT THIS IS--
NO SHIT? AND WHAT ARE YOU NOW?
IT'S ME. ME ME.
ONE OF THOSE TRIED TO KILL ME AND I SOMEHOW ENDED UP IN PRISON!
AND ANOTHER JUST EXPLODED ON MY FRONT LAWN!
I KNOW I DON'T HAVE A LAWN, BUT YOU KNOW WHAT I MEAN!
I'M GOING TO GET BLAMED FOR THAT!
AND NOW ANOTHER ONE OF YOU JUST GREW OUT OF MY FURNACE OR SOMETHING AND HERE YOU ARE?!
IT'S REALLY ME.
OH, SHUT UP.
HERE!

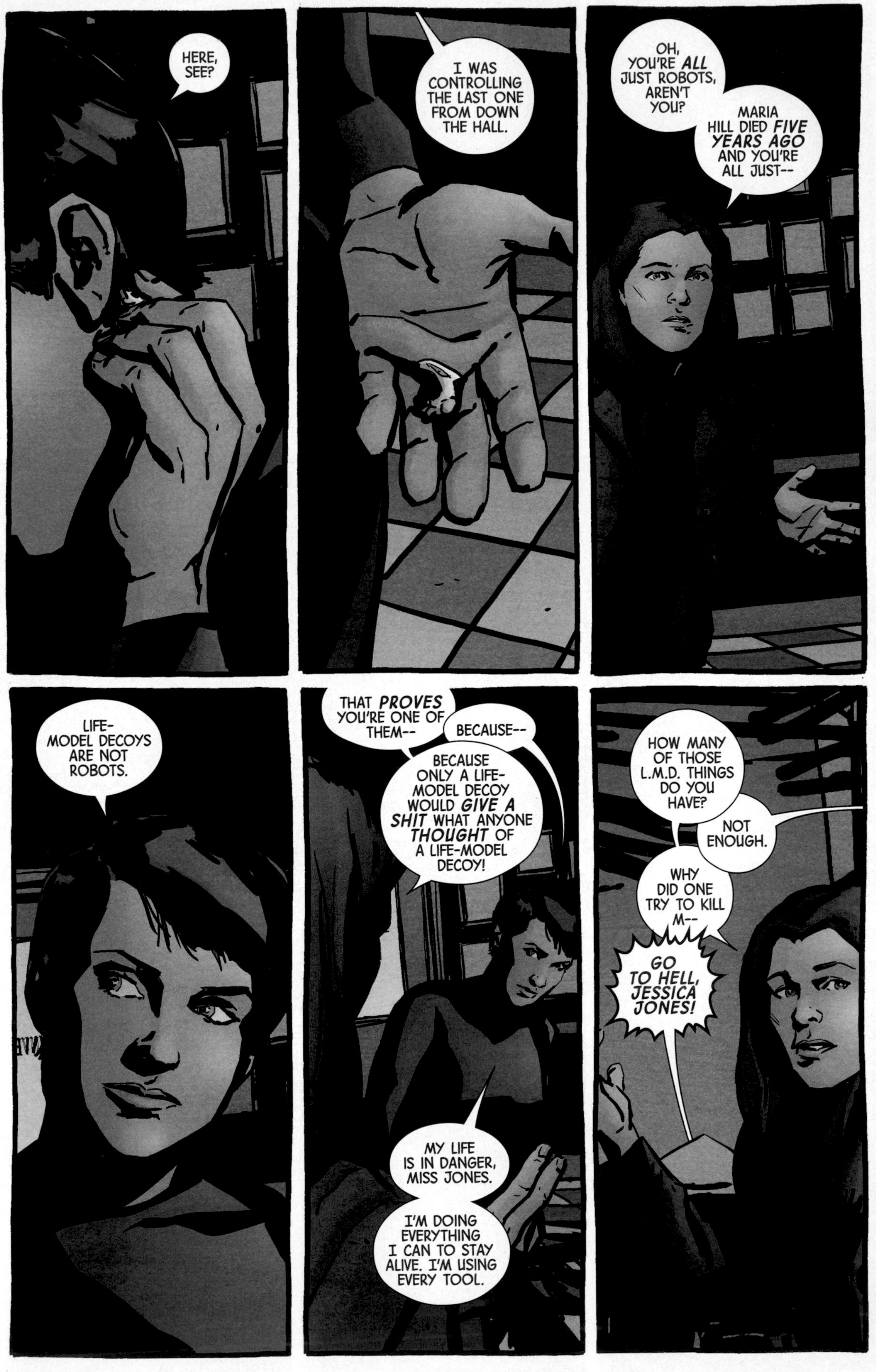
HERE, SEE?
I WAS CONTROLLING THE LAST ONE FROM DOWN THE HALL.
OH, YOU'RE ALL JUST ROBOTS, AREN'T YOU?
MARIA HILL DIED FIVE YEARS AGO AND YOU'RE ALL JUST--
LIFE-MODEL DECOYS ARE NOT ROBOTS.
THAT PROVES YOU'RE ONE OF THEM--
BECAUSE--
BECAUSE ONLY A LIFE-MODEL DECOY WOULD GIVE A SHIT WHAT ANYONE THOUGHT OF A LIFE-MODEL DECOY!
MY LIFE IS IN DANGER, MISS JONES.
I'M DOING EVERYTHING I CAN TO STAY ALIVE. I'M USING EVERY TOOL.
HOW MANY OF THOSE L.M.D. THINGS DO YOU HAVE?
NOT ENOUGH.
WHY DID ONE TRY TO KILL M--
GO TO HELL, JESSICA JONES!

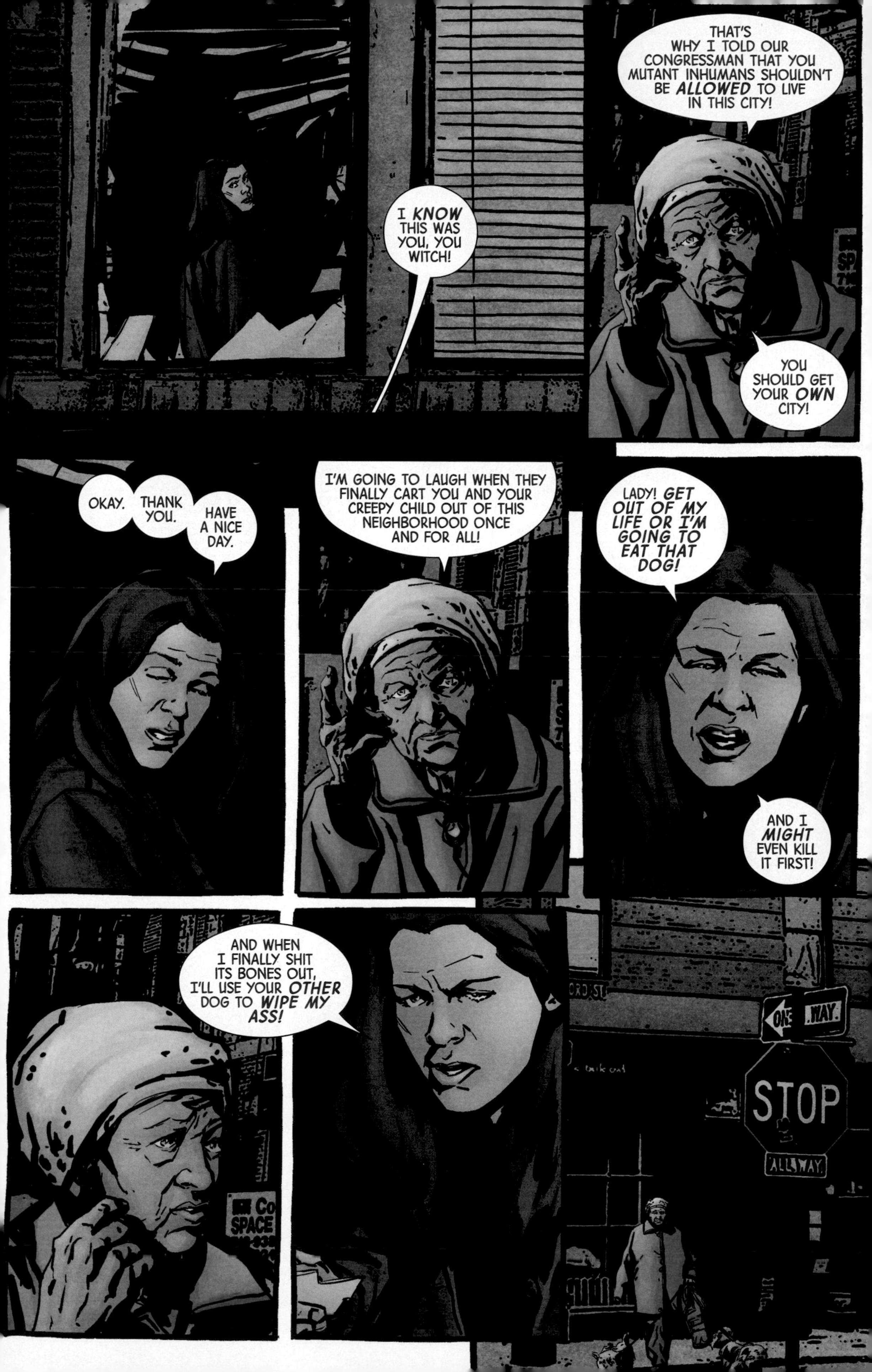
I KNOW THIS WAS YOU, YOU WITCH!
THAT'S WHY I TOLD OUR CONGRESSMAN THAT YOU MUTANT INHUMANS SHOULDN'T BE ALLOWED TO LIVE IN THIS CITY!
YOU SHOULD GET YOUR OWN CITY!
OKAY.
THANK YOU.
HAVE A NICE DAY.
I'M GOING TO LAUGH WHEN THEY FINALLY CART YOU AND YOUR CREEPY CHILD OUT OF THIS NEIGHBORHOOD ONCE AND FOR ALL!
LADY! GET OUT OF MY LIFE OR I'M GOING TO EAT THAT DOG!
AND I MIGHT EVEN KILL IT FIRST!
AND WHEN I FINALLY SHIT ITS BONES OUT, I'LL USE YOUR OTHER DOG TO WIPE MY ASS!
SPACE
ONE WAY
STOP
ALL WAY

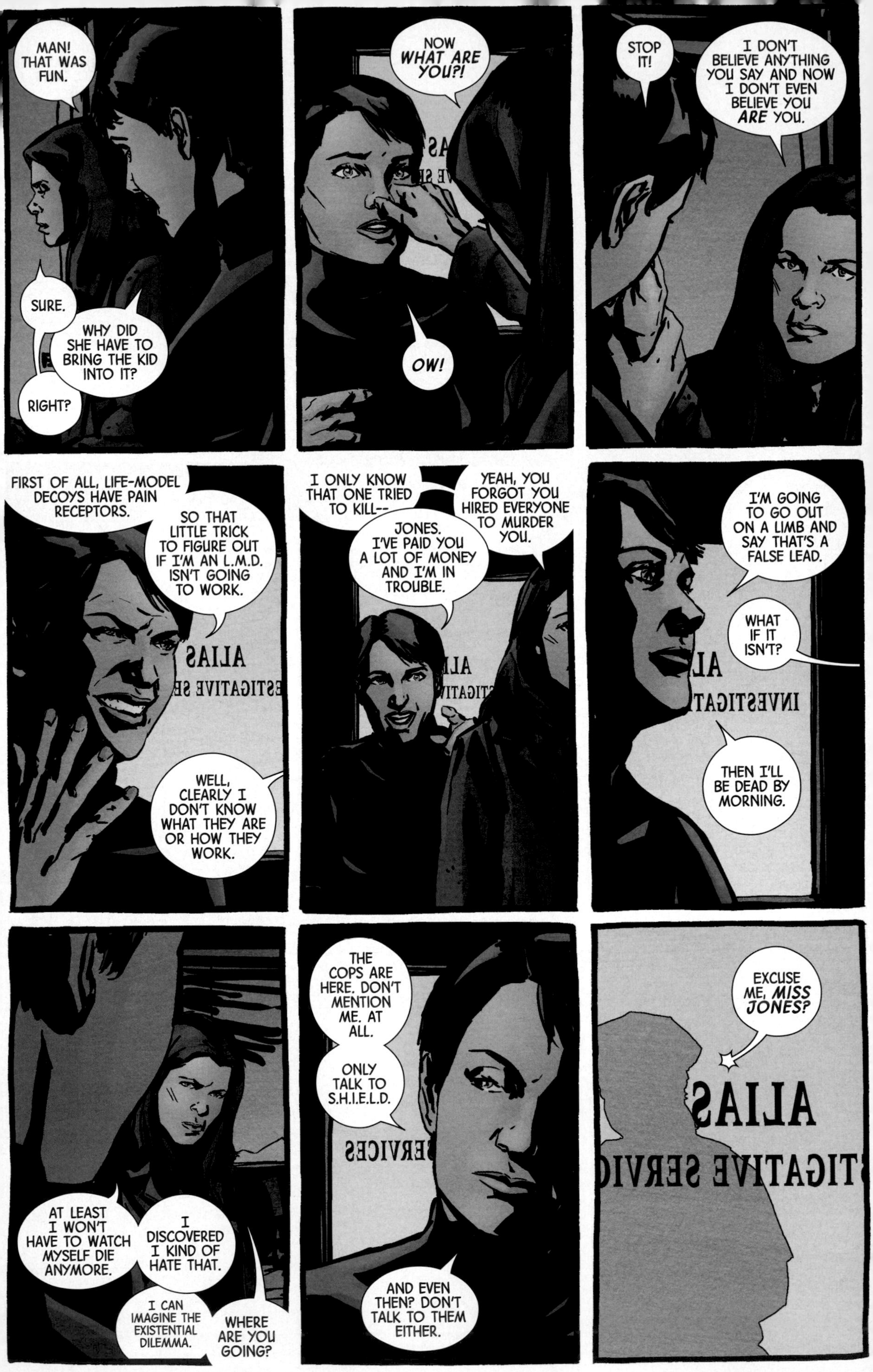
MAN! THAT WAS FUN.
SURE.
WHY DID SHE HAVE TO BRING THE KID INTO IT?
RIGHT?
NOW WHAT ARE YOU?!
OW!
STOP IT!
I DON'T BELIEVE ANYTHING YOU SAY AND NOW I DON'T EVEN BELIEVE YOU ARE YOU.
FIRST OF ALL, LIFE-MODEL DECOYS HAVE PAIN RECEPTORS.
SO THAT LITTLE TRICK TO FIGURE OUT IF I'M AN L.M.D. ISN'T GOING TO WORK.
ALIAS
WELL, CLEARLY I DON'T KNOW WHAT THEY ARE OR HOW THEY WORK.
I ONLY KNOW THAT ONE TRIED TO KILL--
YEAH, YOU FORGOT YOU HIRED EVERYONE TO MURDER YOU.
JONES. I'VE PAID YOU A LOT OF MONEY AND I'M IN TROUBLE.
I'M GOING TO GO OUT ON A LIMB AND SAY THAT'S A FALSE LEAD.
WHAT IF IT ISN'T?
INVESTIGATI
THEN I'LL BE DEAD BY MORNING.
AT LEAST I WON'T HAVE TO WATCH MYSELF DIE ANYMORE.
I DISCOVERED I KIND OF HATE THAT.
I CAN IMAGINE THE EXISTENTIAL DILEMMA.
WHERE ARE YOU GOING?
THE COPS ARE HERE. DON'T MENTION ME. AT ALL.
ONLY TALK TO S.H.I.E.L.D.
AND EVEN THEN? DON'T TALK TO THEM EITHER.
EXCUSE ME, MISS JONES?
ALIAS

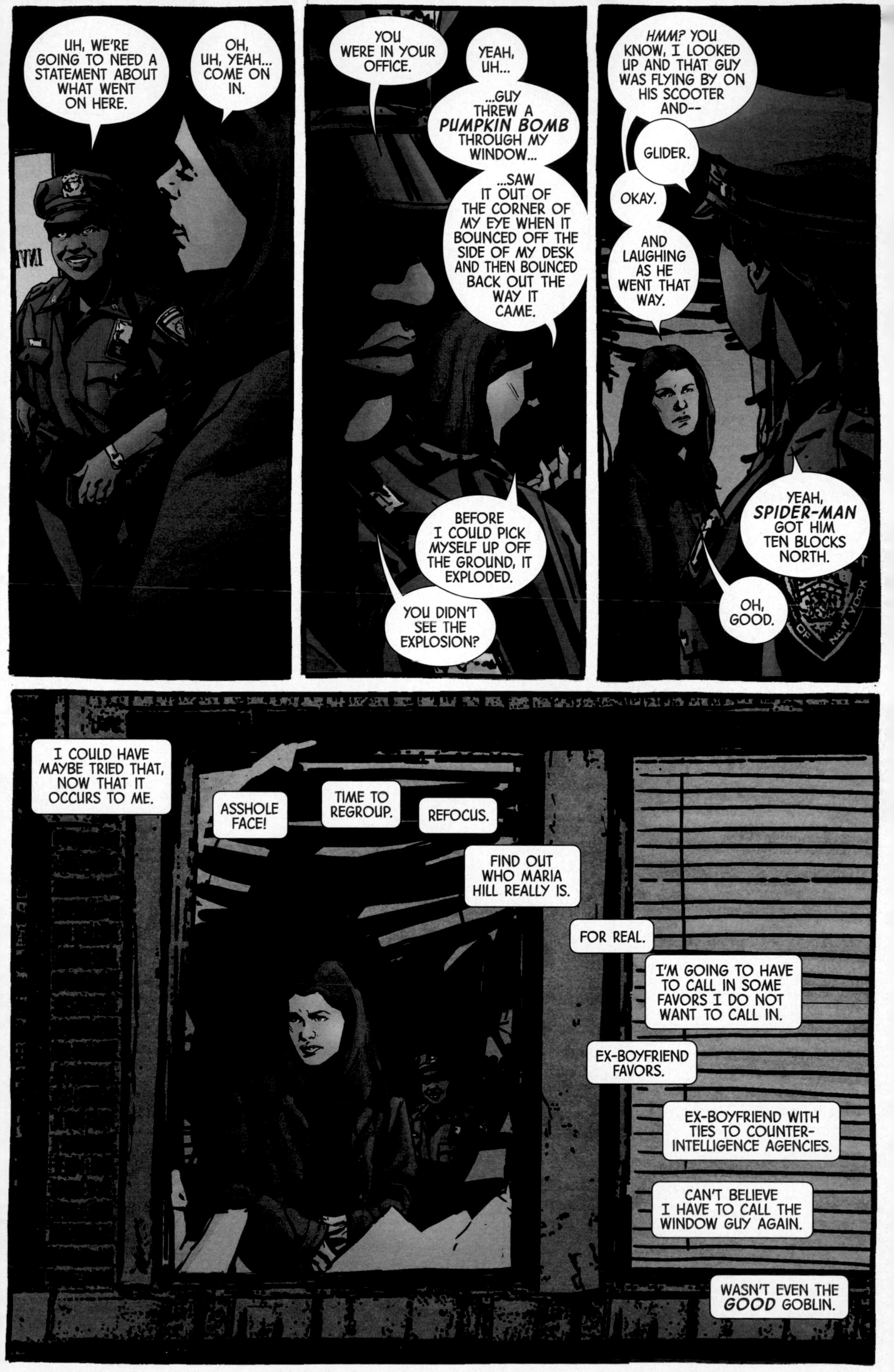
UH, WE'RE GOING TO NEED A STATEMENT ABOUT WHAT WENT ON HERE.
OH, UH, YEAH... COME ON IN.
YOU WERE IN YOUR OFFICE.
YEAH, UH...
...GUY THREW A PUMPKIN BOMB THROUGH MY WINDOW...
...SAW IT OUT OF THE CORNER OF MY EYE WHEN IT BOUNCED OFF THE SIDE OF MY DESK AND THEN BOUNCED BACK OUT THE WAY IT CAME.
BEFORE I COULD PICK MYSELF UP OFF THE GROUND, IT EXPLODED.
YOU DIDN'T SEE THE EXPLOSION?
HMM? YOU KNOW, I LOOKED UP AND THAT GUY WAS FLYING BY ON HIS SCOOTER AND--
GLIDER.
OKAY.
AND LAUGHING AS HE WENT THAT WAY.
YEAH, SPIDER-MAN GOT HIM TEN BLOCKS NORTH.
OH, GOOD.
I COULD HAVE MAYBE TRIED THAT, NOW THAT IT OCCURS TO ME.
ASSHOLE FACE!
TIME TO REGROUP.
REFOCUS.
FIND OUT WHO MARIA HILL REALLY IS.
FOR REAL.
I'M GOING TO HAVE TO CALL IN SOME FAVORS I DO NOT WANT TO CALL IN.
EX-BOYFRIEND FAVORS.
EX-BOYFRIEND WITH TIES TO COUNTER-INTELLIGENCE AGENCIES.
CAN'T BELIEVE I HAVE TO CALL THE WINDOW GUY AGAIN.
WASN'T EVEN THE GOOD GOBLIN.

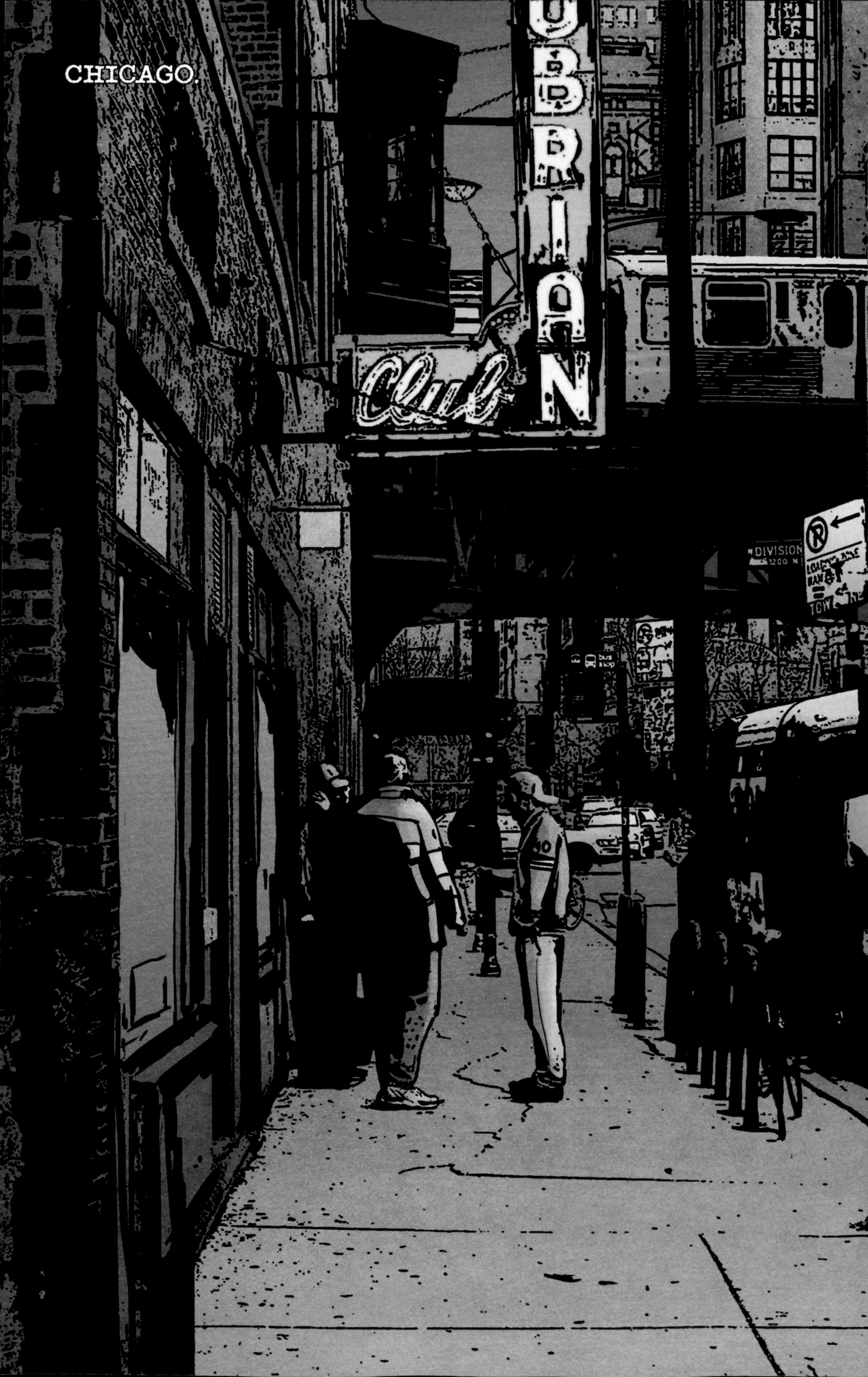
CHICAGO.
Club
DIVISION

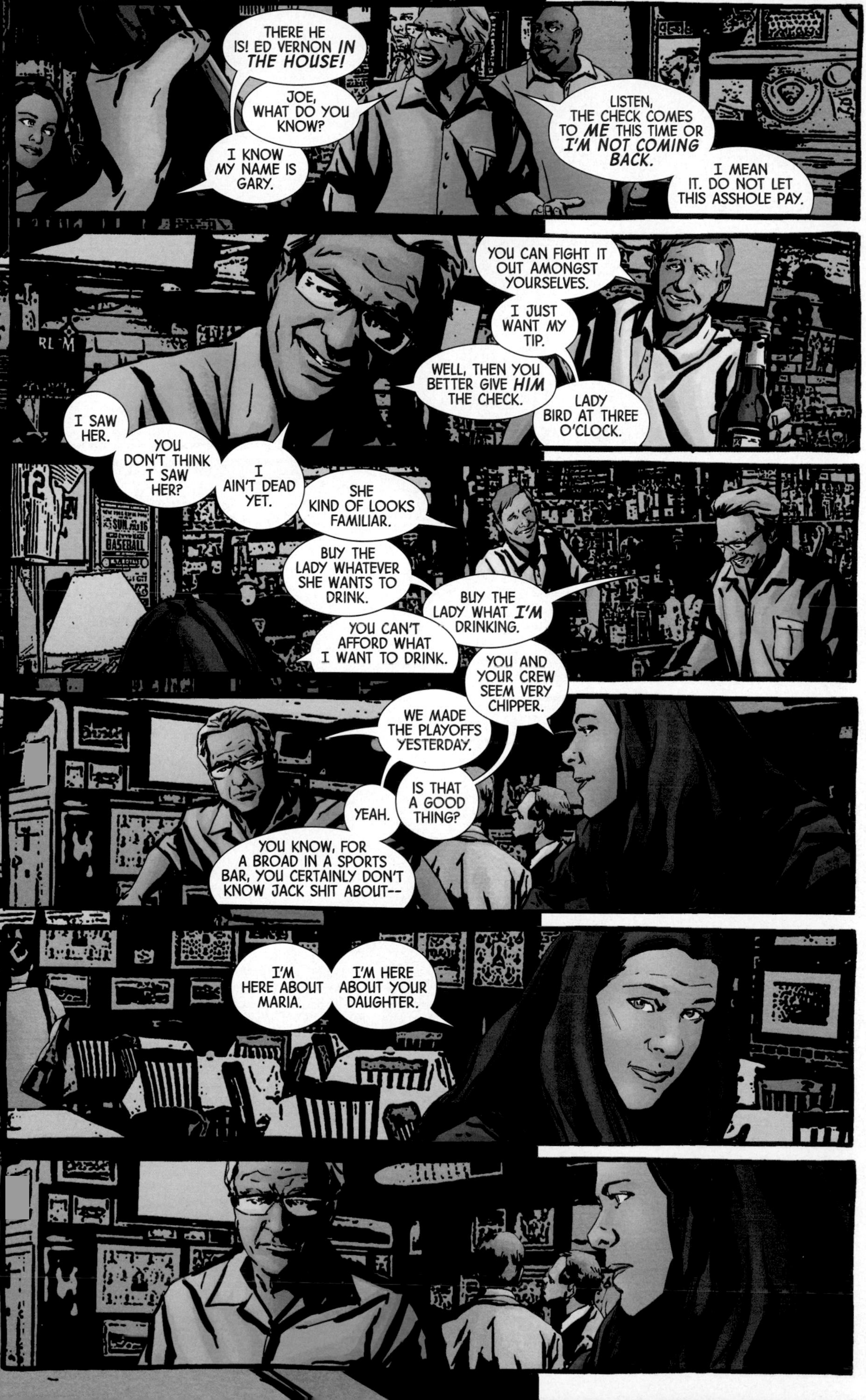
THERE HE IS! ED VERNON IN THE HOUSE!
JOE, WHAT DO YOU KNOW?
I KNOW MY NAME IS GARY.
LISTEN, THE CHECK COMES TO ME THIS TIME OR I'M NOT COMING BACK.
I MEAN IT. DO NOT LET THIS ASSHOLE PAY.
YOU CAN FIGHT IT OUT AMONGST YOURSELVES.
I JUST WANT MY TIP.
WELL, THEN YOU BETTER GIVE HIM THE CHECK.
LADY BIRD AT THREE O'CLOCK.
I SAW HER.
YOU DON'T THINK I SAW HER?
I AIN'T DEAD YET.
SHE KIND OF LOOKS FAMILIAR.
BUY THE LADY WHATEVER SHE WANTS TO DRINK.
BUY THE LADY WHAT I'M DRINKING.
YOU CAN'T AFFORD WHAT I WANT TO DRINK.
YOU AND YOUR CREW SEEM VERY CHIPPER.
WE MADE THE PLAYOFFS YESTERDAY.
IS THAT A GOOD THING?
YEAH.
YOU KNOW, FOR A BROAD IN A SPORTS BAR, YOU CERTAINLY DON'T KNOW JACK SHIT ABOUT--
I'M HERE ABOUT MARIA.
I'M HERE ABOUT YOUR DAUGHTER.

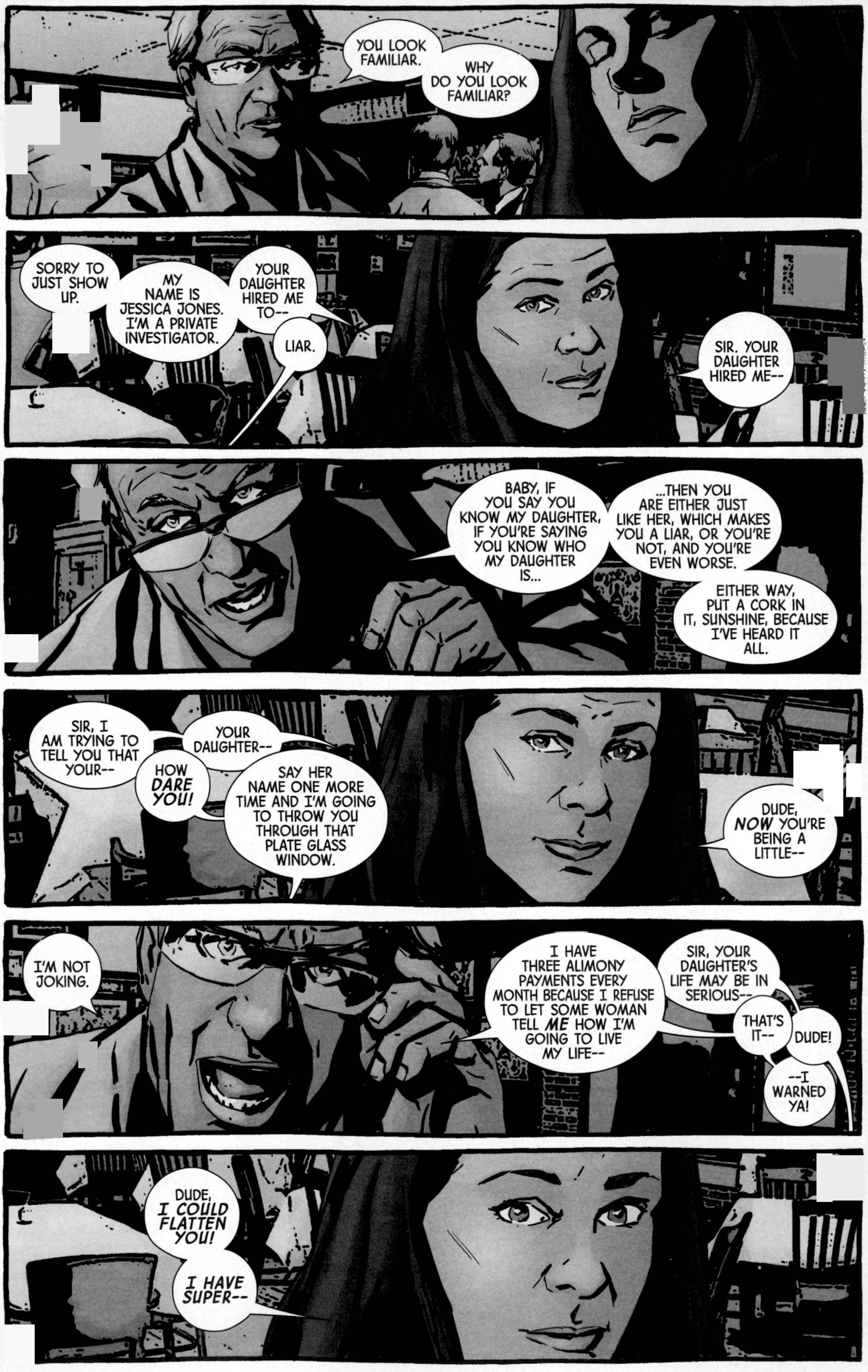

YOU LOOK FAMILIAR.
WHY DO YOU LOOK FAMILIAR?
SORRY TO JUST SHOW UP.
MY NAME IS JESSICA JONES. I'M A PRIVATE INVESTIGATOR.
YOUR DAUGHTER HIRED ME TO--
LIAR.
SIR. YOUR DAUGHTER HIRED ME--
BABY, IF YOU SAY YOU KNOW MY DAUGHTER, IF YOU'RE SAYING YOU KNOW WHO MY DAUGHTER IS...
...THEN YOU ARE EITHER JUST LIKE HER, WHICH MAKES YOU A LIAR, OR YOU'RE NOT, AND YOU'RE EVEN WORSE.
EITHER WAY, PUT A CORK IN IT, SUNSHINE, BECAUSE I'VE HEARD IT ALL.
SIR, I AM TRYING TO TELL YOU THAT YOUR--
YOUR DAUGHTER--
HOW *DARE YOU!*
SAY HER NAME ONE MORE TIME AND I'M GOING TO THROW YOU THROUGH THAT PLATE GLASS WINDOW.
DUDE, ***NOW*** YOU'RE BEING A LITTLE--
I'M NOT JOKING.
I HAVE THREE ALIMONY PAYMENTS EVERY MONTH BECAUSE I REFUSE TO LET SOME WOMAN TELL ***ME*** HOW I'M GOING TO LIVE MY LIFE--
SIR, YOUR DAUGHTER'S LIFE MAY BE IN SERIOUS--
THAT'S IT--
DUDE!
--I WARNED YA!
DUDE, ***I COULD FLATTEN YOU!***
I HAVE SUPER--

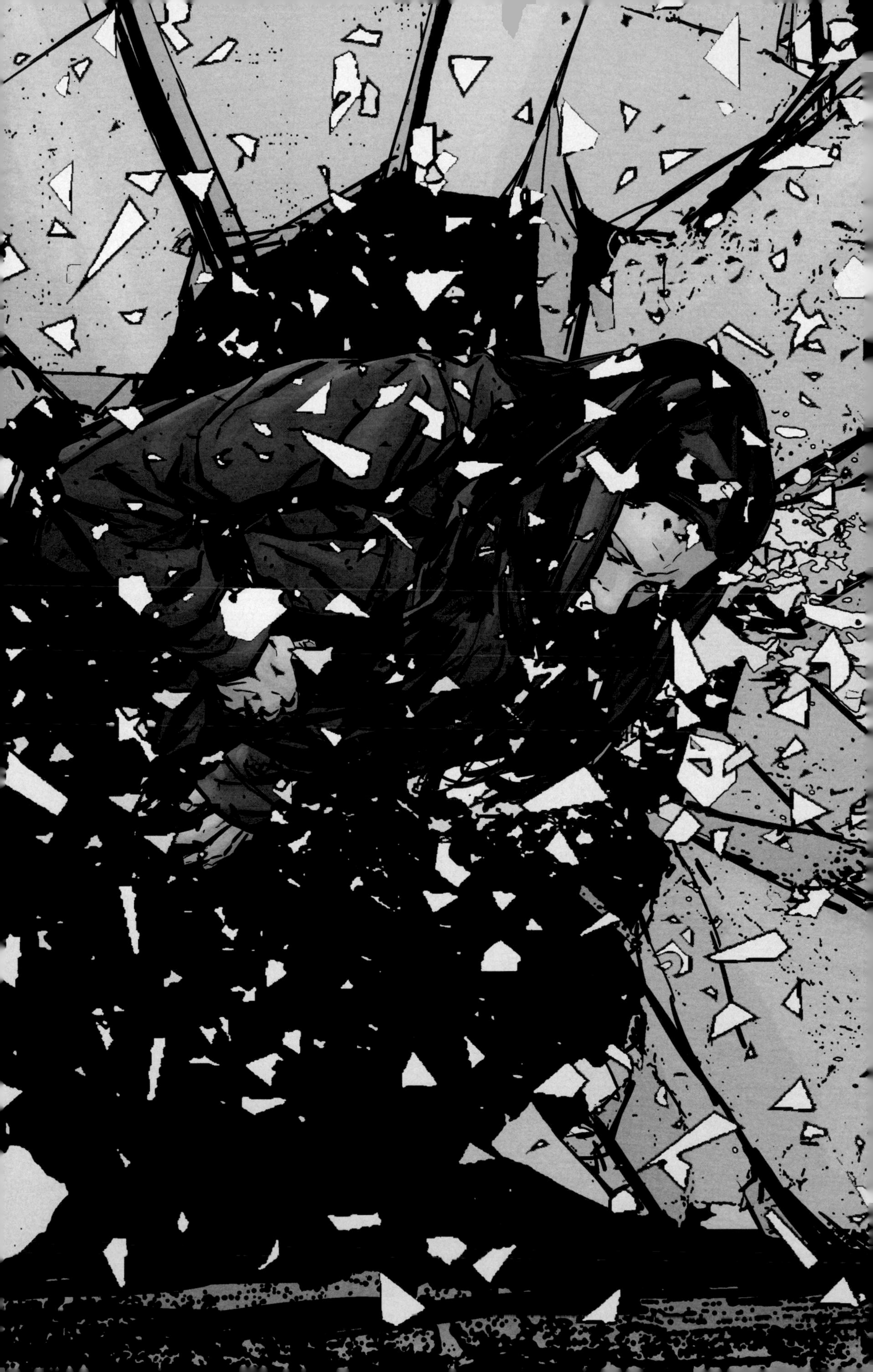

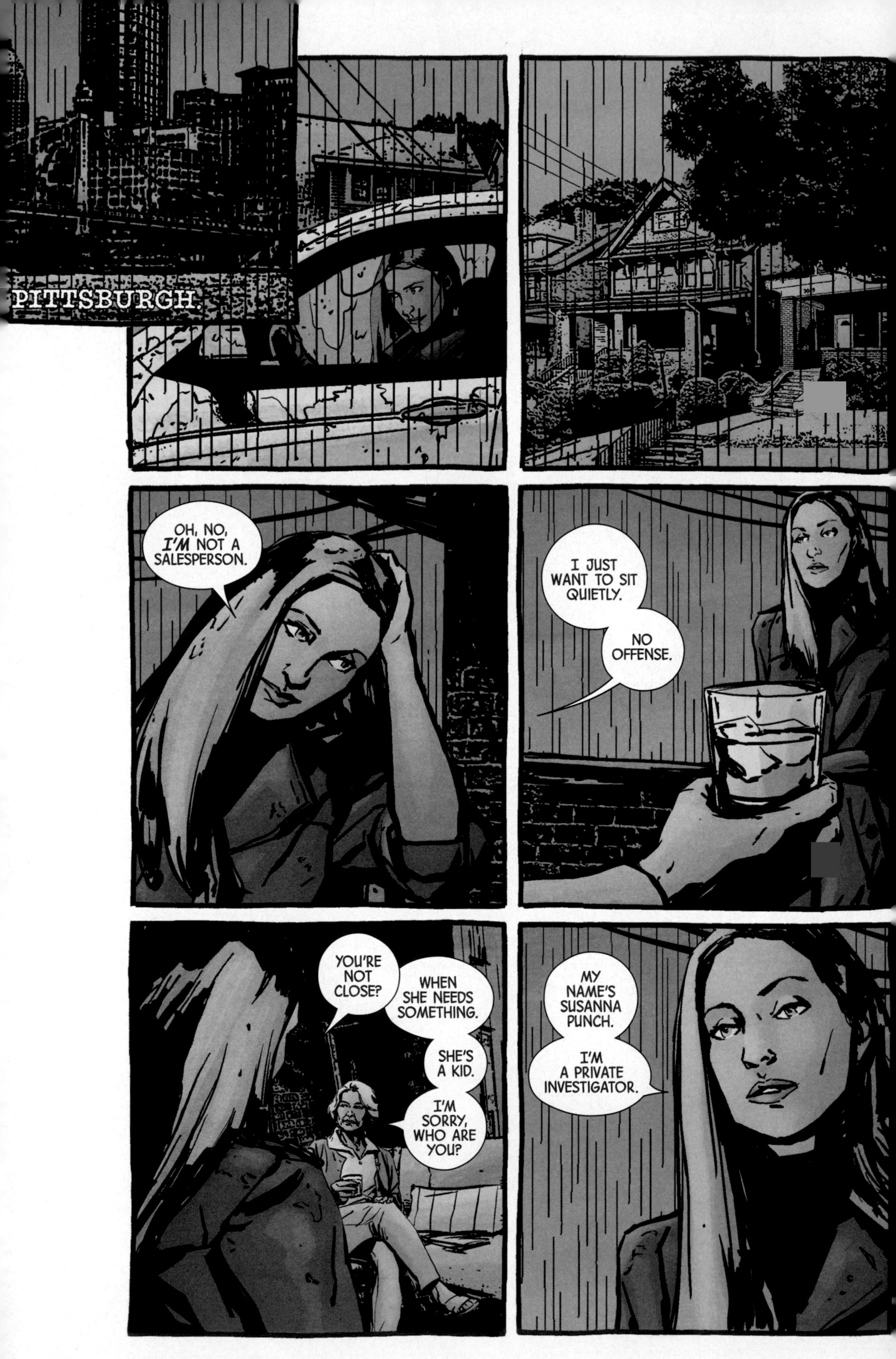
PITTSBURGH.
OH, NO, I'M NOT A SALESPERSON.
I JUST WANT TO SIT QUIETLY.
NO OFFENSE.
YOU'RE NOT CLOSE?
WHEN SHE NEEDS SOMETHING.
SHE'S A KID.
I'M SORRY, WHO ARE YOU?
MY NAME'S SUSANNA PUNCH.
I'M A PRIVATE INVESTIGATOR.

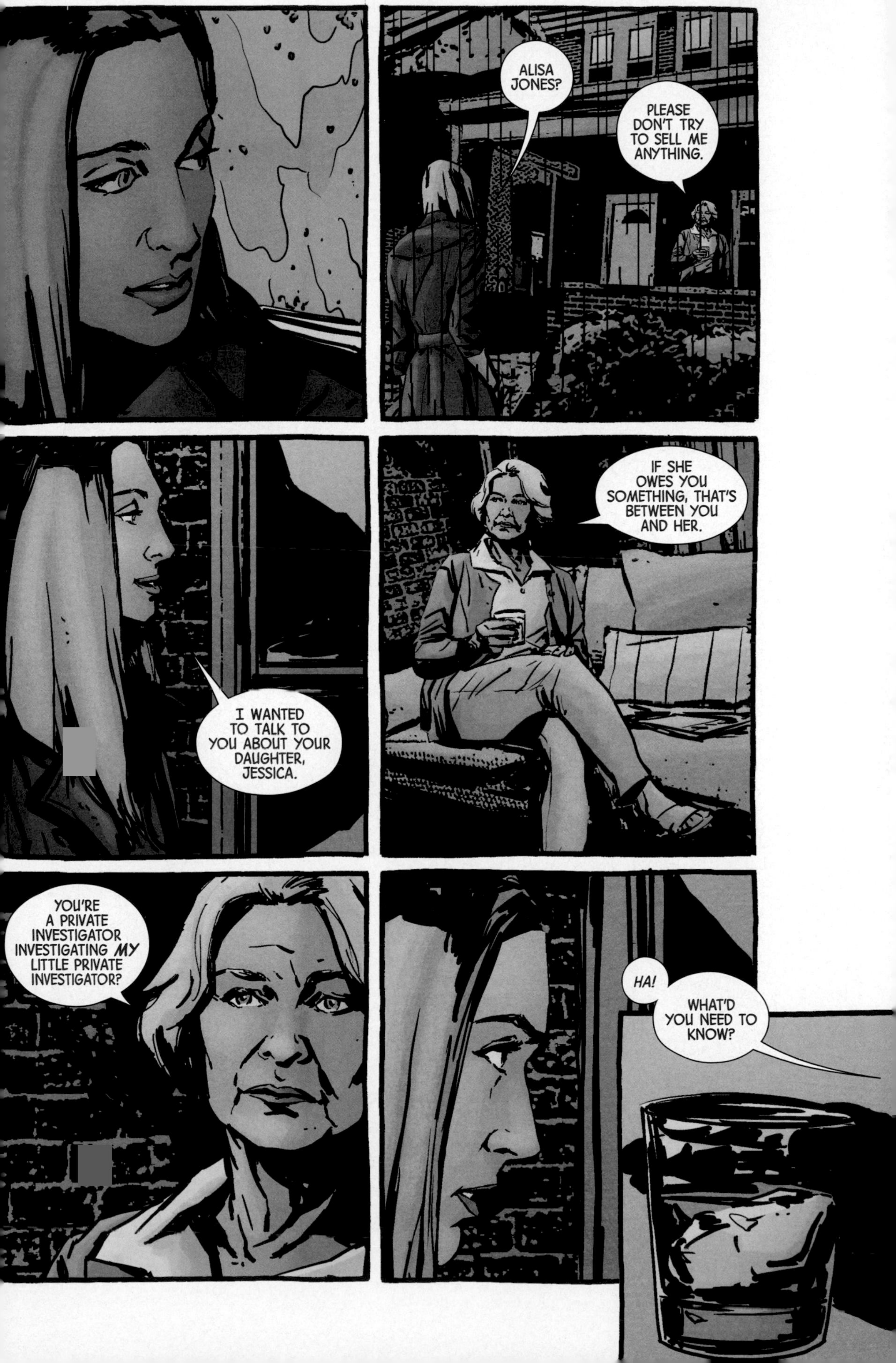
ALISA JONES?
PLEASE DON'T TRY TO SELL ME ANYTHING.
I WANTED TO TALK TO YOU ABOUT YOUR DAUGHTER, JESSICA.
IF SHE OWES YOU SOMETHING, THAT'S BETWEEN YOU AND HER.
YOU'RE A PRIVATE INVESTIGATOR INVESTIGATING *MY* LITTLE PRIVATE INVESTIGATOR?
HA!
WHAT'D YOU NEED TO KNOW?

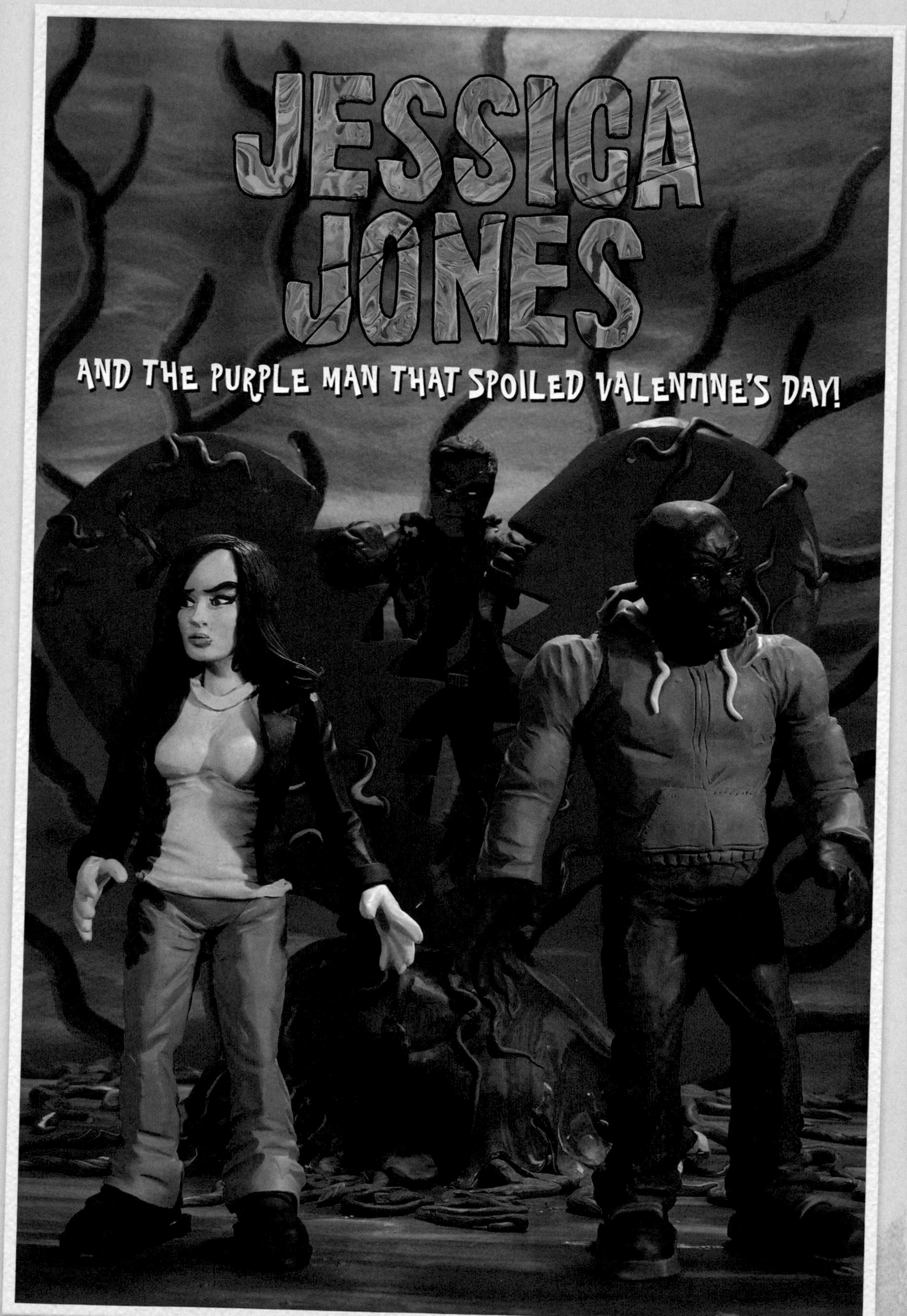
JESSICA JONES
AND THE PURPLE MAN THAT SPOILED VALENTINE'S DAY!

#11 variant by **Mr.Oz**

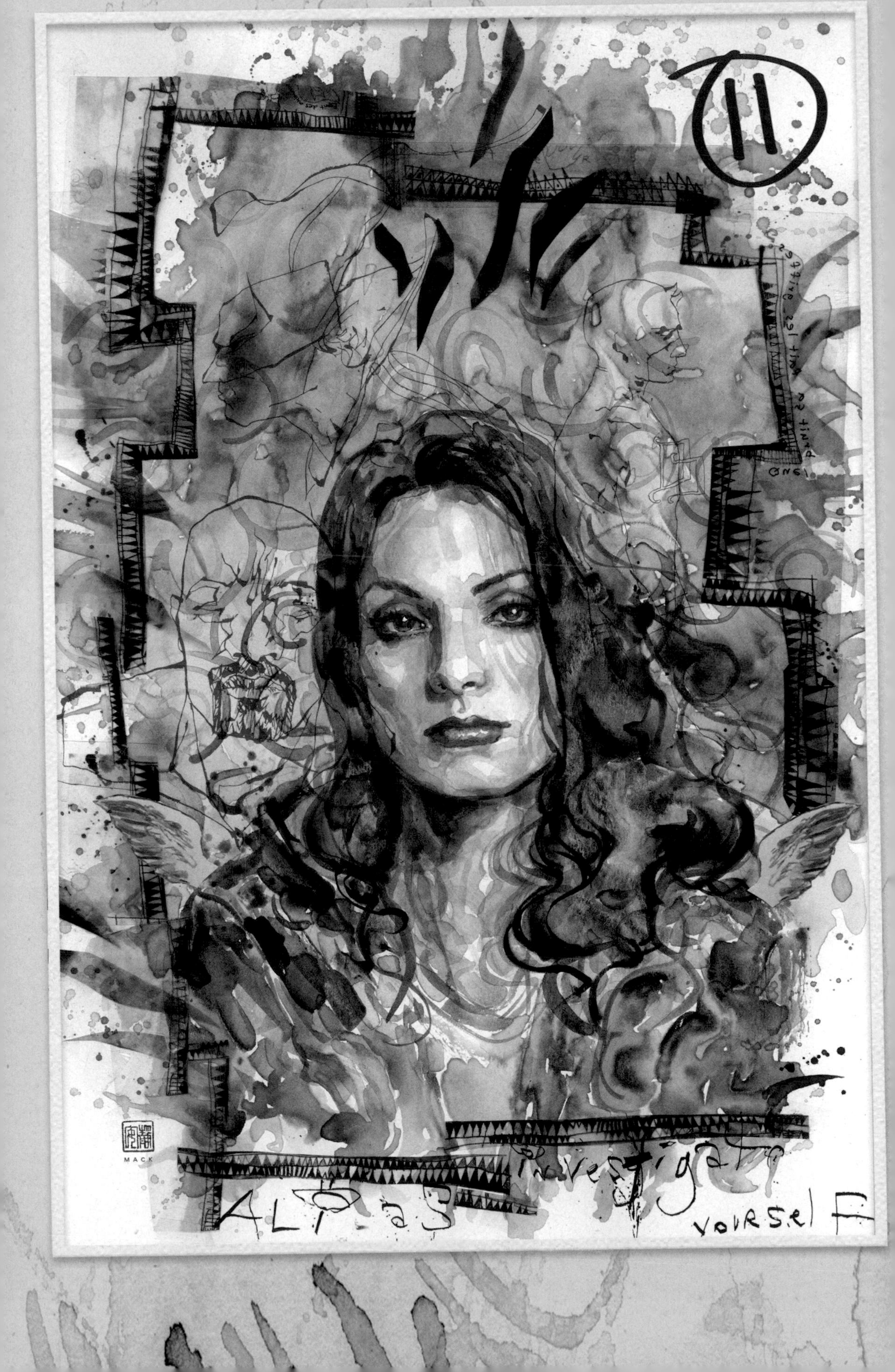
11
MACK
ALIAS
investigate
yourself

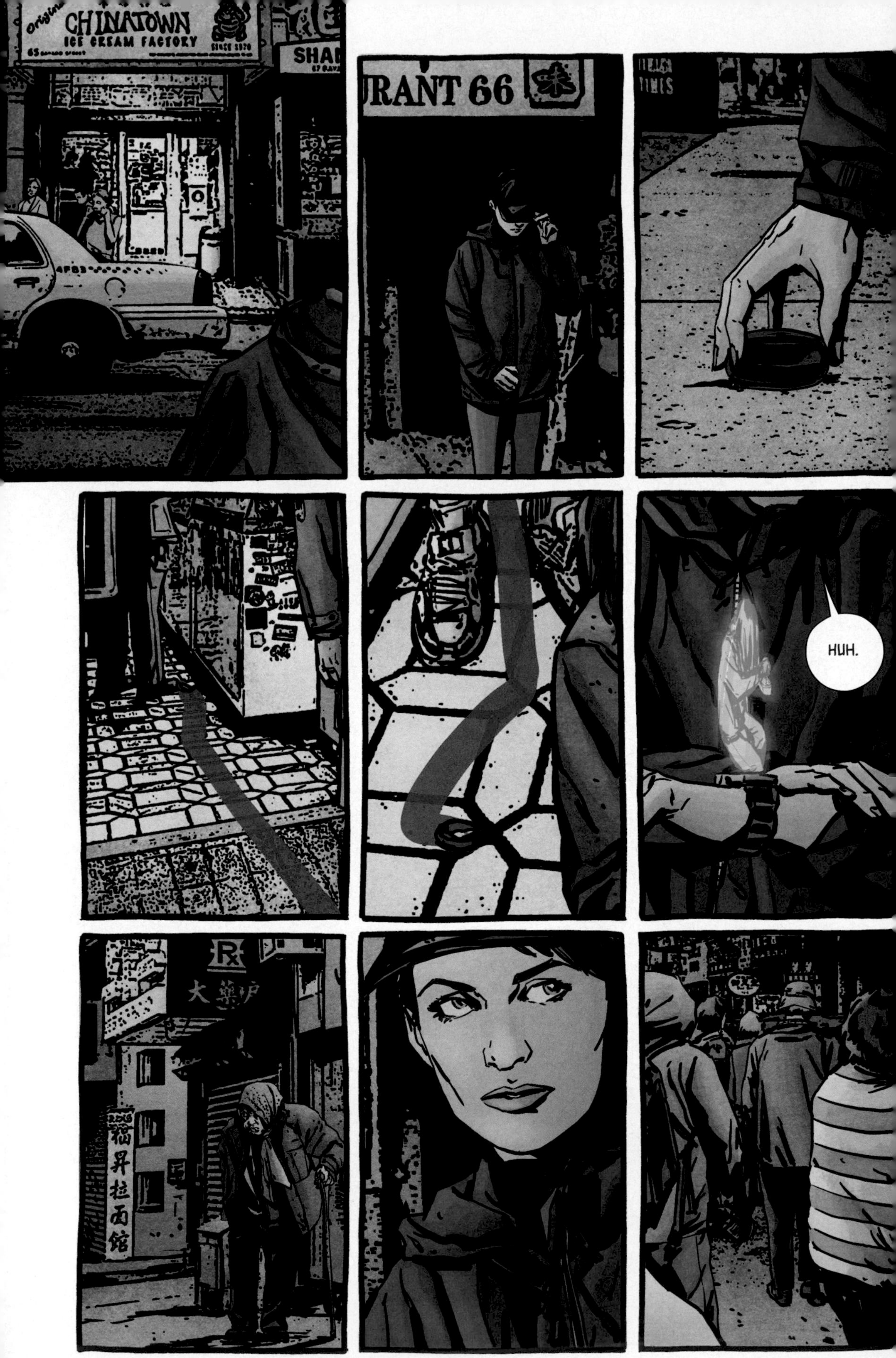
Original
CHINATOWN
ICE CREAM FACTORY
URANT 66
HUH.

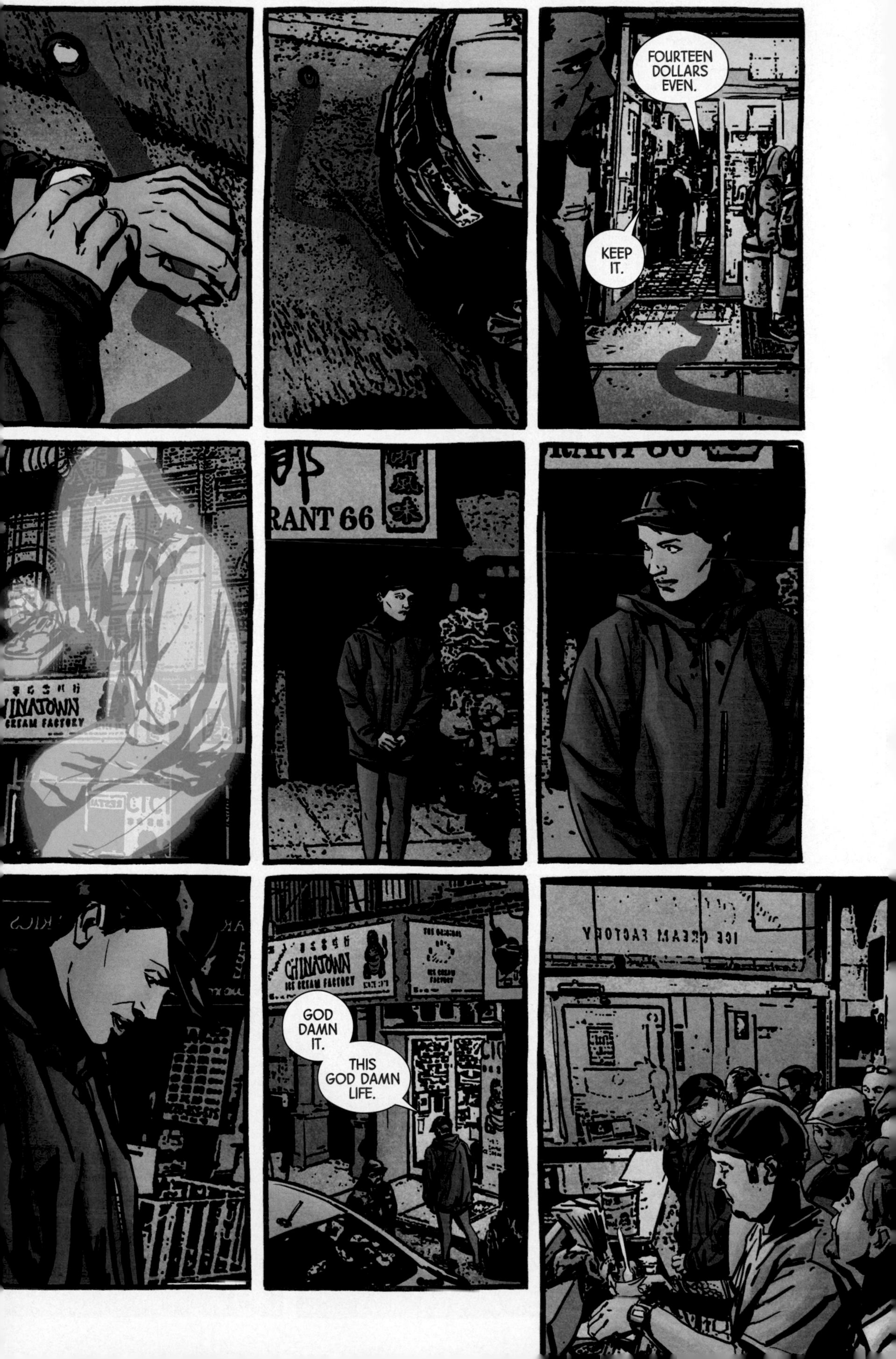
FOURTEEN DOLLARS EVEN.
KEEP IT.
RANT 66
CHINATOWN
ICE CREAM FACTORY
GOD DAMN IT.
THIS GOD DAMN LIFE.

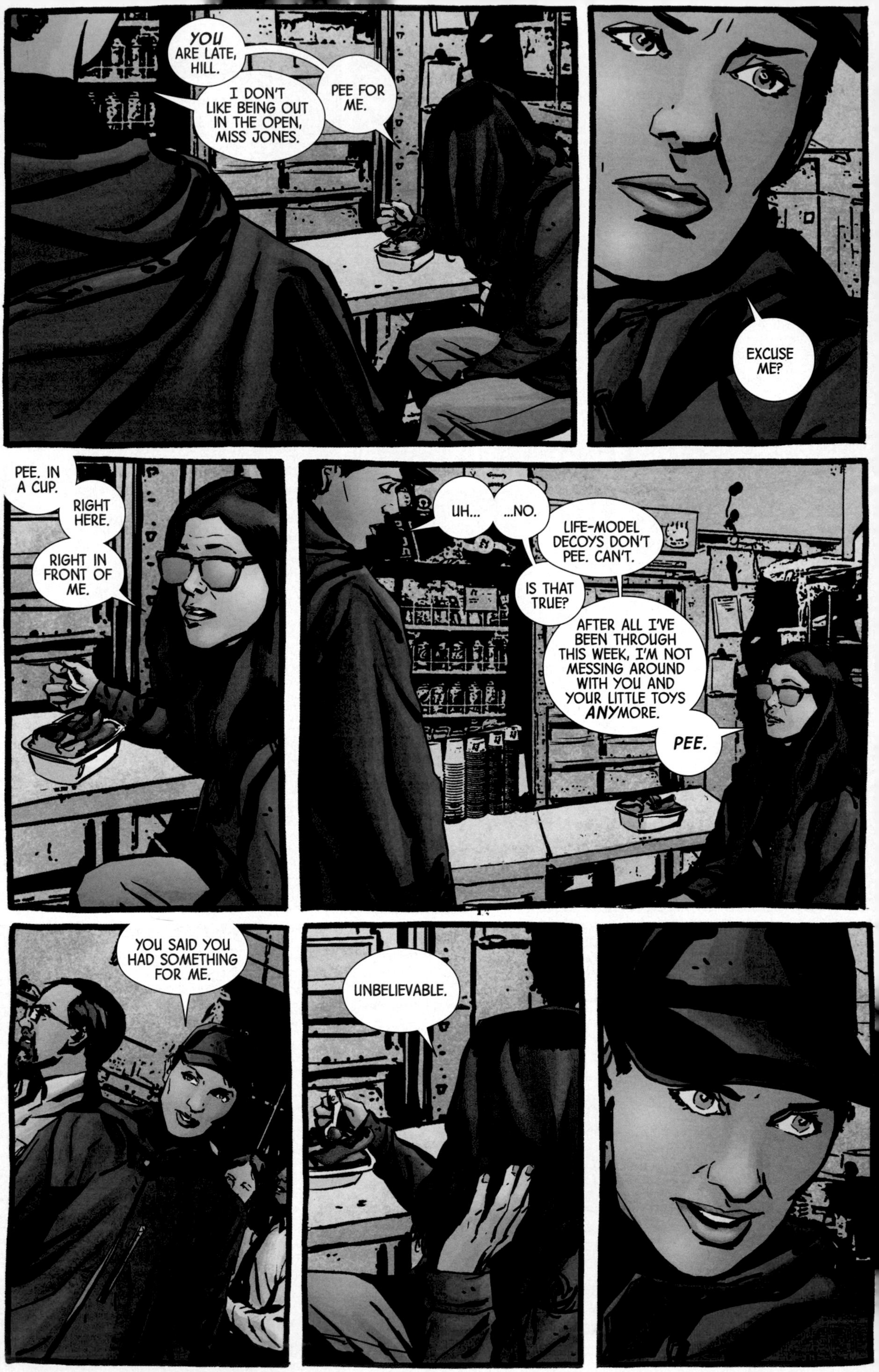
YOU ARE LATE, HILL.
I DON'T LIKE BEING OUT IN THE OPEN, MISS JONES.
PEE FOR ME.
EXCUSE ME?
PEE. IN A CUP.
RIGHT HERE.
RIGHT IN FRONT OF ME.
UH...
...NO.
LIFE-MODEL DECOYS DON'T PEE. CAN'T.
IS THAT TRUE?
AFTER ALL I'VE BEEN THROUGH THIS WEEK, I'M NOT MESSING AROUND WITH YOU AND YOUR LITTLE TOYS ANYMORE.
PEE.
YOU SAID YOU HAD SOMETHING FOR ME.
UNBELIEVABLE.

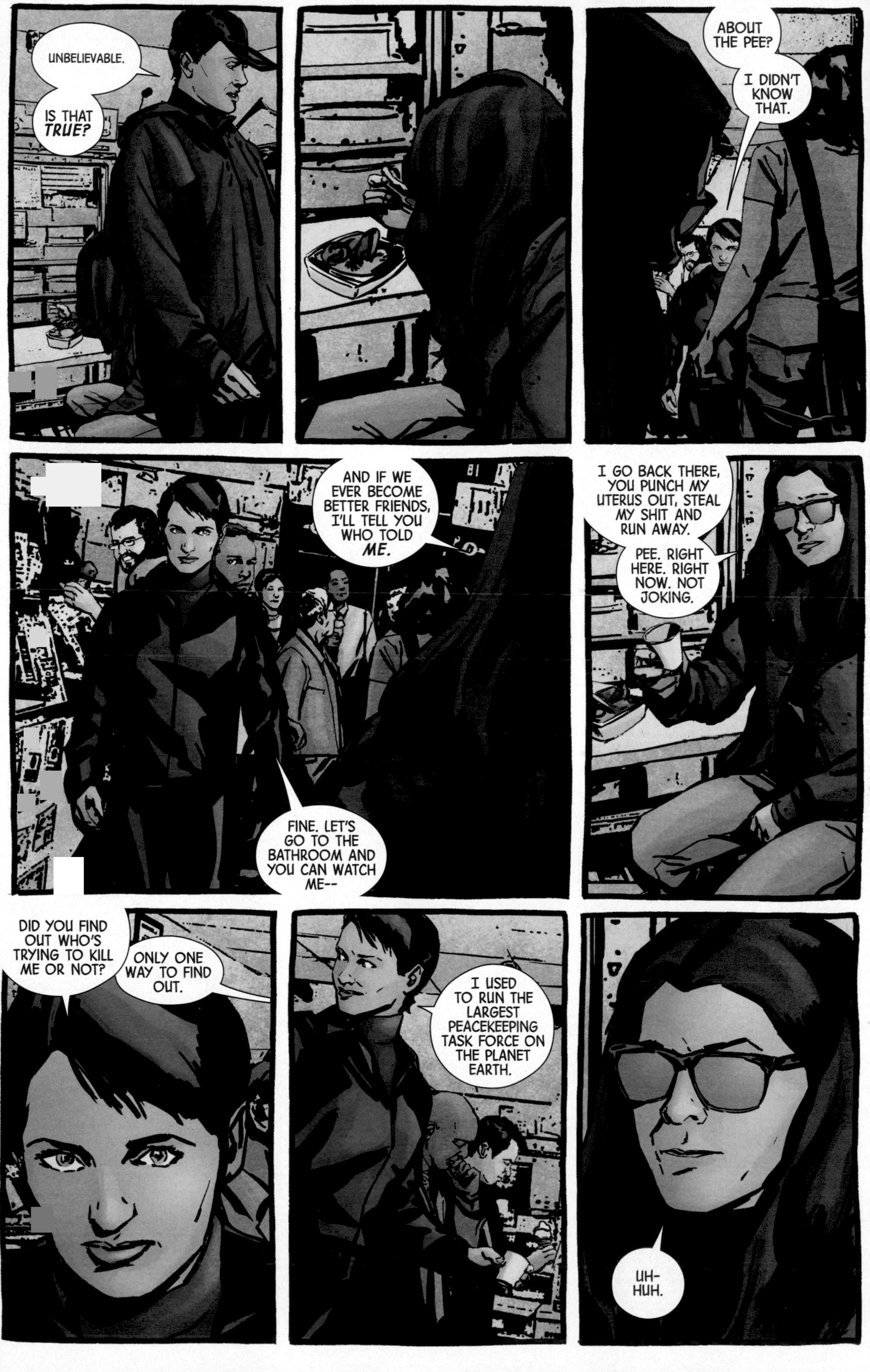
UNBELIEVABLE.
IS THAT TRUE?
ABOUT THE PEE?
I DIDN'T KNOW THAT.
AND IF WE EVER BECOME BETTER FRIENDS, I'LL TELL YOU WHO TOLD ME.
FINE. LET'S GO TO THE BATHROOM AND YOU CAN WATCH ME--
I GO BACK THERE, YOU PUNCH MY UTERUS OUT, STEAL MY SHIT AND RUN AWAY.
PEE. RIGHT HERE. RIGHT NOW. NOT JOKING.
DID YOU FIND OUT WHO'S TRYING TO KILL ME OR NOT?
ONLY ONE WAY TO FIND OUT.
I USED TO RUN THE LARGEST PEACEKEEPING TASK FORCE ON THE PLANET EARTH.
UH-HUH.

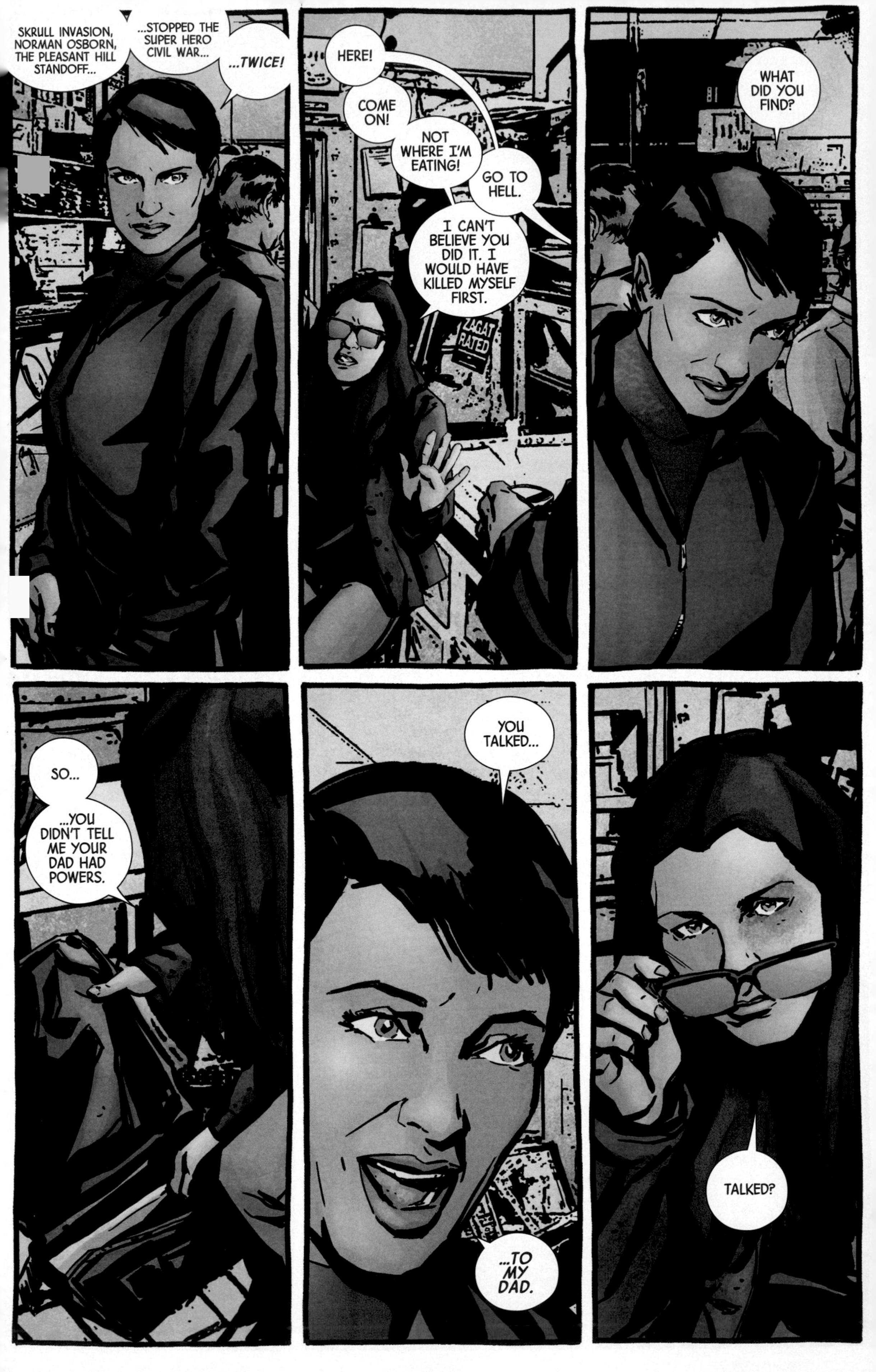
SKRULL INVASION, NORMAN OSBORN, THE PLEASANT HILL STANDOFF...
...STOPPED THE SUPER HERO CIVIL WAR...
...TWICE!
HERE!
COME ON!
NOT WHERE I'M EATING!
GO TO HELL.
I CAN'T BELIEVE YOU DID IT. I WOULD HAVE KILLED MYSELF FIRST.
ZAGAT RATED
WHAT DID YOU FIND?
SO...
...YOU DIDN'T TELL ME YOUR DAD HAD POWERS.
YOU TALKED...
...TO MY DAD.
TALKED?

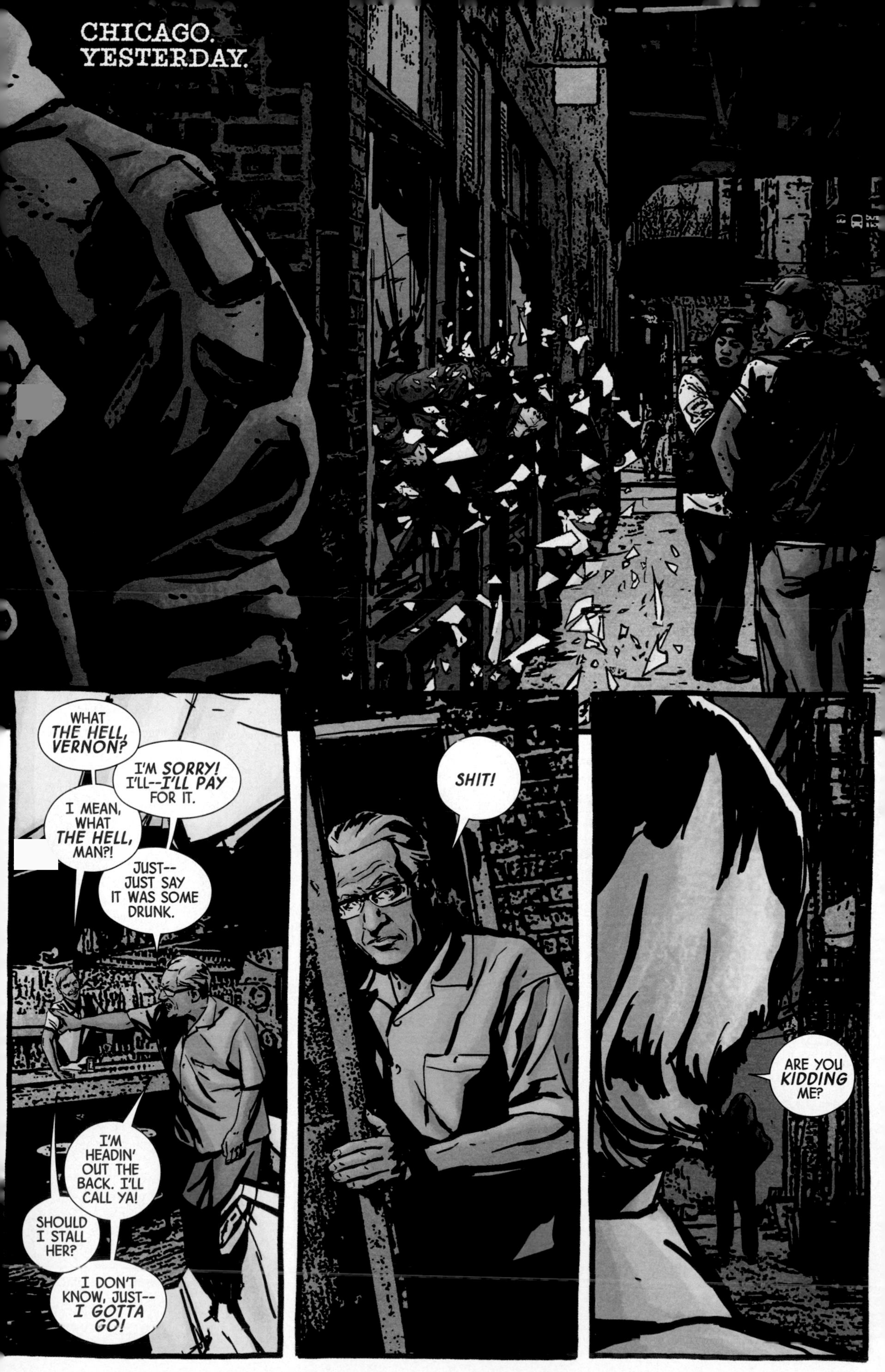
CHICAGO. YESTERDAY.
WHAT THE HELL, VERNON?
I'M SORRY! I'LL--I'LL PAY FOR IT.
I MEAN, WHAT THE HELL, MAN?!
JUST-- JUST SAY IT WAS SOME DRUNK.
I'M HEADIN' OUT THE BACK. I'LL CALL YA!
SHOULD I STALL HER?
I DON'T KNOW, JUST-- I GOTTA GO!
SHIT!
ARE YOU KIDDING ME?

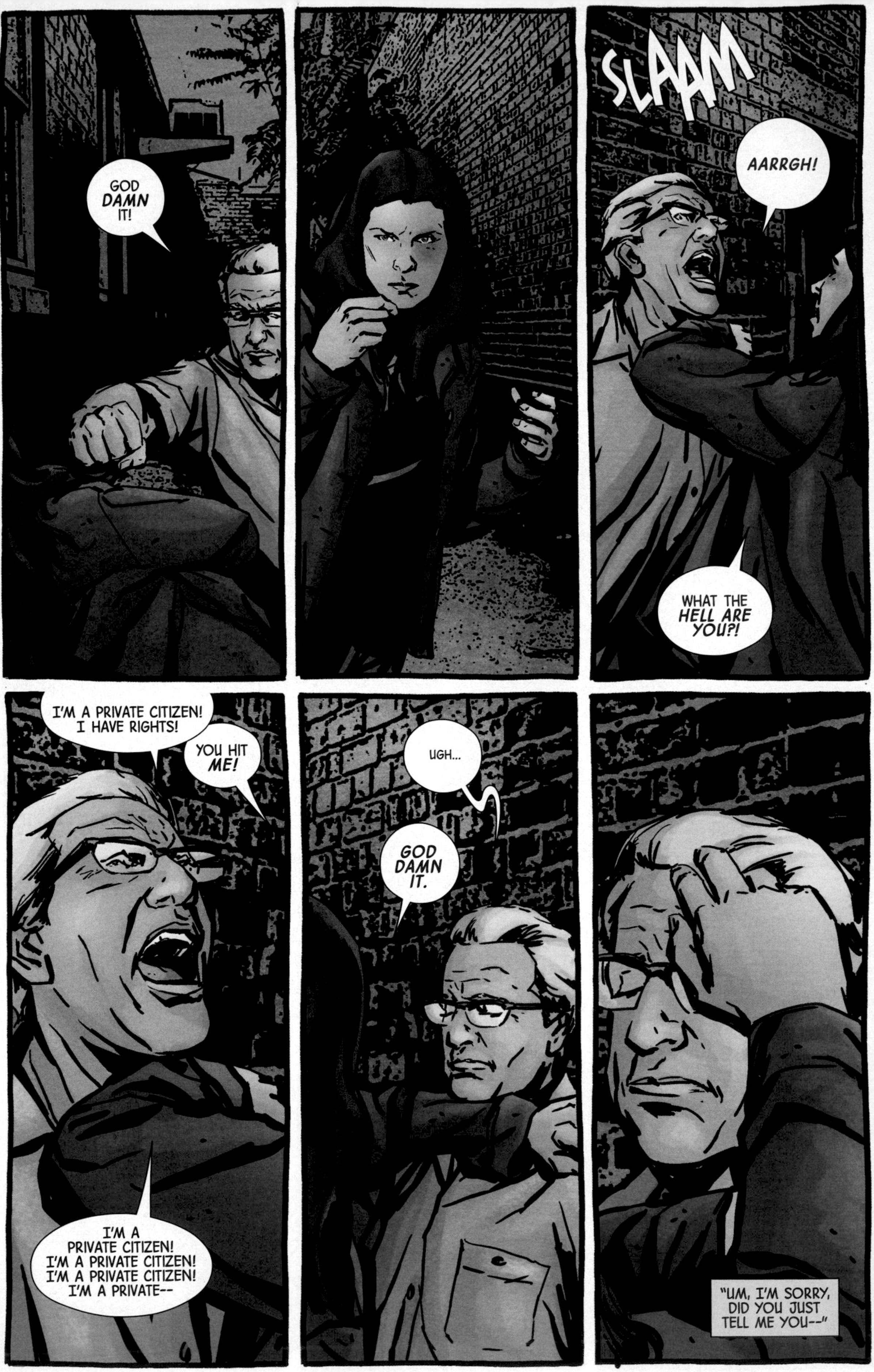
GOD DAMN IT!
SLAAM
AARRGH!
WHAT THE HELL ARE YOU?!
I'M A PRIVATE CITIZEN! I HAVE RIGHTS!
YOU HIT ME!
I'M A PRIVATE CITIZEN! I'M A PRIVATE CITIZEN! I'M A PRIVATE CITIZEN! I'M A PRIVATE--
UGH...
GOD DAMN IT.
"UM, I'M SORRY, DID YOU JUST TELL ME YOU--"

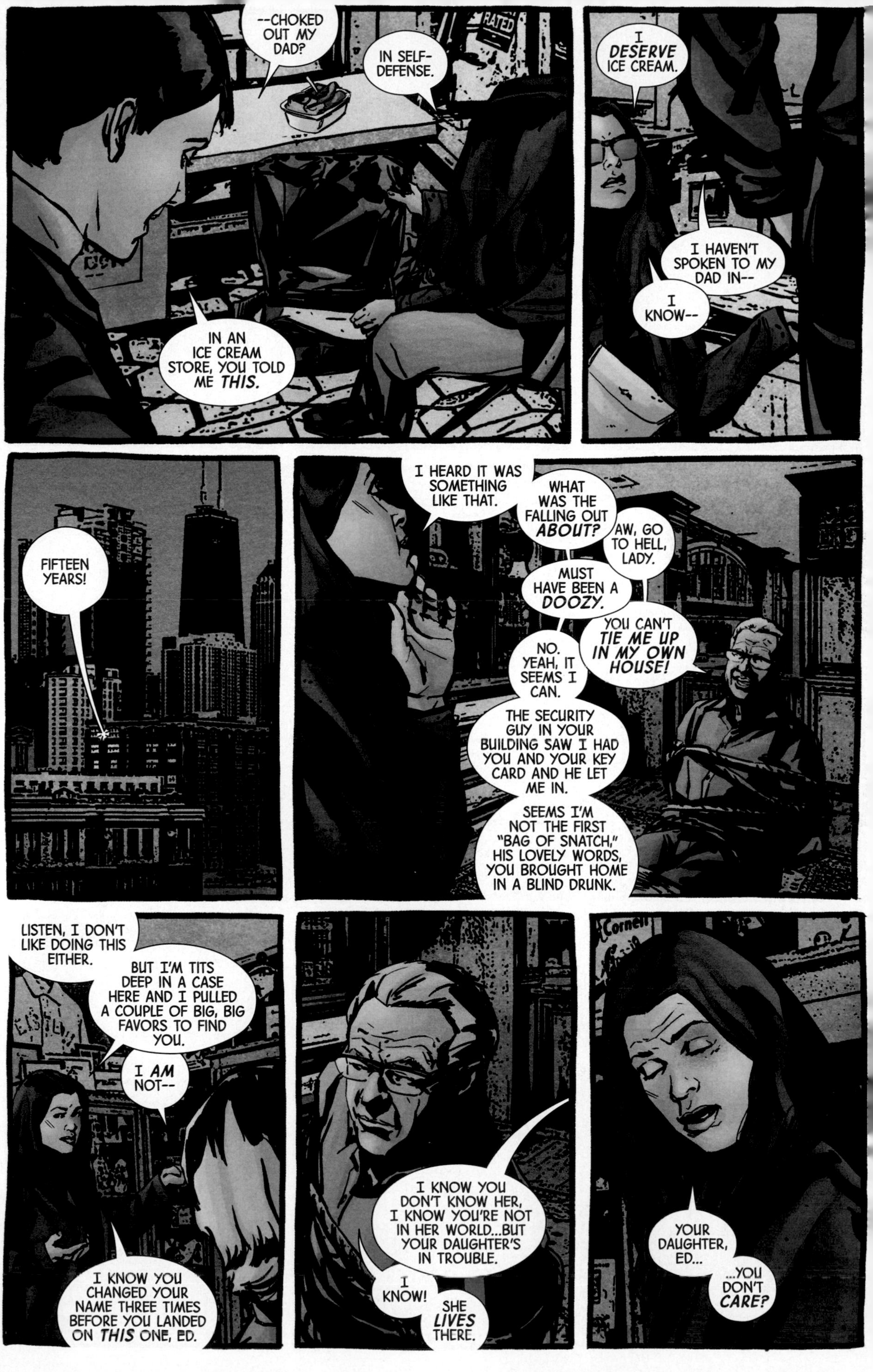
--CHOKED OUT MY DAD?
IN SELF-DEFENSE.
IN AN ICE CREAM STORE, YOU TOLD ME *THIS.*
I *DESERVE* ICE CREAM.
I HAVEN'T SPOKEN TO MY DAD IN--
I KNOW--
FIFTEEN YEARS!
I HEARD IT WAS SOMETHING LIKE THAT.
WHAT WAS THE FALLING OUT *ABOUT?*
AW, GO TO HELL, LADY.
MUST HAVE BEEN A *DOOZY.*
YOU CAN'T *TIE ME UP IN MY OWN HOUSE!*
NO. YEAH, IT SEEMS I CAN.
THE SECURITY GUY IN YOUR BUILDING SAW I HAD YOU AND YOUR KEY CARD AND HE LET ME IN.
SEEMS I'M NOT THE FIRST "BAG OF SNATCH," HIS LOVELY WORDS, YOU BROUGHT HOME IN A BLIND DRUNK.
LISTEN, I DON'T LIKE DOING THIS EITHER.
BUT I'M TITS DEEP IN A CASE HERE AND I PULLED A COUPLE OF BIG, BIG FAVORS TO FIND YOU.
I *AM* NOT--
I KNOW YOU CHANGED YOUR NAME THREE TIMES BEFORE YOU LANDED ON *THIS* ONE, ED.
I KNOW YOU DON'T KNOW HER, I KNOW YOU'RE NOT IN HER WORLD...BUT YOUR DAUGHTER'S IN TROUBLE.
I KNOW!
SHE *LIVES* THERE.
YOUR DAUGHTER, ED...
...YOU DON'T *CARE?*

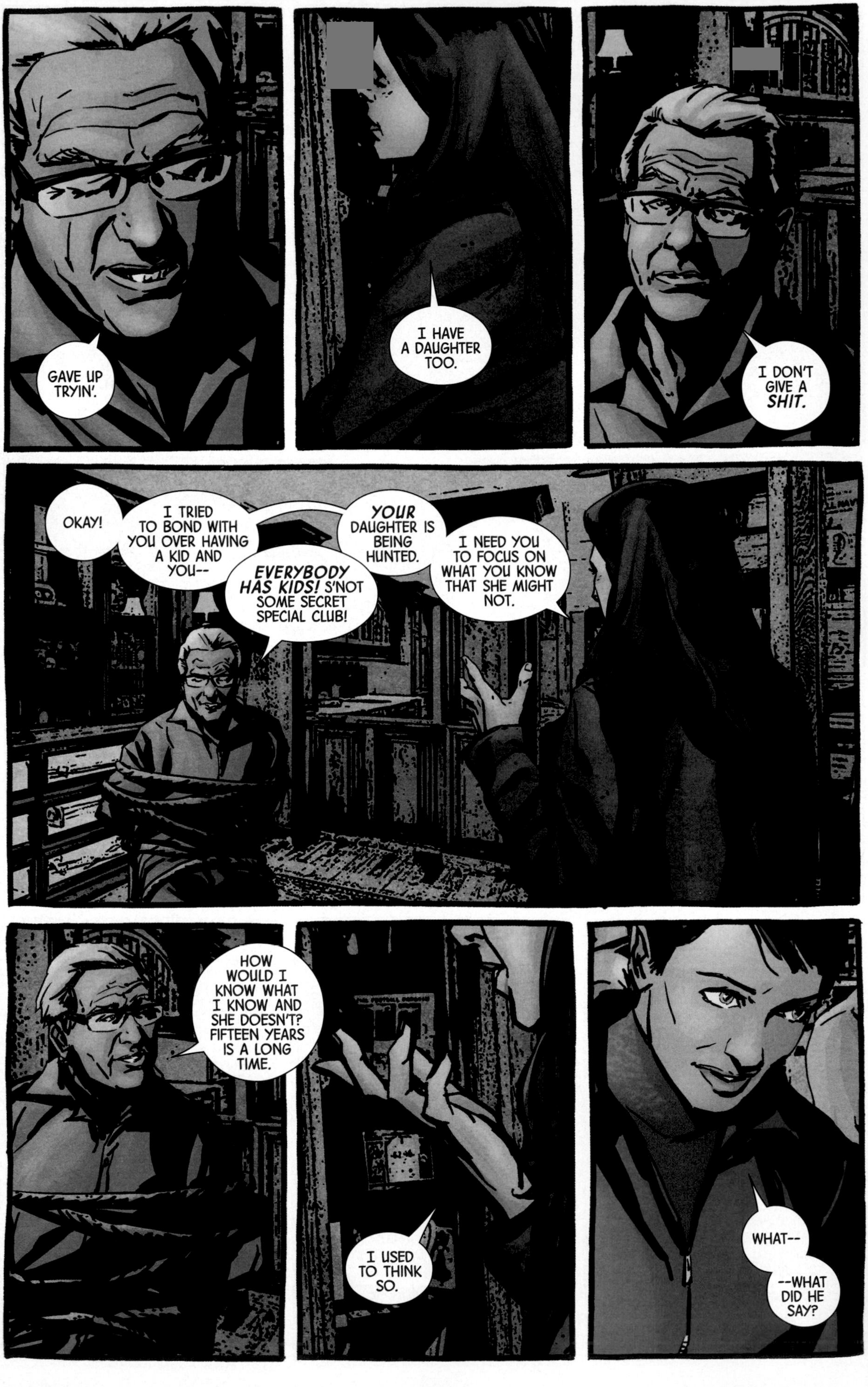
GAVE UP TRYIN'.
I HAVE A DAUGHTER TOO.
I DON'T GIVE A ***SHIT.***
OKAY!
I TRIED TO BOND WITH YOU OVER HAVING A KID AND YOU--
EVERYBODY HAS KIDS! S'NOT SOME SECRET SPECIAL CLUB!
YOUR DAUGHTER IS BEING HUNTED.
I NEED YOU TO FOCUS ON WHAT YOU KNOW THAT SHE MIGHT NOT.
HOW WOULD I KNOW WHAT I KNOW AND SHE DOESN'T? FIFTEEN YEARS IS A LONG TIME.
I USED TO THINK SO.
WHAT--
--WHAT DID HE SAY?

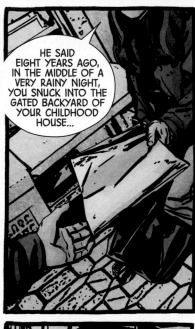

HE SAID EIGHT YEARS AGO, IN THE MIDDLE OF A VERY RAINY NIGHT, YOU SNUCK INTO THE GATED BACKYARD OF YOUR CHILDHOOD HOUSE...

"...AND YOU BURIED SOMETHING IN A LITTLE CHILDHOOD GARDEN.

"HE SAW YOU DO IT.

"HE SAID IT WAS THE LAST TIME HE EVER SAW YOU IN PERSON.

"SO WHEN HE MOVED, HE DUG IT UP, AND HE PUT IT IN HIS SAFE ALONG WITH HIS PATIENCE AND GOOD NATURE, I'M ASSUMING."

I--I HAVE NO MEMORY OF DOING THAT.

WHICH IS WHAT YOU TOLD ME TO LOOK OUT FOR. SO I DID.

YOU OPENED IT.

NICK FUR
EYES ONL

mission
failure repor
ROJECT: bootleg

HELL YES, I DID.

I GOT PUNCHED IN THE EYE FOR THAT...I LOOKED.

WHAT IS IT?

OH, NO...

CRHAS
HSS

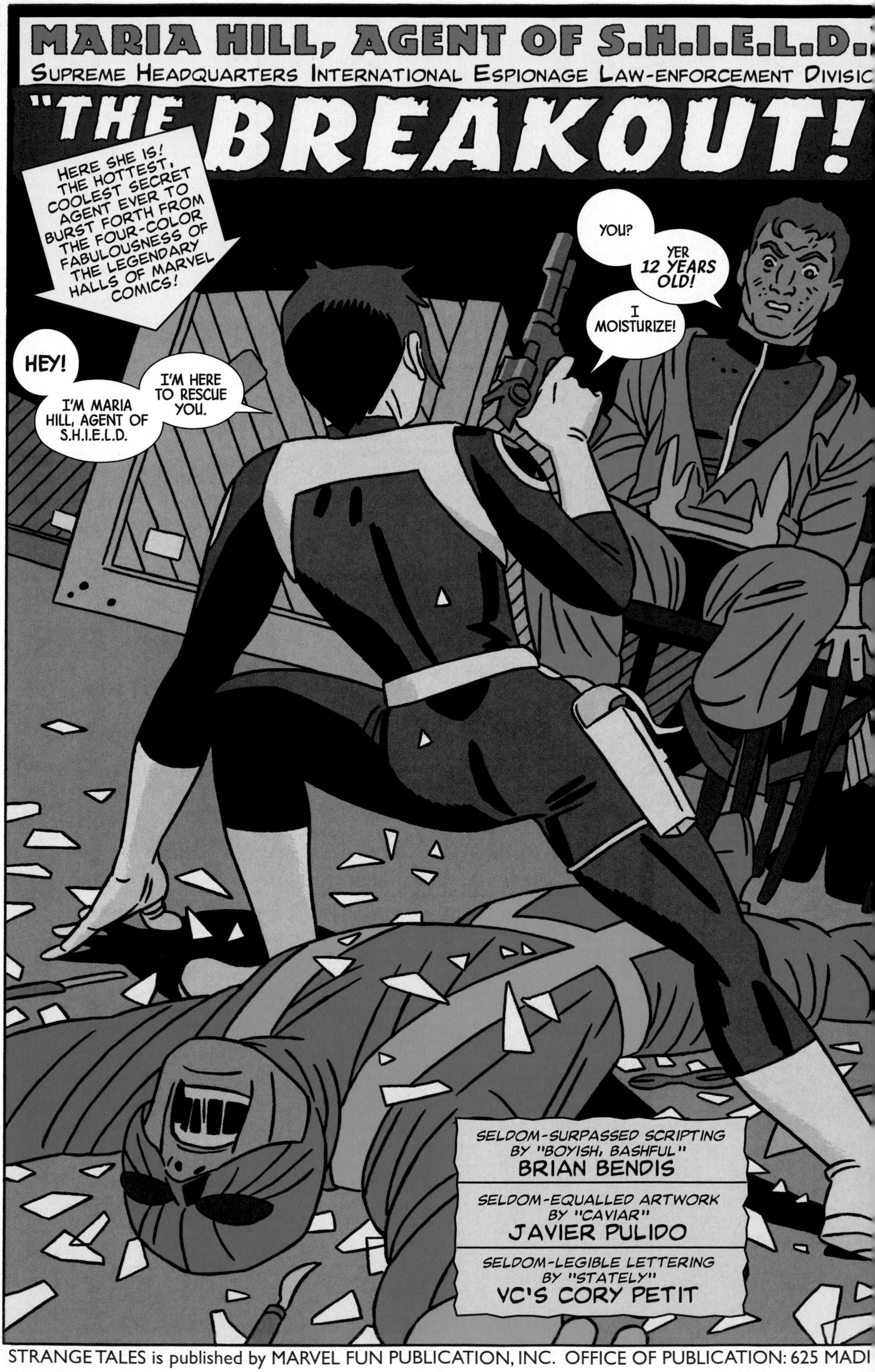
MARIA HILL, AGENT OF S.H.I.E.L.D.
SUPREME HEADQUARTERS INTERNATIONAL ESPIONAGE LAW-ENFORCEMENT DIVISIC
"THE BREAKOUT!
HERE SHE IS! THE HOTTEST, COOLEST SECRET AGENT EVER TO BURST FORTH FROM THE FOUR-COLOR FABULOUSNESS OF THE LEGENDARY HALLS OF MARVEL COMICS!
HEY!
I'M MARIA HILL, AGENT OF S.H.I.E.L.D.
I'M HERE TO RESCUE YOU.
YOU?
YER 12 YEARS OLD!
I MOISTURIZE!
SELDOM-SURPASSED SCRIPTING BY "BOYISH, BASHFUL" BRIAN BENDIS
SELDOM-EQUALLED ARTWORK BY "CAVIAR" JAVIER PULIDO
SELDOM-LEGIBLE LETTERING BY "STATELY" VC'S CORY PETIT

STRANGE TALES is published by MARVEL FUN PUBLICATION, INC. OFFICE OF PUBLICATION: 625 MADI

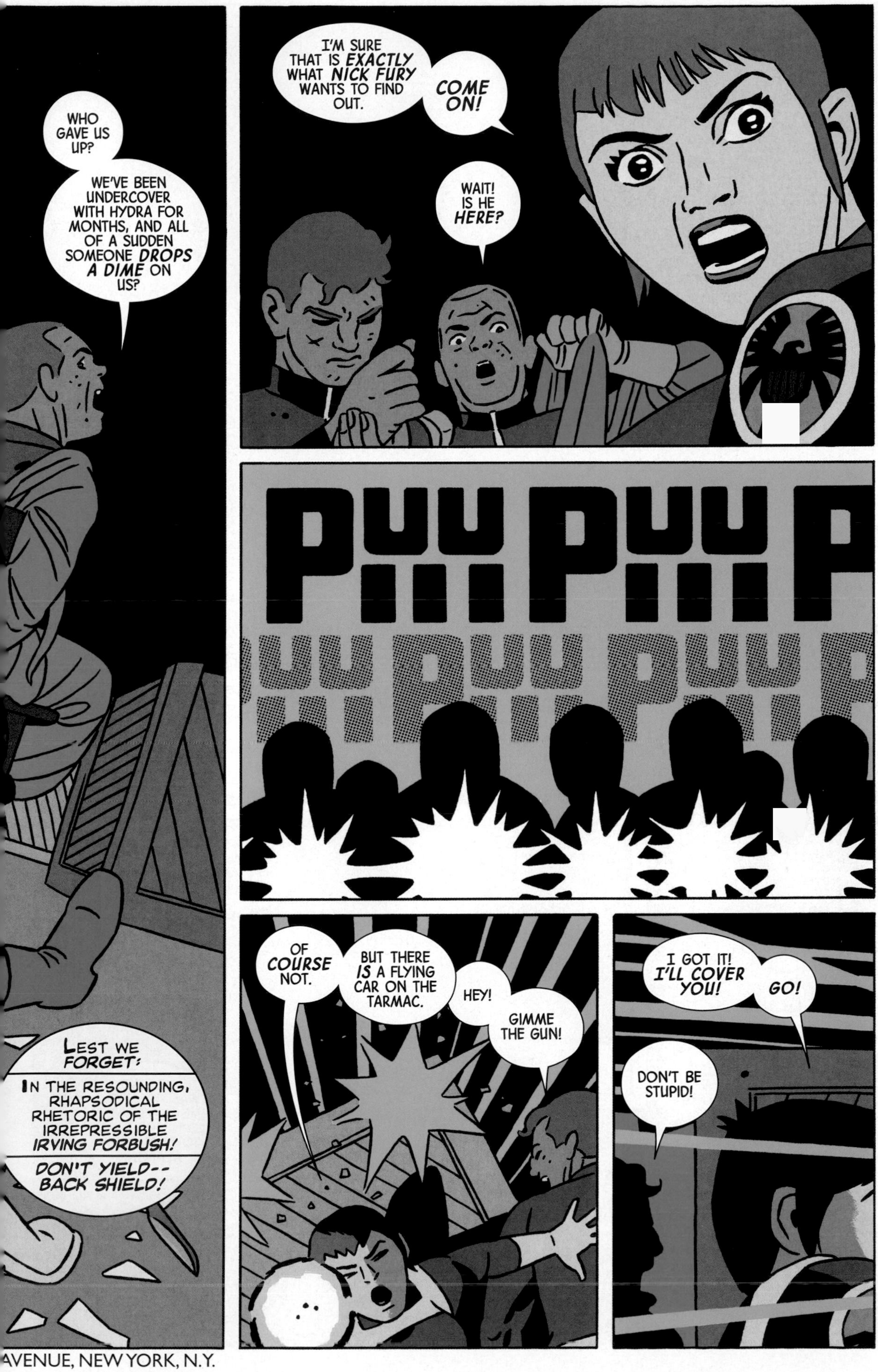
WHO GAVE US UP?
WE'VE BEEN UNDERCOVER WITH HYDRA FOR MONTHS, AND ALL OF A SUDDEN SOMEONE DROPS A DIME ON US?
I'M SURE THAT IS EXACTLY WHAT NICK FURY WANTS TO FIND OUT.
COME ON!
WAIT! IS HE HERE?
PIIIPIIIP
OF COURSE NOT.
BUT THERE IS A FLYING CAR ON THE TARMAC.
HEY!
GIMME THE GUN!
I GOT IT! I'LL COVER YOU!
GO!
DON'T BE STUPID!
LEST WE FORGET:
IN THE RESOUNDING, RHAPSODICAL RHETORIC OF THE IRREPRESSIBLE IRVING FORBUSH!
DON'T YIELD-- BACK SHIELD!

AVENUE, NEW YORK, N.Y.

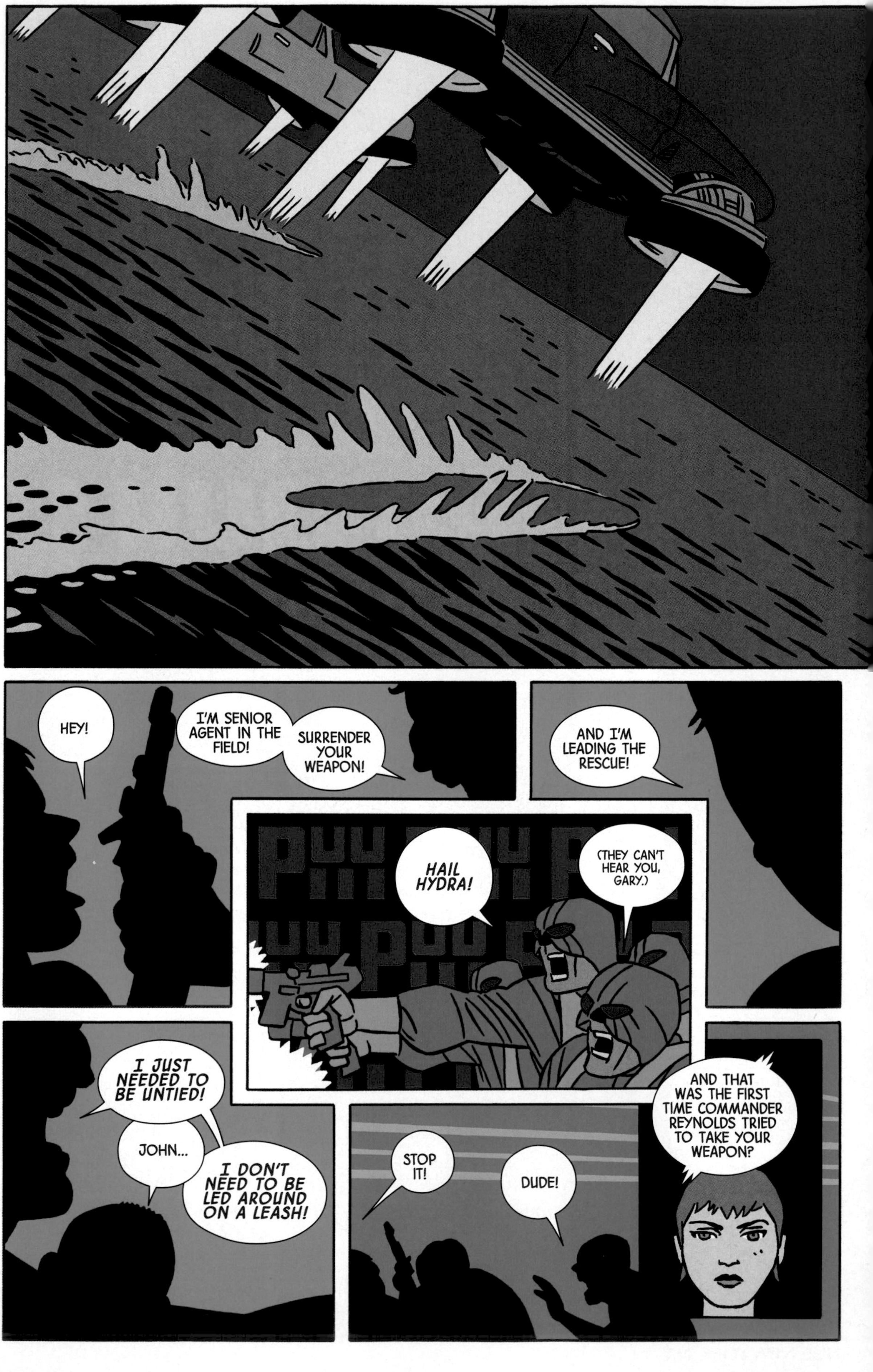
HEY!
I'M SENIOR AGENT IN THE FIELD!
SURRENDER YOUR WEAPON!
AND I'M LEADING THE RESCUE!
HAIL HYDRA!
(THEY CAN'T HEAR YOU, GARY.)
I JUST NEEDED TO BE UNTIED!
JOHN...
I DON'T NEED TO BE LED AROUND ON A LEASH!
STOP IT!
DUDE!
AND THAT WAS THE FIRST TIME COMMANDER REYNOLDS TRIED TO TAKE YOUR WEAPON?

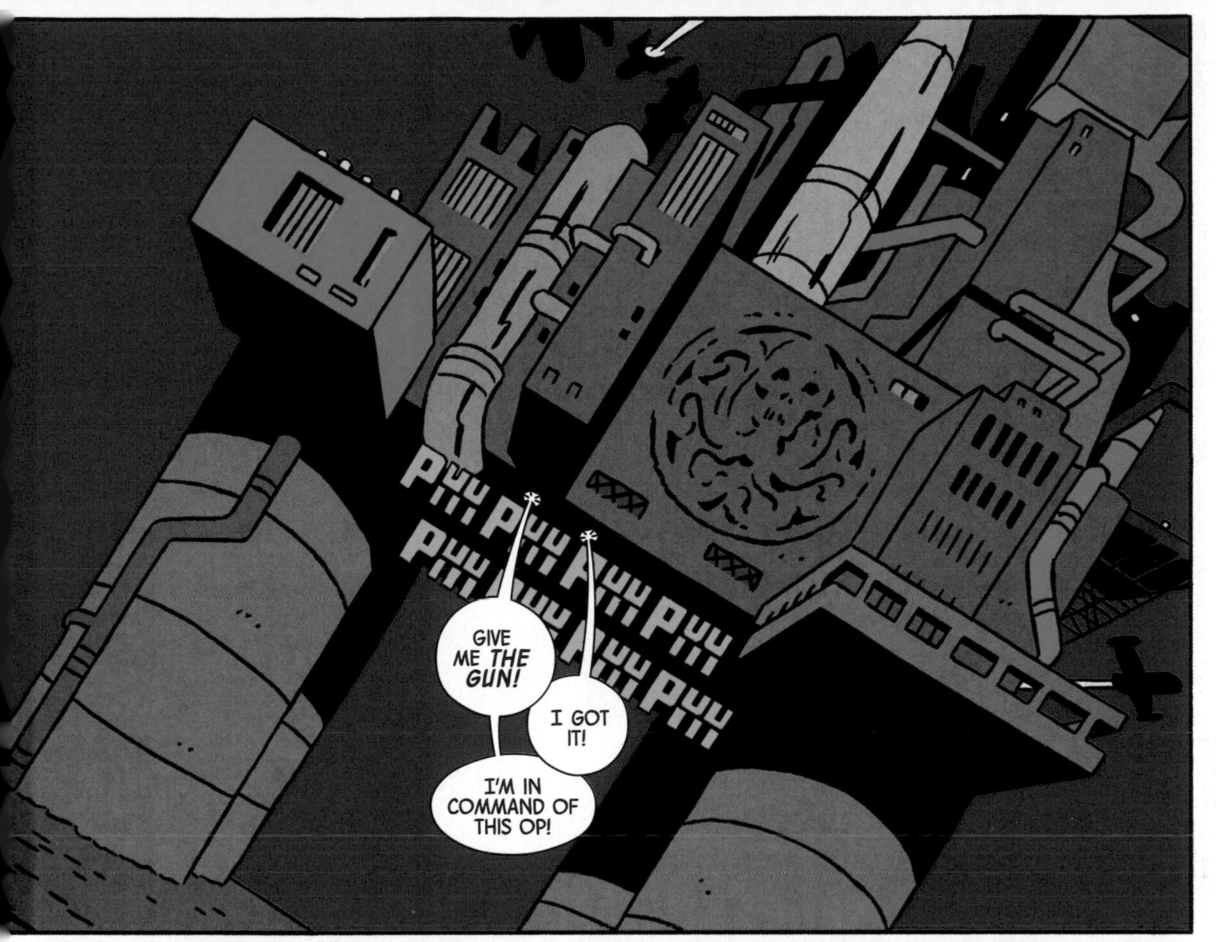
PUU PUU PUU PUU PUU PUU PUU PUU PUU
GIVE ME THE GUN!
I GOT IT!
I'M IN COMMAND OF THIS OP!

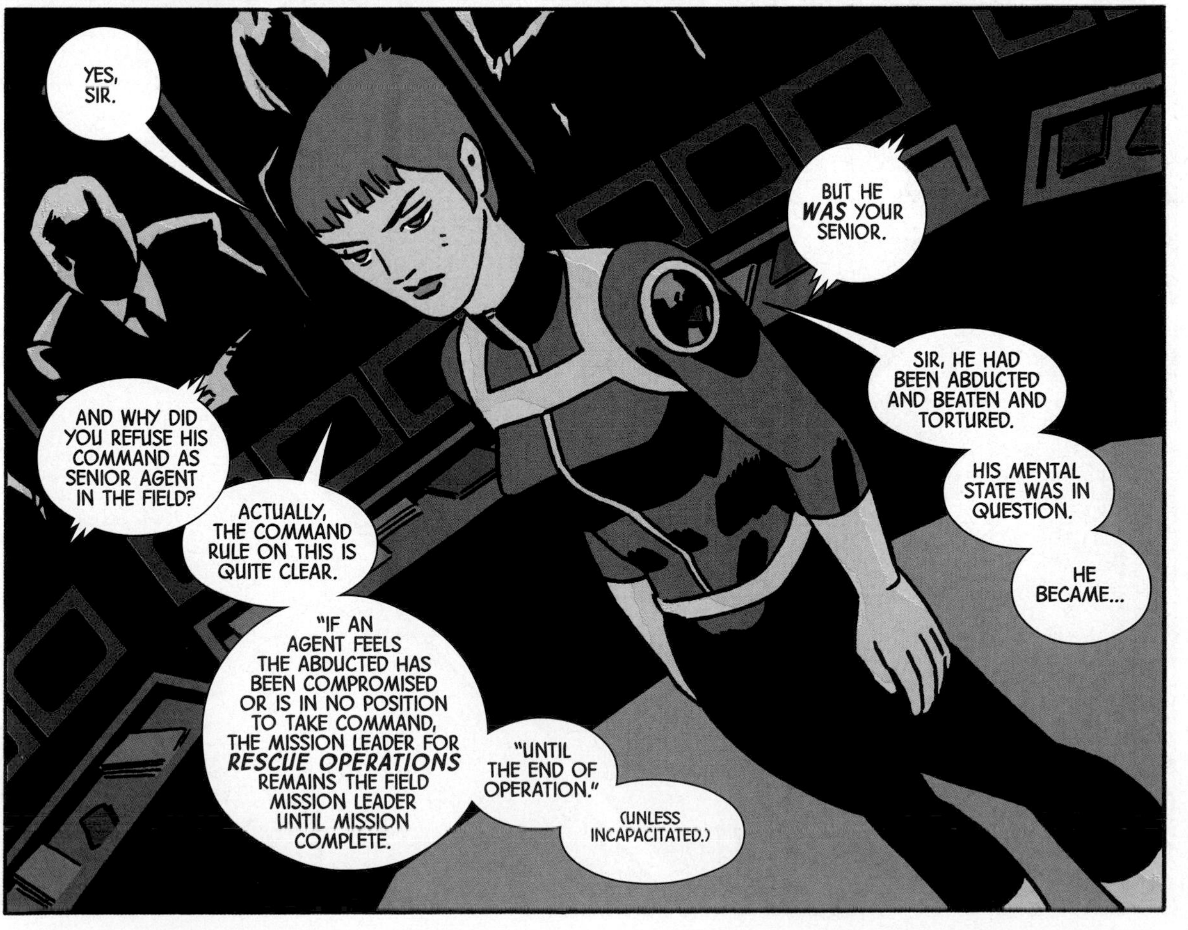
YES, SIR.
BUT HE WAS YOUR SENIOR.
SIR, HE HAD BEEN ABDUCTED AND BEATEN AND TORTURED.
HIS MENTAL STATE WAS IN QUESTION.
HE BECAME...
AND WHY DID YOU REFUSE HIS COMMAND AS SENIOR AGENT IN THE FIELD?
ACTUALLY, THE COMMAND RULE ON THIS IS QUITE CLEAR.
"IF AN AGENT FEELS THE ABDUCTED HAS BEEN COMPROMISED OR IS IN NO POSITION TO TAKE COMMAND, THE MISSION LEADER FOR RESCUE OPERATIONS REMAINS THE FIELD MISSION LEADER UNTIL MISSION COMPLETE.
"UNTIL THE END OF OPERATION."
(UNLESS INCAPACITATED.)

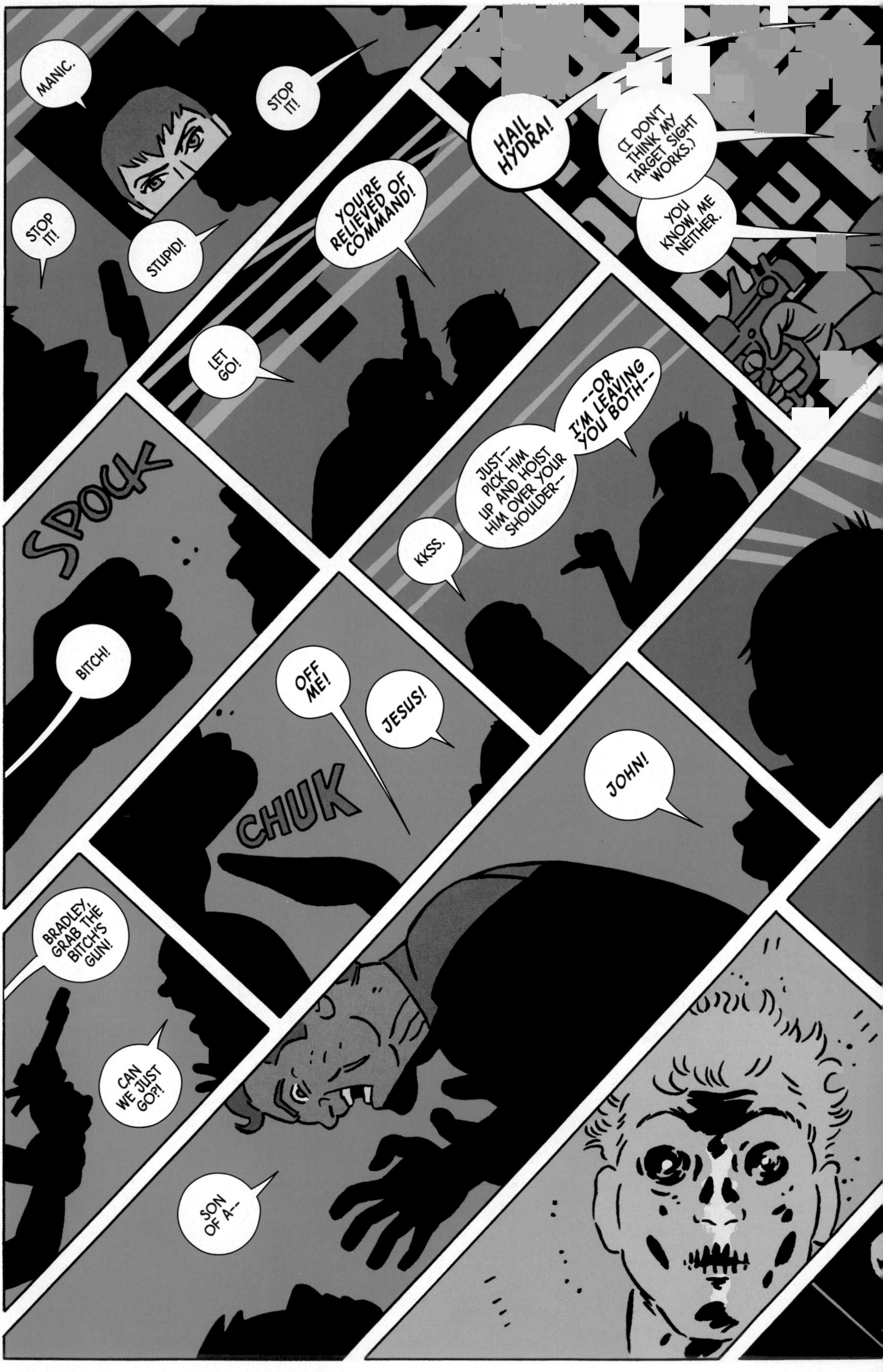

MANIC.
STOP IT!
STOP IT!
STUPID!
YOU'RE RELIEVED OF COMMAND!
LET GO!
HAIL HYDRA!
(I DON'T THINK MY TARGET SIGHT WORKS.)
YOU KNOW, ME NEITHER.
SPOCK
JUST-- PICK HIM UP AND HOIST HIM OVER YOUR SHOULDER--
--OR I'M LEAVING YOU BOTH--
KKSS.
BITCH!
OFF ME!
JESUS!
CHUK
JOHN!
BRADLEY, GRAB THE BITCH'S GUN!
CAN WE JUST GO?!
SON OF A--

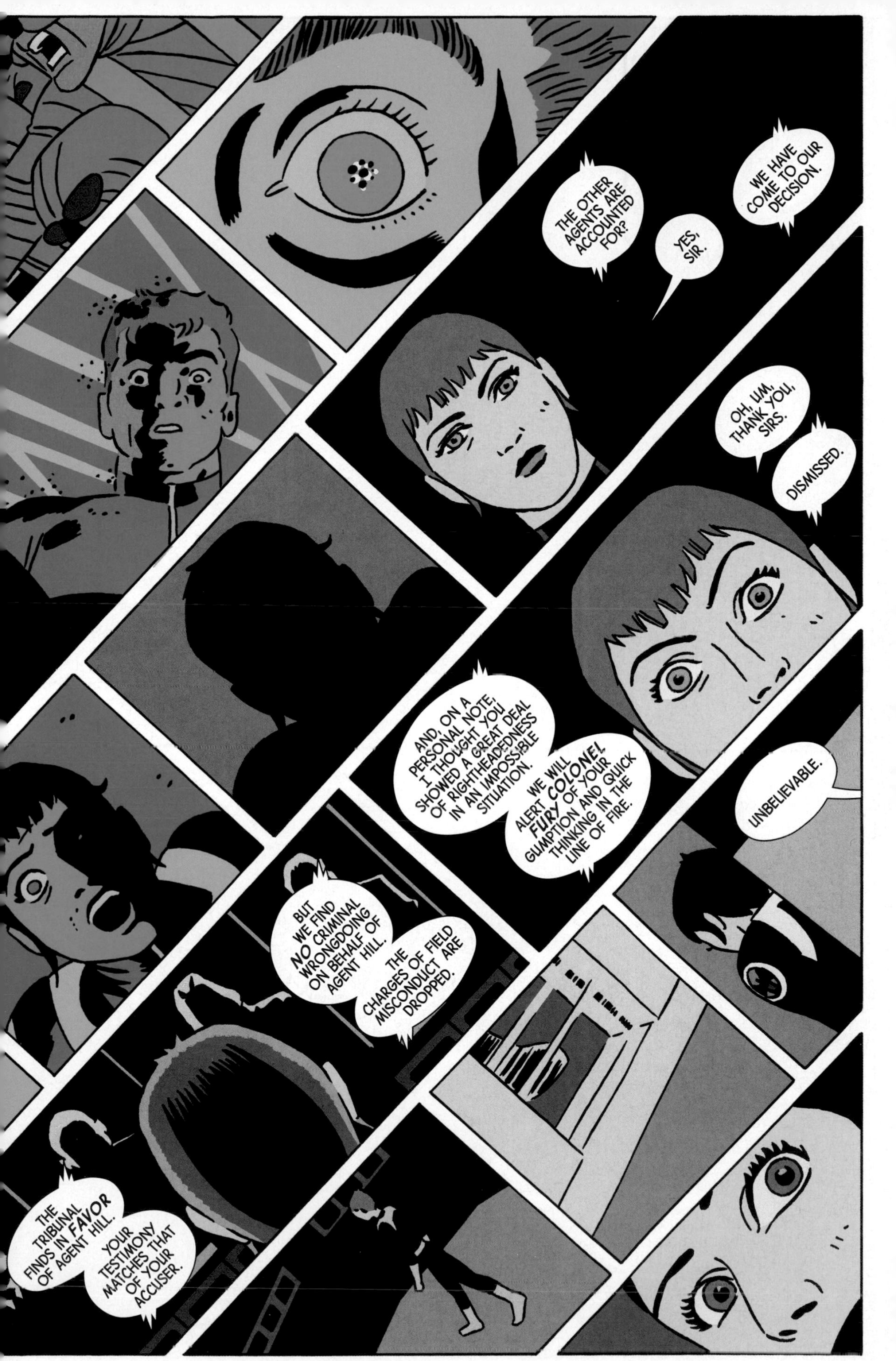
WE HAVE COME TO OUR DECISION.
THE TRIBUNAL FINDS IN FAVOR OF AGENT HILL.
YOUR TESTIMONY MATCHES THAT OF YOUR ACCUSER.
BUT WE FIND NO CRIMINAL WRONGDOING ON BEHALF OF AGENT HILL.
THE CHARGES OF FIELD MISCONDUCT ARE DROPPED.
AND, ON A PERSONAL NOTE, I THOUGHT YOU SHOWED A GREAT DEAL OF RIGHTHEADEDNESS IN AN IMPOSSIBLE SITUATION.
WE WILL ALERT COLONEL FURY OF YOUR GUMPTION AND QUICK THINKING IN THE LINE OF FIRE.
OH, UM, THANK YOU, SIRS.
DISMISSED.
THE OTHER AGENTS ARE ACCOUNTED FOR?
YES, SIR.
UNBELIEVABLE.

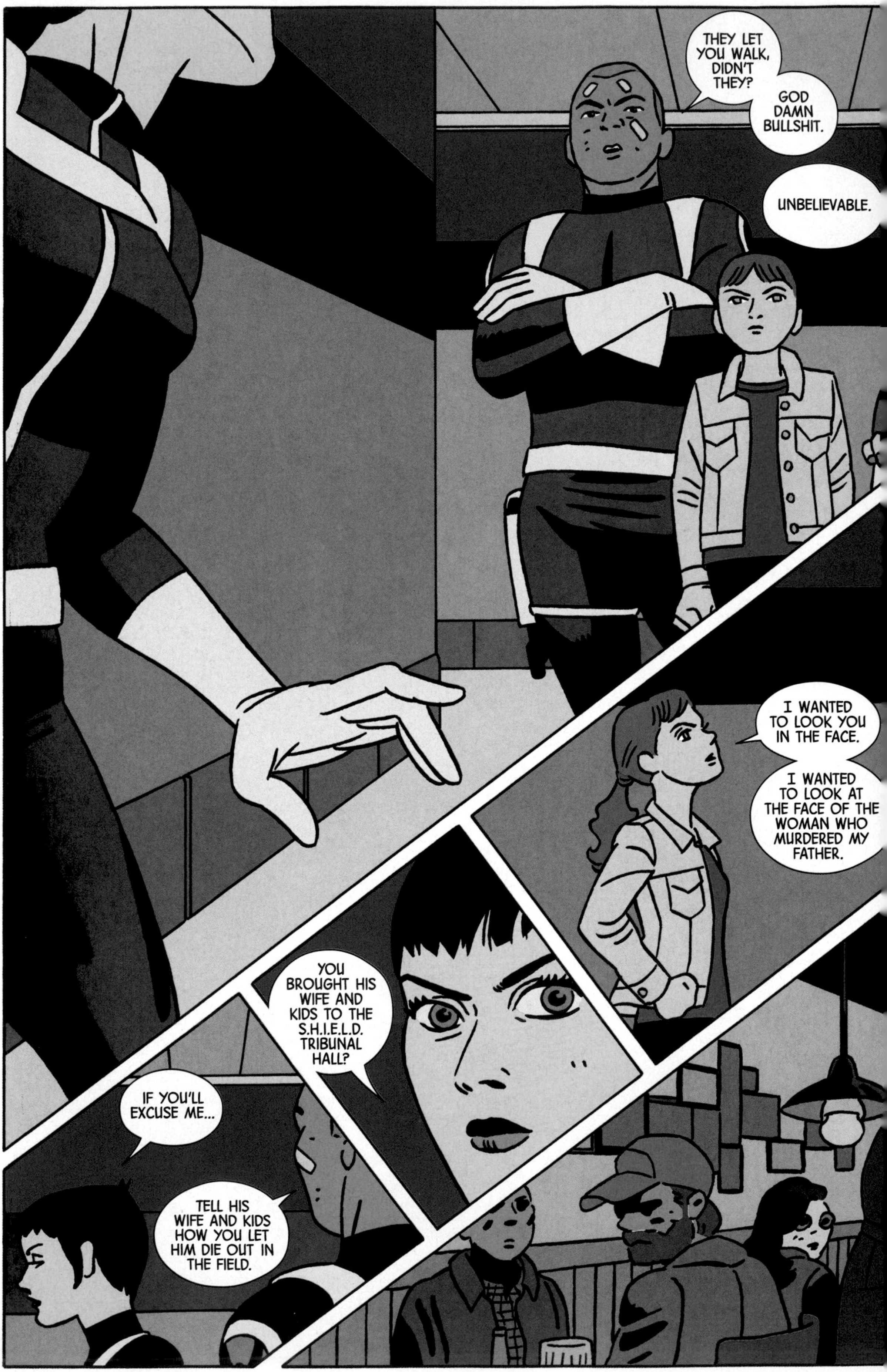
THEY LET YOU WALK, DIDN'T THEY?
GOD DAMN BULLSHIT.
UNBELIEVABLE.
I WANTED TO LOOK YOU IN THE FACE.
I WANTED TO LOOK AT THE FACE OF THE WOMAN WHO MURDERED MY FATHER.
YOU BROUGHT HIS WIFE AND KIDS TO THE S.H.I.E.L.D. TRIBUNAL HALL?
IF YOU'LL EXCUSE ME...
TELL HIS WIFE AND KIDS HOW YOU LET HIM DIE OUT IN THE FIELD.

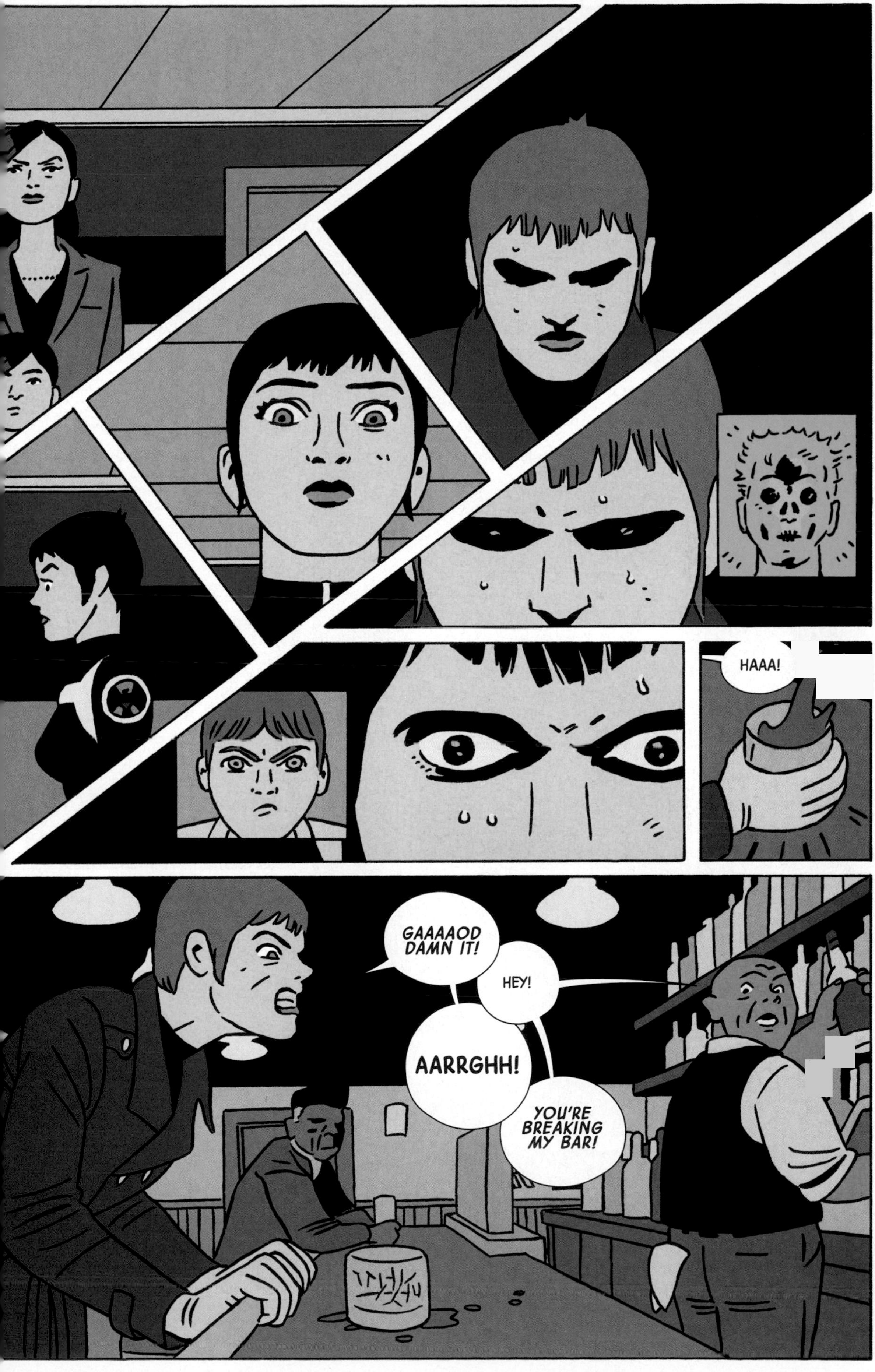
HAAA!
GAAAAOD DAMN IT!
HEY!
AARRGHH!
YOU'RE BREAKING MY BAR!

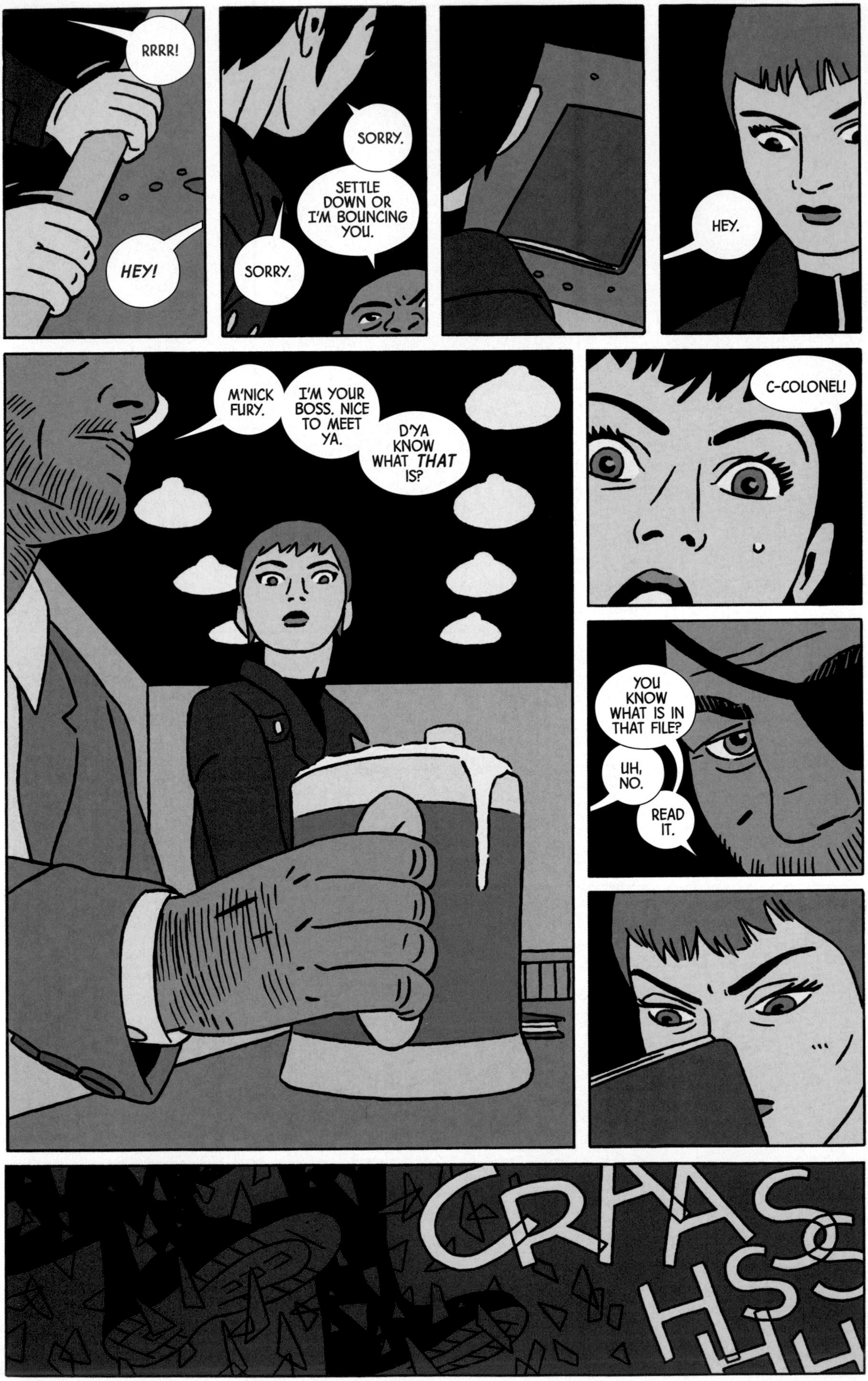
RRRR!
HEY!
SORRY.
SETTLE DOWN OR I'M BOUNCING YOU.
SORRY.
HEY.
M'NICK FURY.
I'M YOUR BOSS. NICE TO MEET YA.
D'YA KNOW WHAT *THAT* IS?
C-COLONEL!
YOU KNOW WHAT IS IN THAT FILE?
UH, NO.
READ IT.
CRASSHH

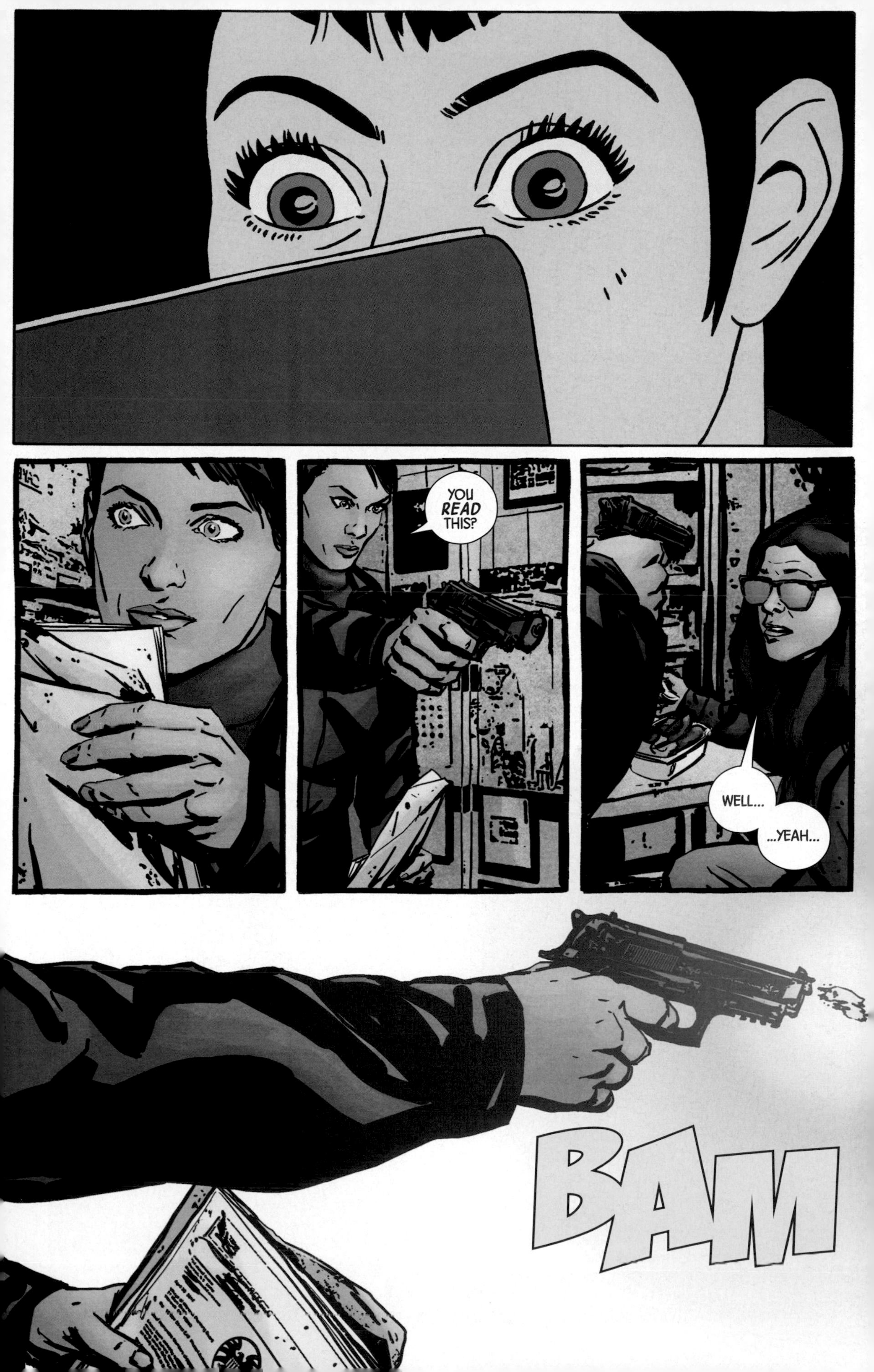
YOU READ THIS?
WELL...
...YEAH...
BAM

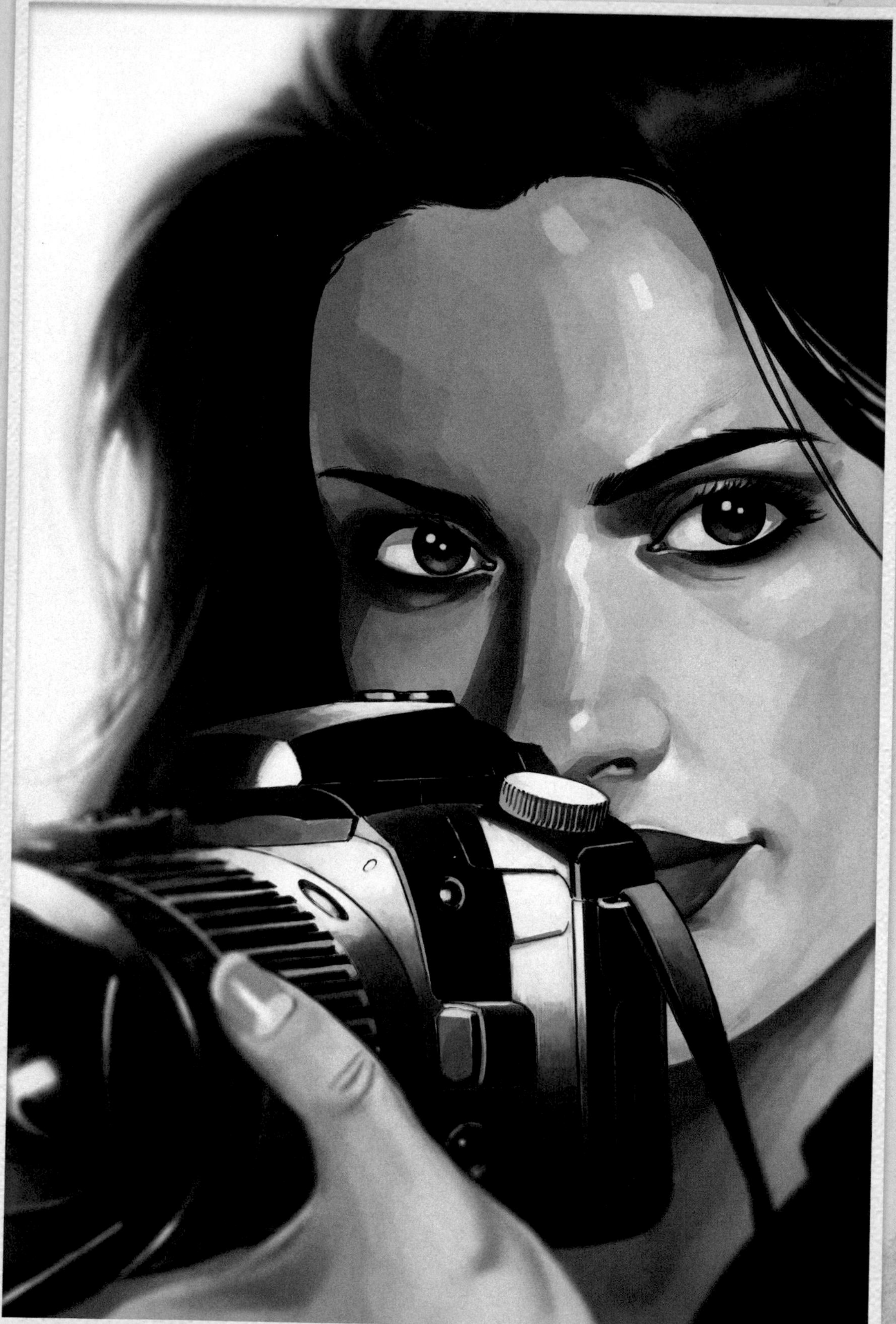

#12 variant by **Djibril Morissette-Phan**

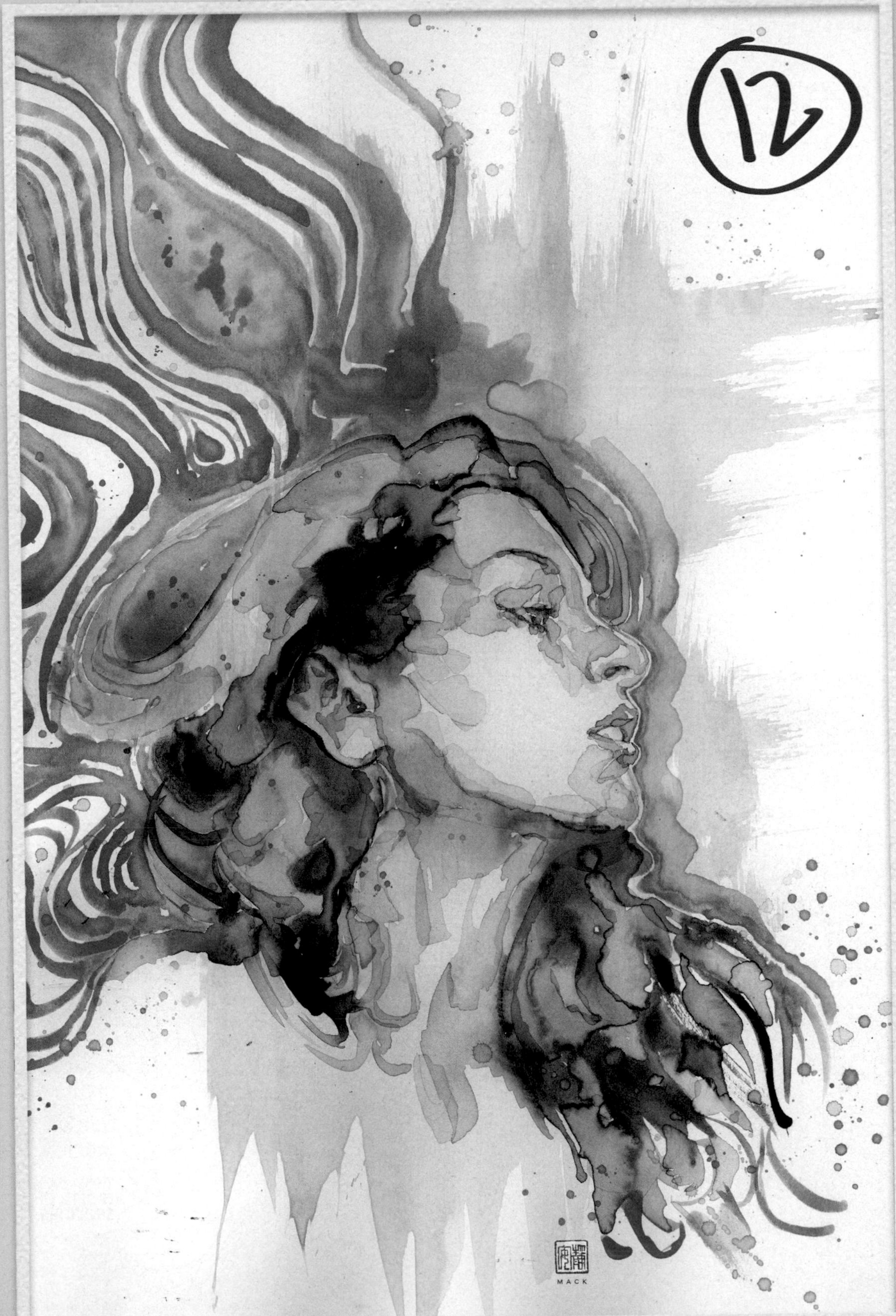
12
MACK

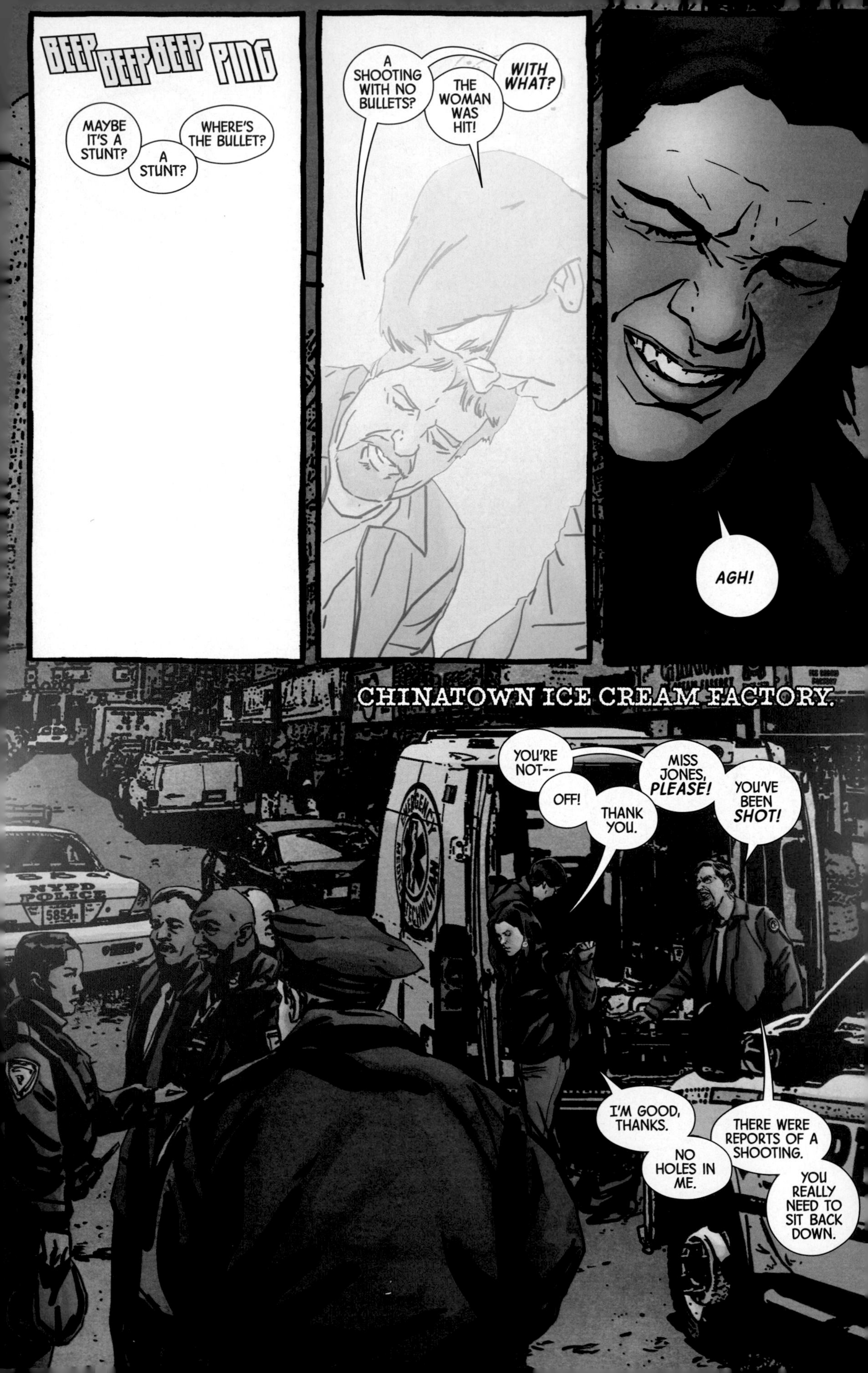
BEEP BEEP BEEP PING
MAYBE IT'S A STUNT?
A STUNT?
WHERE'S THE BULLET?
A SHOOTING WITH NO BULLETS?
THE WOMAN WAS HIT!
WITH WHAT?
AGH!
CHINATOWN ICE CREAM FACTORY.
YOU'RE NOT--
OFF!
MISS JONES, PLEASE!
THANK YOU.
YOU'VE BEEN SHOT!
I'M GOOD, THANKS.
NO HOLES IN ME.
THERE WERE REPORTS OF A SHOOTING.
YOU REALLY NEED TO SIT BACK DOWN.

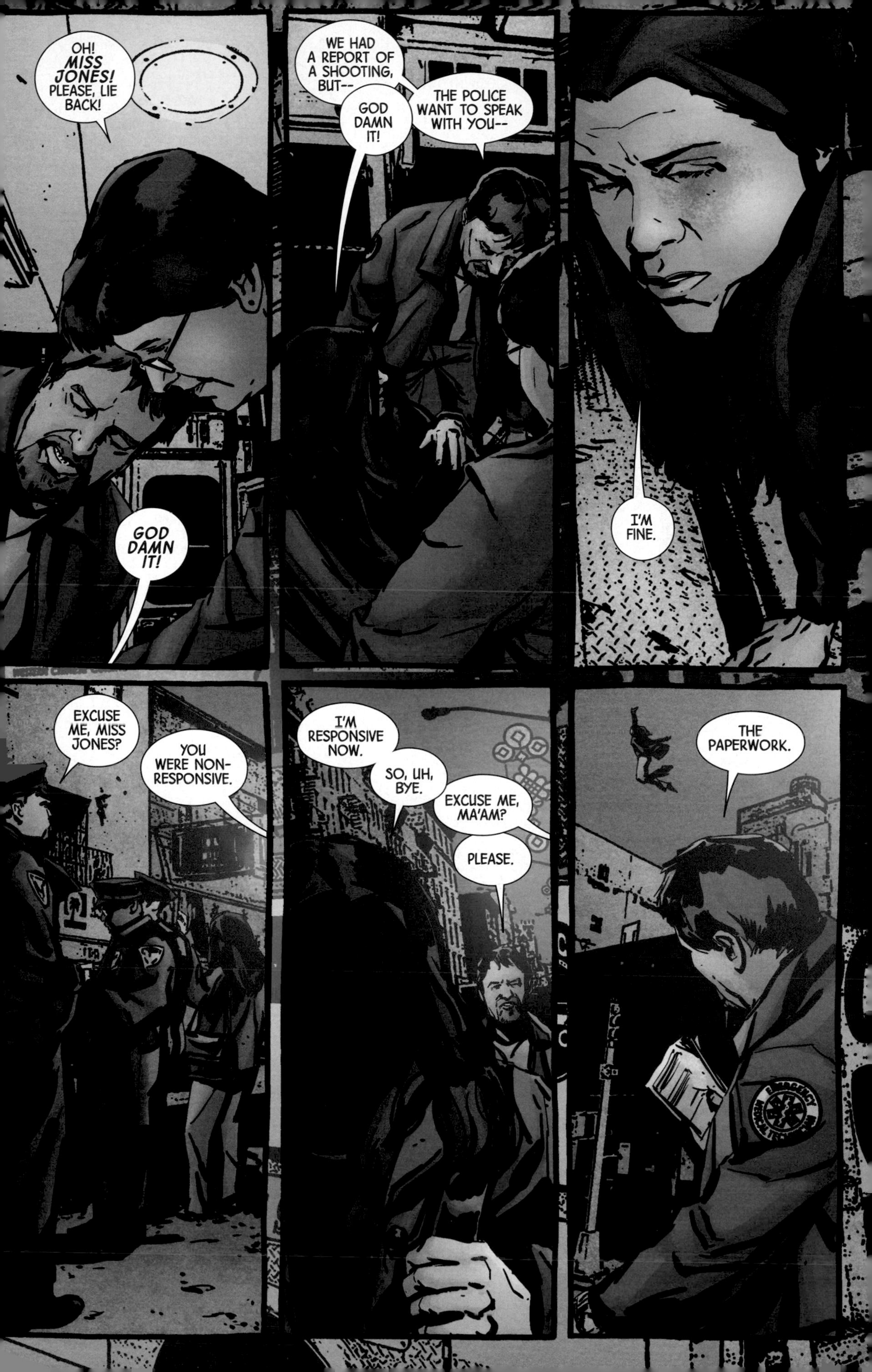
OH! MISS JONES! PLEASE, LIE BACK!
GOD DAMN IT!
WE HAD A REPORT OF A SHOOTING, BUT--
GOD DAMN IT!
THE POLICE WANT TO SPEAK WITH YOU--
I'M FINE.
EXCUSE ME, MISS JONES?
YOU WERE NON-RESPONSIVE.
I'M RESPONSIVE NOW.
SO, UH, BYE.
EXCUSE ME, MA'AM?
PLEASE.
THE PAPERWORK.

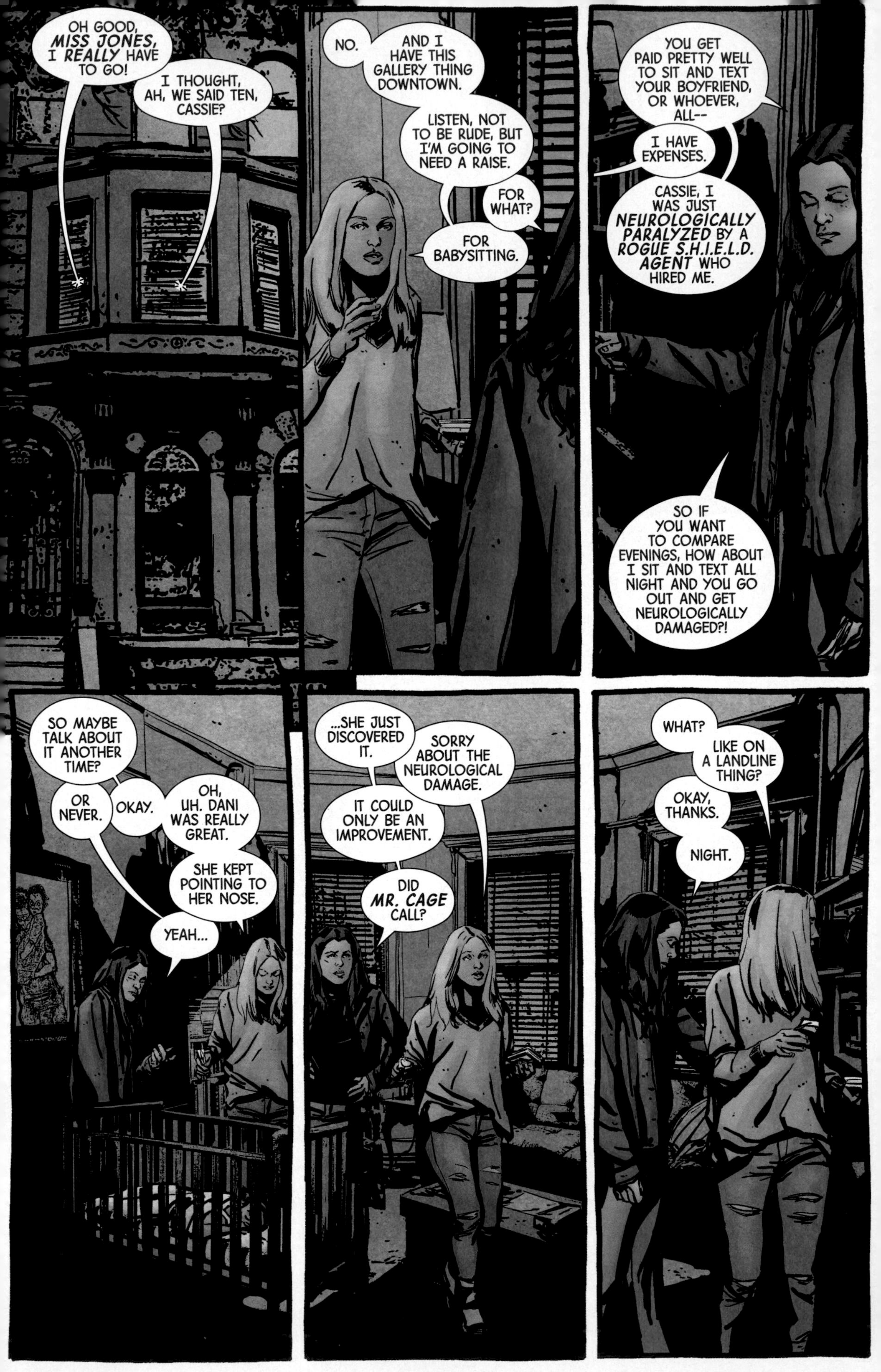
OH GOOD, MISS JONES, I REALLY HAVE TO GO!
I THOUGHT, AH, WE SAID TEN, CASSIE?
NO.
AND I HAVE THIS GALLERY THING DOWNTOWN.
LISTEN, NOT TO BE RUDE, BUT I'M GOING TO NEED A RAISE.
FOR WHAT?
FOR BABYSITTING.
YOU GET PAID PRETTY WELL TO SIT AND TEXT YOUR BOYFRIEND, OR WHOEVER, ALL--
I HAVE EXPENSES.
CASSIE, I WAS JUST NEUROLOGICALLY PARALYZED BY A ROGUE S.H.I.E.L.D. AGENT WHO HIRED ME.
SO IF YOU WANT TO COMPARE EVENINGS, HOW ABOUT I SIT AND TEXT ALL NIGHT AND YOU GO OUT AND GET NEUROLOGICALLY DAMAGED?!
SO MAYBE TALK ABOUT IT ANOTHER TIME?
OR NEVER.
OKAY.
OH, UH. DANI WAS REALLY GREAT.
SHE KEPT POINTING TO HER NOSE.
YEAH...
...SHE JUST DISCOVERED IT.
SORRY ABOUT THE NEUROLOGICAL DAMAGE.
IT COULD ONLY BE AN IMPROVEMENT.
DID MR. CAGE CALL?
WHAT?
LIKE ON A LANDLINE THING?
OKAY, THANKS.
NIGHT.

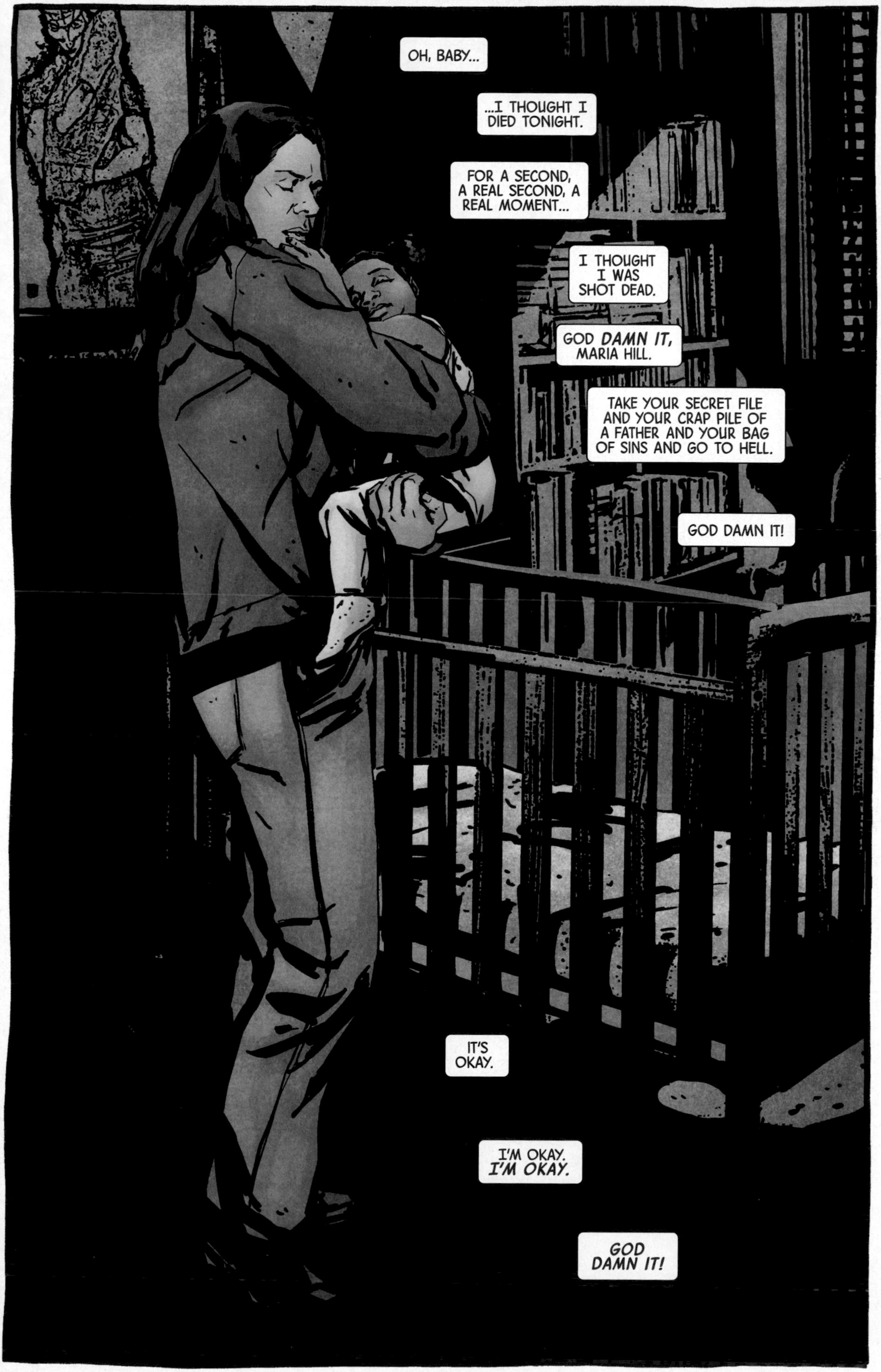
OH, BABY...
...I THOUGHT I DIED TONIGHT.
FOR A SECOND, A REAL SECOND, A REAL MOMENT...
I THOUGHT I WAS SHOT DEAD.
GOD *DAMN IT,* MARIA HILL.
TAKE YOUR SECRET FILE AND YOUR CRAP PILE OF A FATHER AND YOUR BAG OF SINS AND GO TO HELL.
GOD DAMN IT!
IT'S OKAY.
I'M OKAY. *I'M OKAY.*
GOD DAMN IT!

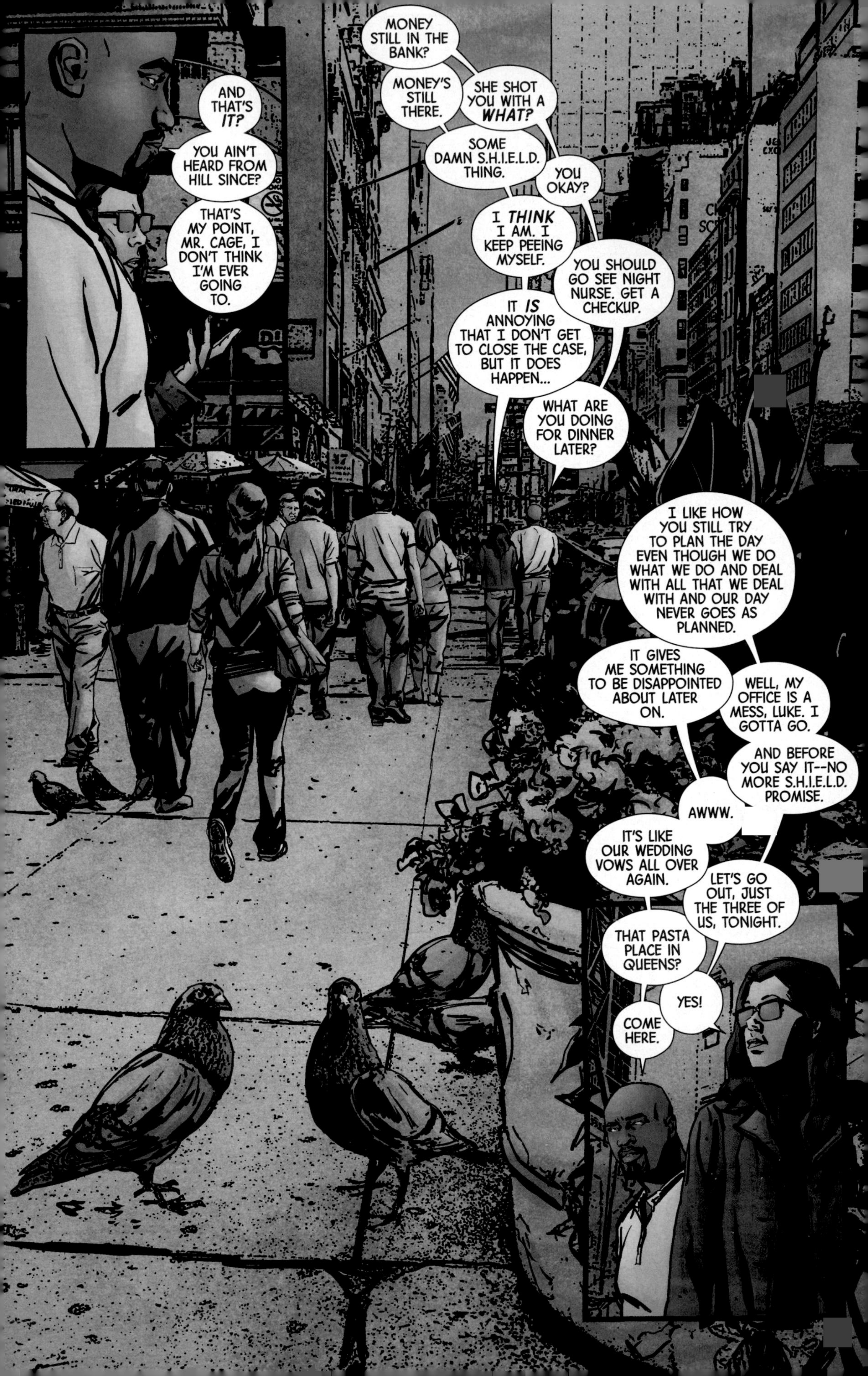
AND THAT'S IT?
YOU AIN'T HEARD FROM HILL SINCE?
THAT'S MY POINT, MR. CAGE, I DON'T THINK I'M EVER GOING TO.
MONEY STILL IN THE BANK?
MONEY'S STILL THERE.
SHE SHOT YOU WITH A WHAT?
SOME DAMN S.H.I.E.L.D. THING.
YOU OKAY?
I THINK I AM. I KEEP PEEING MYSELF.
YOU SHOULD GO SEE NIGHT NURSE. GET A CHECKUP.
IT IS ANNOYING THAT I DON'T GET TO CLOSE THE CASE, BUT IT DOES HAPPEN...
WHAT ARE YOU DOING FOR DINNER LATER?
I LIKE HOW YOU STILL TRY TO PLAN THE DAY EVEN THOUGH WE DO WHAT WE DO AND DEAL WITH ALL THAT WE DEAL WITH AND OUR DAY NEVER GOES AS PLANNED.
IT GIVES ME SOMETHING TO BE DISAPPOINTED ABOUT LATER ON.
WELL, MY OFFICE IS A MESS, LUKE. I GOTTA GO.
AND BEFORE YOU SAY IT--NO MORE S.H.I.E.L.D. PROMISE.
AWWW.
IT'S LIKE OUR WEDDING VOWS ALL OVER AGAIN.
LET'S GO OUT, JUST THE THREE OF US, TONIGHT.
THAT PASTA PLACE IN QUEENS?
YES!
COME HERE.

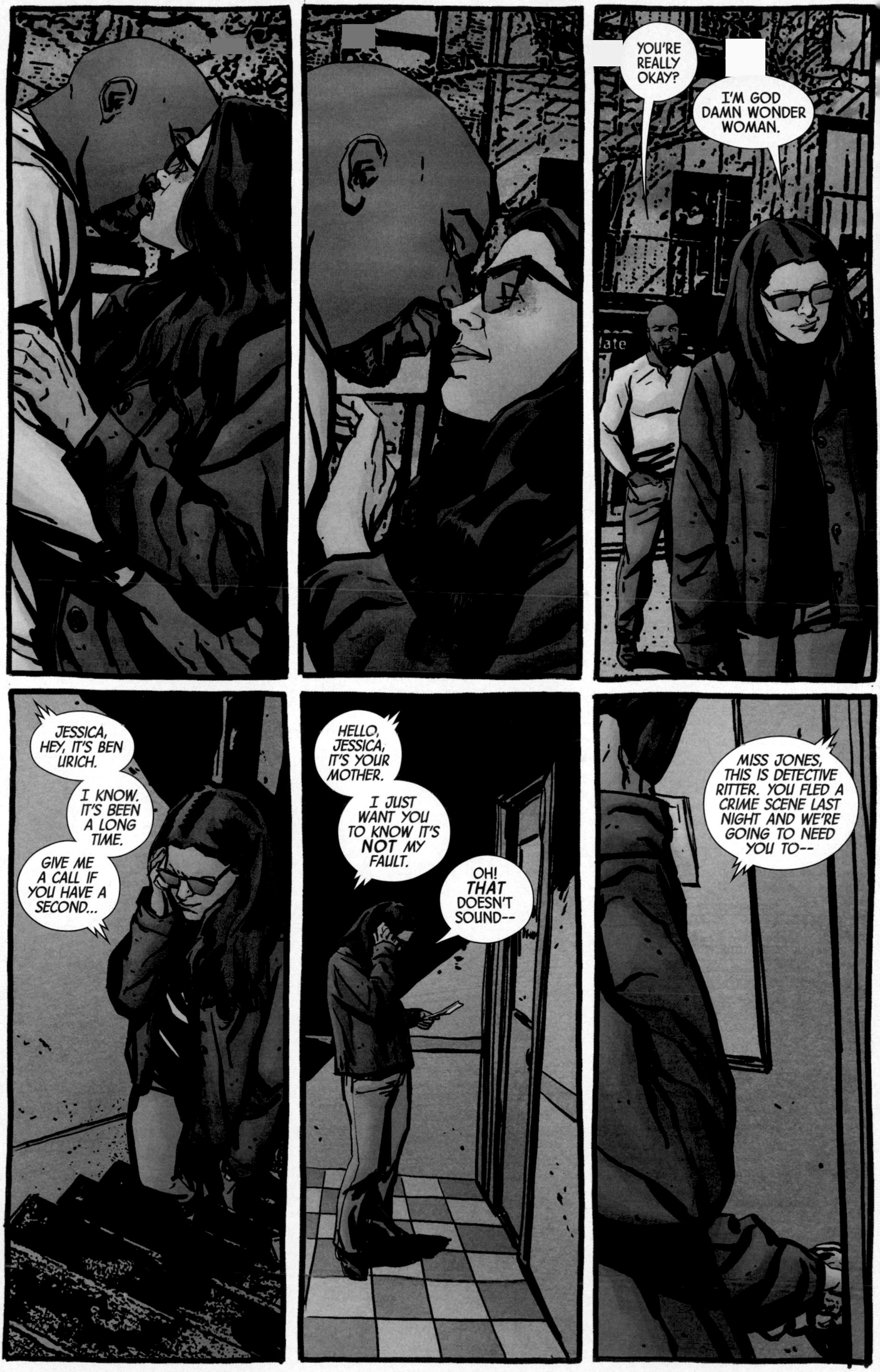
YOU'RE REALLY OKAY?
I'M GOD DAMN WONDER WOMAN.
JESSICA, HEY, IT'S BEN URICH.
I KNOW. IT'S BEEN A LONG TIME.
GIVE ME A CALL IF YOU HAVE A SECOND...
HELLO, JESSICA, IT'S YOUR MOTHER.
I JUST WANT YOU TO KNOW IT'S NOT MY FAULT.
OH! THAT DOESN'T SOUND--
MISS JONES, THIS IS DETECTIVE RITTER. YOU FLED A CRIME SCENE LAST NIGHT AND WE'RE GOING TO NEED YOU TO--

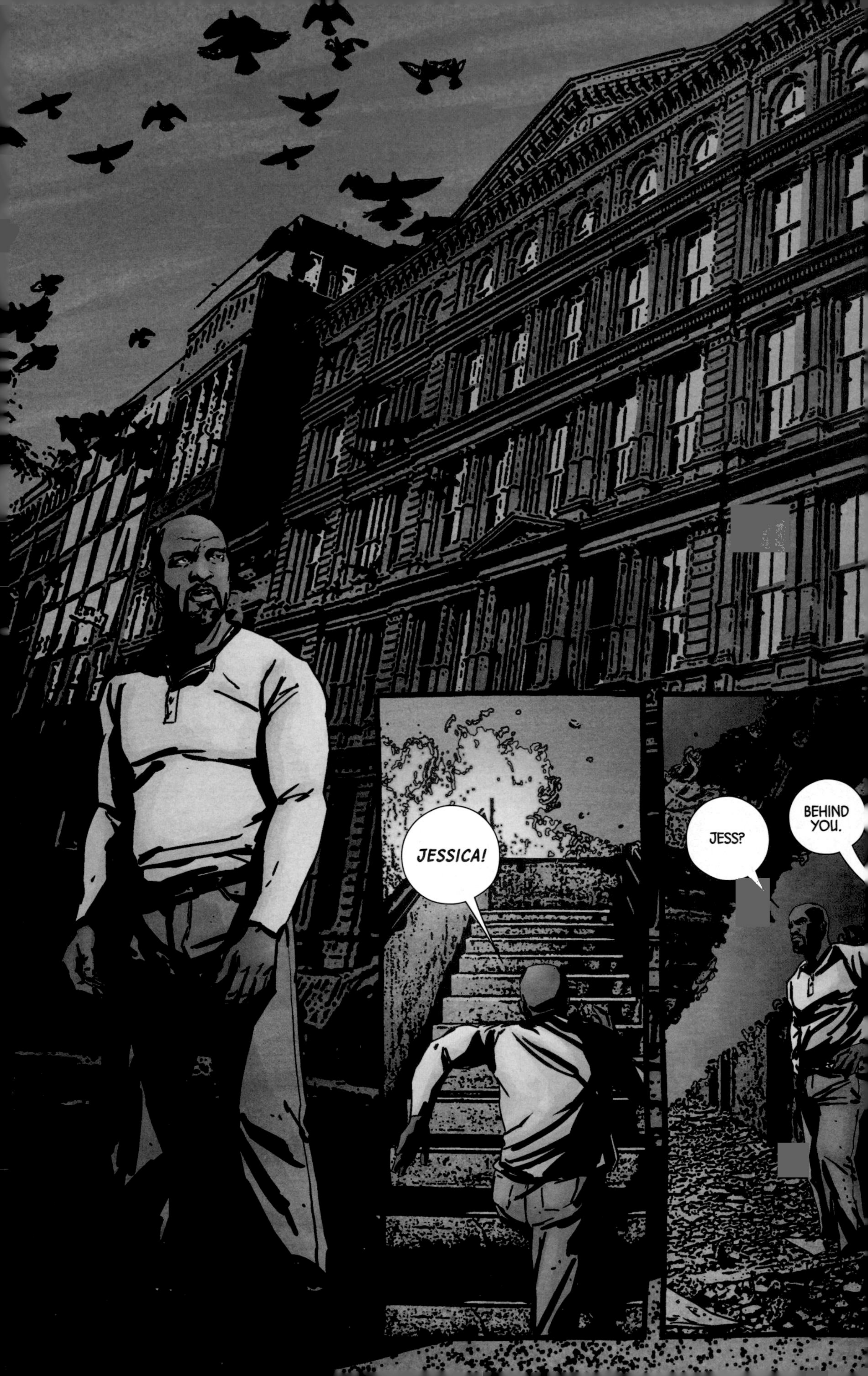
JESSICA!
JESS?
BEHIND YOU.

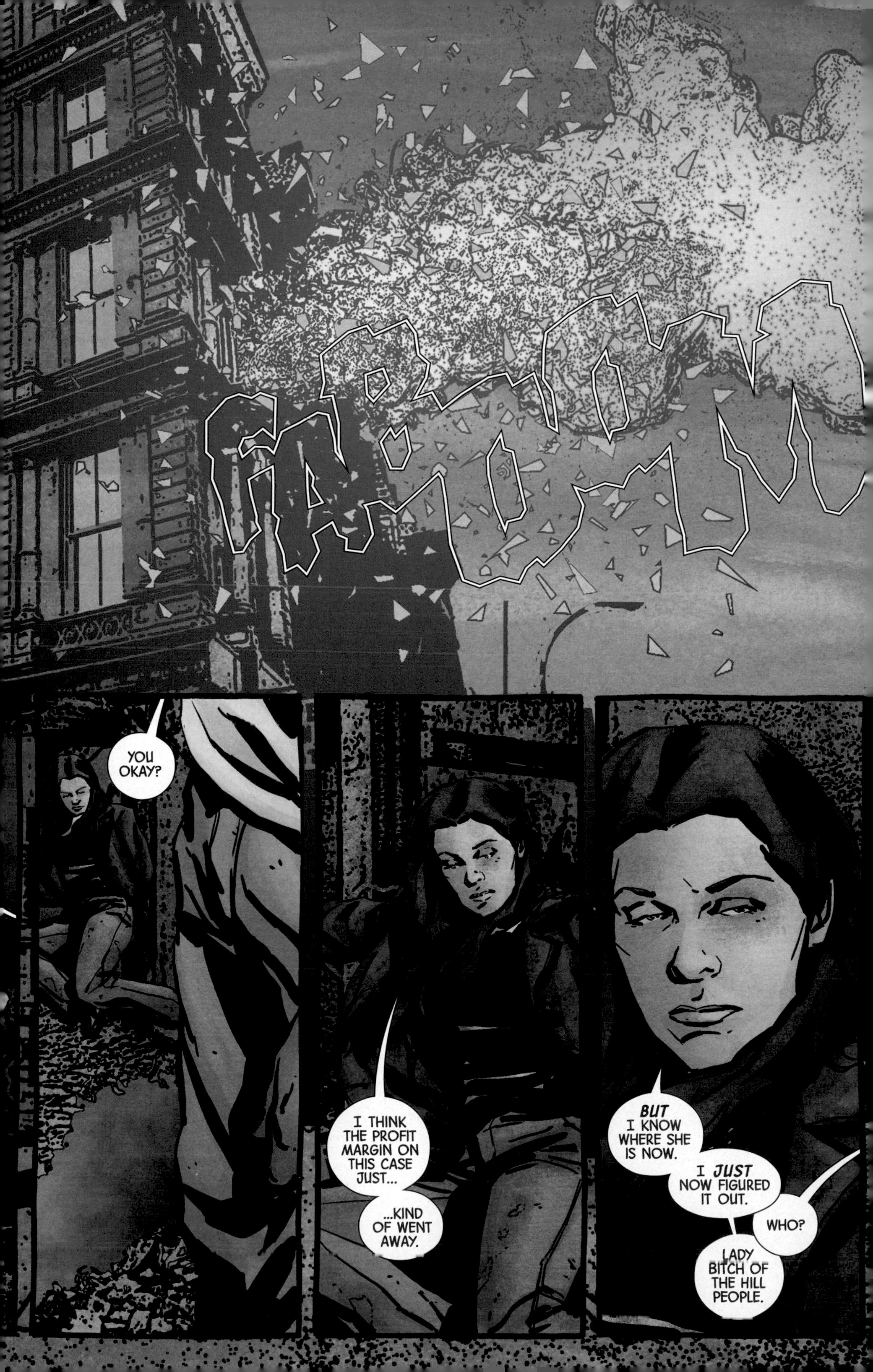
FRA-BOOOM
YOU OKAY?
I THINK THE PROFIT MARGIN ON THIS CASE JUST...
...KIND OF WENT AWAY.
BUT I KNOW WHERE SHE IS NOW.
I *JUST* NOW FIGURED IT OUT.
WHO?
LADY BITCH OF THE HILL PEOPLE.

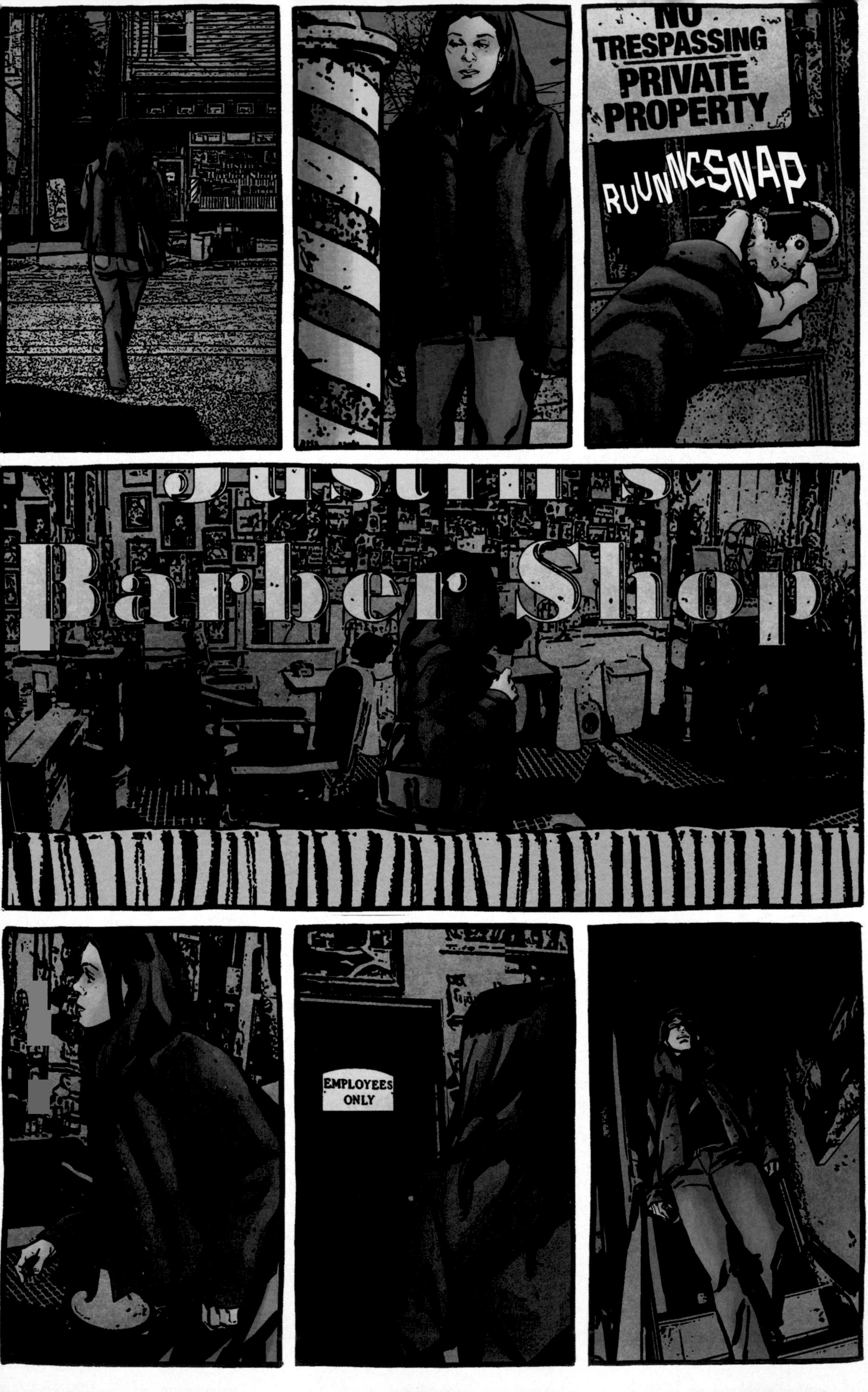
NO TRESPASSING PRIVATE PROPERTY
RUUNNCSNAP
Barber Shop
EMPLOYEES ONLY

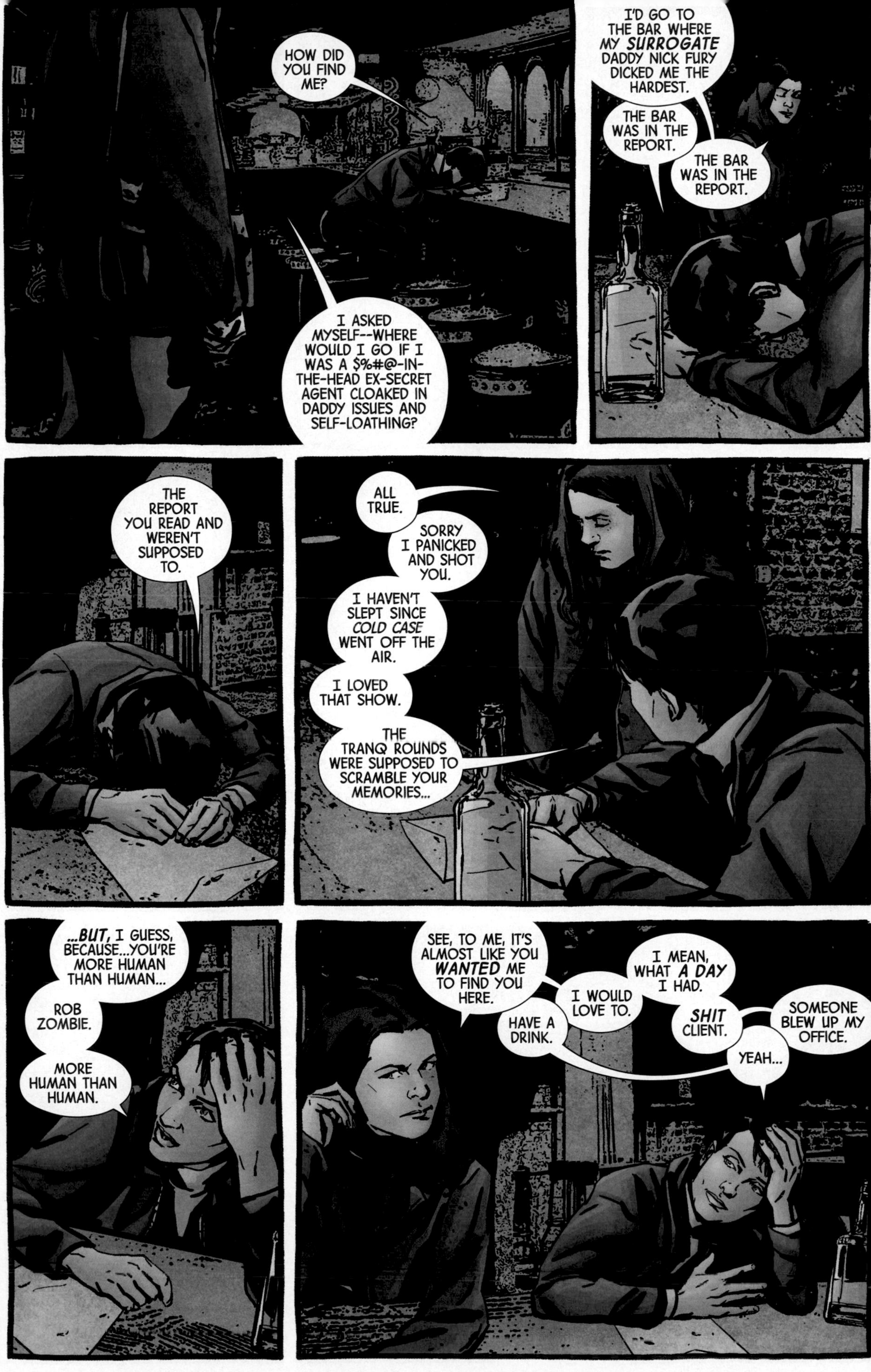
HOW DID YOU FIND ME?
I ASKED MYSELF--WHERE WOULD I GO IF I WAS A $%#@-IN-THE-HEAD EX-SECRET AGENT CLOAKED IN DADDY ISSUES AND SELF-LOATHING?
I'D GO TO THE BAR WHERE MY SURROGATE DADDY NICK FURY DICKED ME THE HARDEST.
THE BAR WAS IN THE REPORT.
THE BAR WAS IN THE REPORT.
THE REPORT YOU READ AND WEREN'T SUPPOSED TO.
ALL TRUE.
SORRY I PANICKED AND SHOT YOU.
I HAVEN'T SLEPT SINCE COLD CASE WENT OFF THE AIR.
I LOVED THAT SHOW.
THE TRANQ ROUNDS WERE SUPPOSED TO SCRAMBLE YOUR MEMORIES...
...BUT, I GUESS, BECAUSE...YOU'RE MORE HUMAN THAN HUMAN...
ROB ZOMBIE.
MORE HUMAN THAN HUMAN.
SEE, TO ME, IT'S ALMOST LIKE YOU WANTED ME TO FIND YOU HERE.
HAVE A DRINK.
I WOULD LOVE TO.
I MEAN, WHAT A DAY I HAD.
SHIT CLIENT.
SOMEONE BLEW UP MY OFFICE.
YEAH...

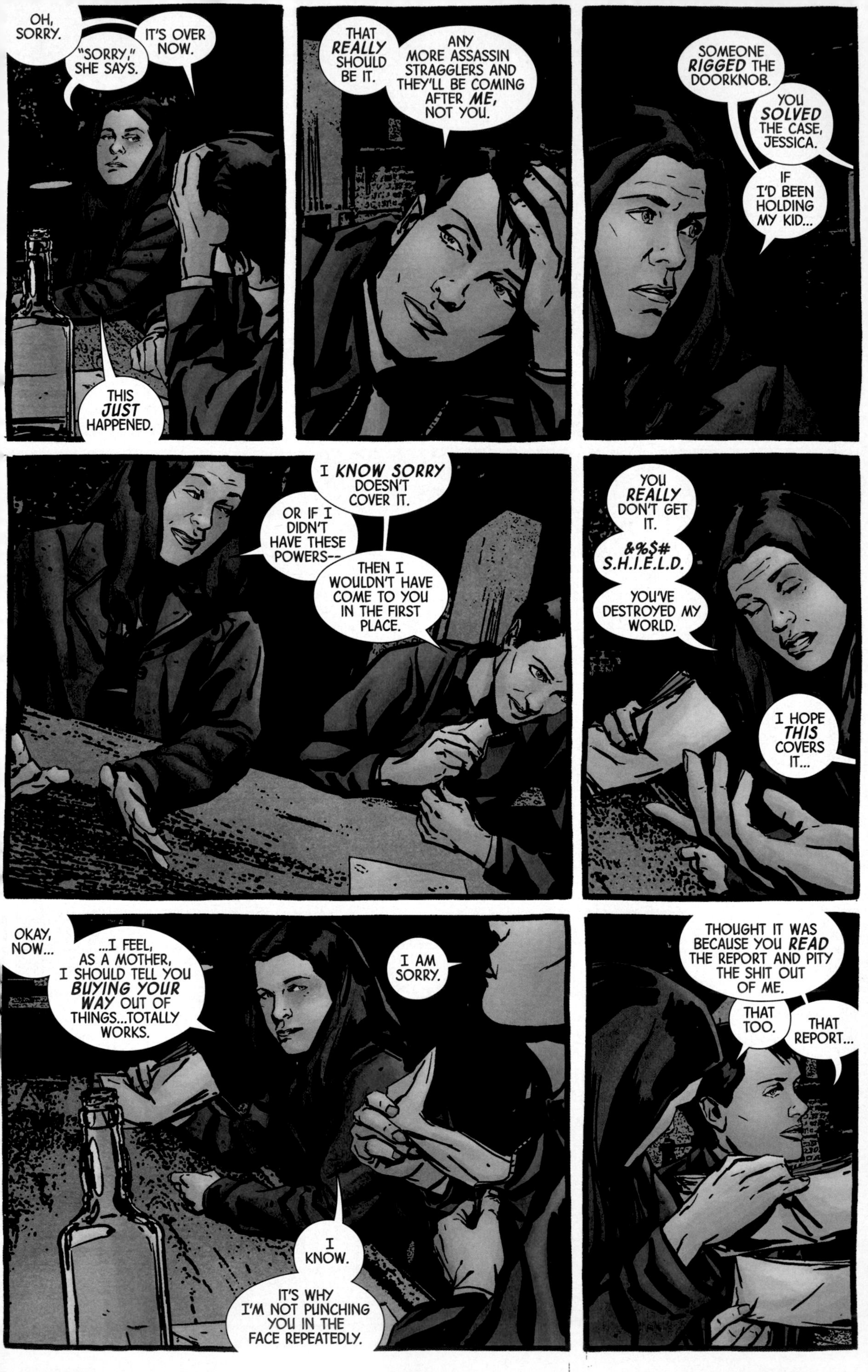
OH, SORRY.
IT'S OVER NOW.
"SORRY," SHE SAYS.
THIS JUST HAPPENED.
THAT REALLY SHOULD BE IT.
ANY MORE ASSASSIN STRAGGLERS AND THEY'LL BE COMING AFTER ME, NOT YOU.
SOMEONE RIGGED THE DOORKNOB.
YOU SOLVED THE CASE, JESSICA.
IF I'D BEEN HOLDING MY KID...
OR IF I DIDN'T HAVE THESE POWERS--
I KNOW SORRY DOESN'T COVER IT.
THEN I WOULDN'T HAVE COME TO YOU IN THE FIRST PLACE.
YOU REALLY DON'T GET IT.
&%$# S.H.I.E.L.D.
YOU'VE DESTROYED MY WORLD.
I HOPE THIS COVERS IT...
OKAY, NOW...
...I FEEL, AS A MOTHER, I SHOULD TELL YOU BUYING YOUR WAY OUT OF THINGS...TOTALLY WORKS.
I AM SORRY.
I KNOW.
IT'S WHY I'M NOT PUNCHING YOU IN THE FACE REPEATEDLY.
THOUGHT IT WAS BECAUSE YOU READ THE REPORT AND PITY THE SHIT OUT OF ME.
THAT TOO.
THAT REPORT...

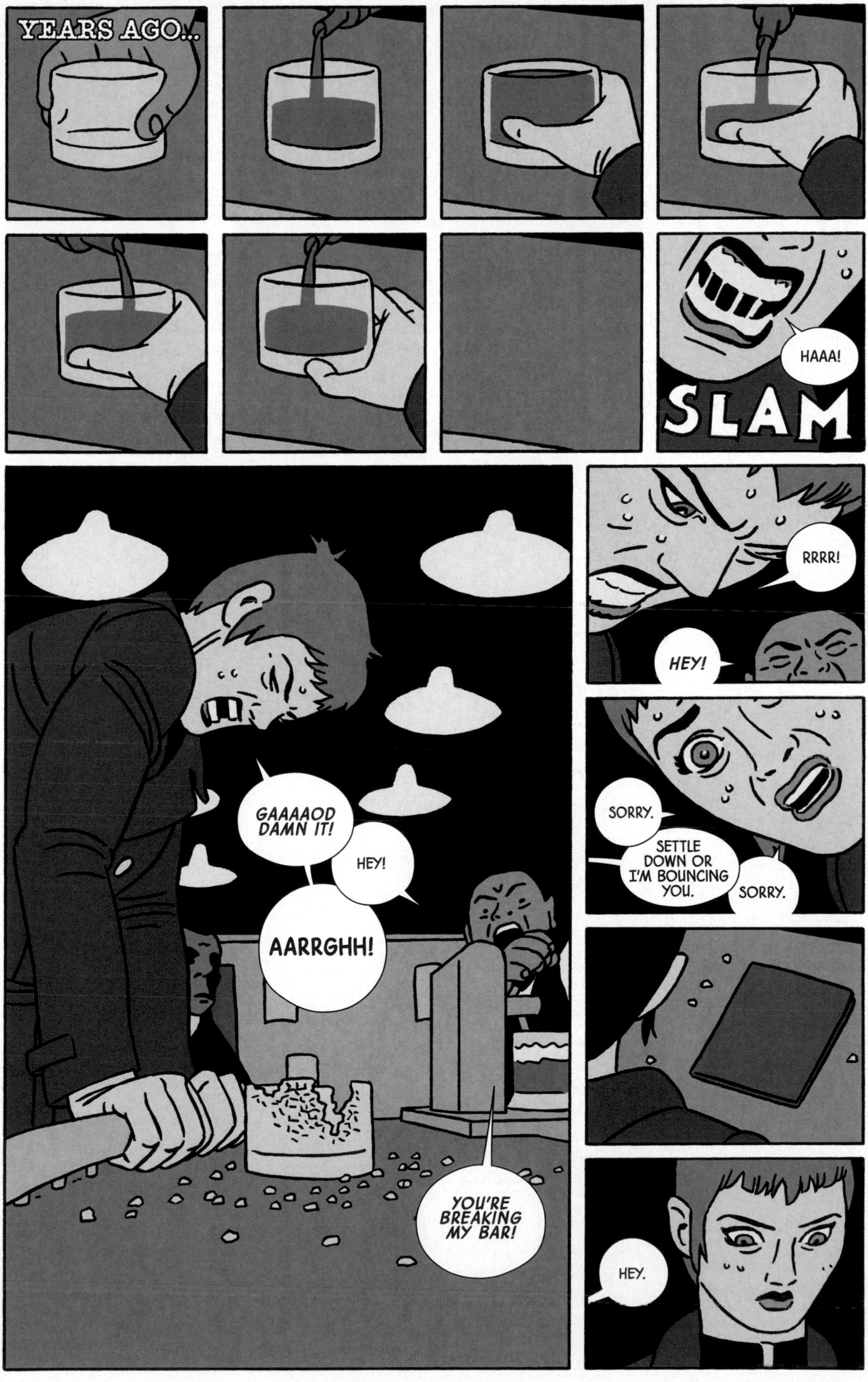
YEARS AGO...
HAAA!
SLAM
RRRR!
HEY!
GAAAAOD DAMN IT!
HEY!
AARRGHH!
YOU'RE BREAKING MY BAR!
SORRY.
SETTLE DOWN OR I'M BOUNCING YOU.
SORRY.
HEY.

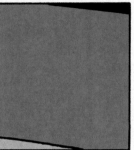

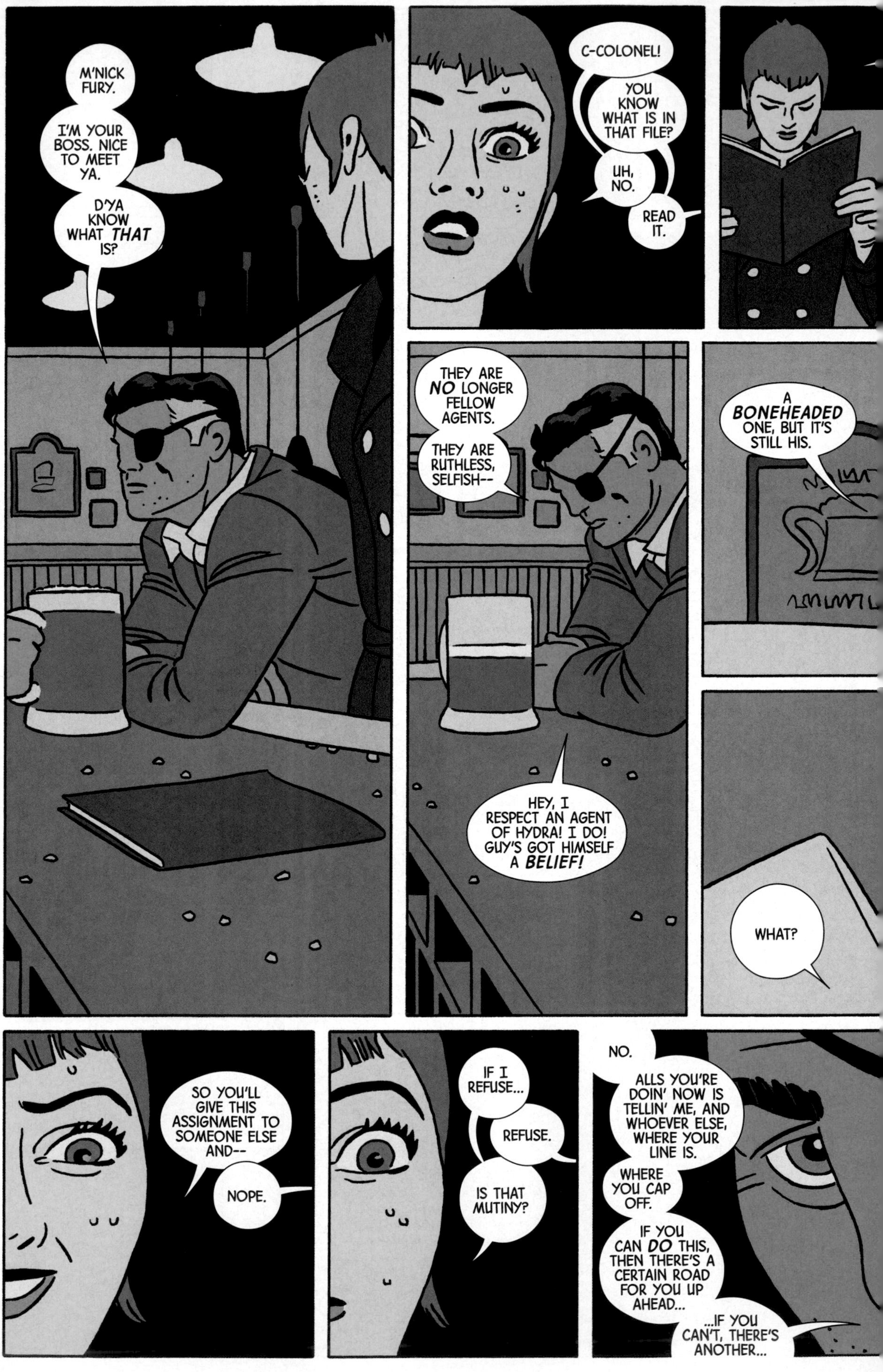
M'NICK FURY.
I'M YOUR BOSS. NICE TO MEET YA.
D'YA KNOW WHAT THAT IS?
C-COLONEL!
YOU KNOW WHAT IS IN THAT FILE?
UH, NO.
READ IT.
THEY ARE NO LONGER FELLOW AGENTS.
THEY ARE RUTHLESS, SELFISH--
HEY, I RESPECT AN AGENT OF HYDRA! I DO! GUY'S GOT HIMSELF A BELIEF!
A BONEHEADED ONE, BUT IT'S STILL HIS.
WHAT?
SO YOU'LL GIVE THIS ASSIGNMENT TO SOMEONE ELSE AND--
NOPE.
IF I REFUSE...
REFUSE.
IS THAT MUTINY?
NO.
ALLS YOU'RE DOIN' NOW IS TELLIN' ME, AND WHOEVER ELSE, WHERE YOUR LINE IS.
WHERE YOU CAP OFF.
IF YOU CAN DO THIS, THEN THERE'S A CERTAIN ROAD FOR YOU UP AHEAD...
...IF YOU CAN'T, THERE'S ANOTHER...

THIS IS A KILL ORDER.

YES.

THE MEN YOU RESCUED-- AND THAT, IN TURN, TRIED TO BURN YOUR ASS-- ARE NOW CONFIRMED HYDRA TRIPLE AGENTS.

THEY'RE WORKING FOR US, REPORTING IT TO HYDRA AND SELLING ALL THE SECRETS OF BOTH ORGANIZATIONS ON THE DARK WEB.

AND IT WAS *THERE* WE CAUGHT ONE OF *THEM* ACTIVELY TRYING TO PUT A HIT OUT ON *YOU.*

KILL ORDER IS GIVEN.

THEY ARE ALL YOURS.

FELLOW AGENTS.

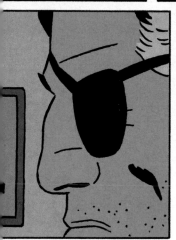

BUT THIS STUFF, IT'S AGAINST MY RELIGION AND IT'S DANGEROUS.

IT'S GAD-BLANGED MURDEROUS.

THIS--THIS ISN'T WHAT I SIGNED ON FOR.

YES, IT IS.

KILLING FELLOW AGENTS.

I'M CONFUSED.

I MET THEIR FAMILIES.

WIVES. CHILDREN.

AH! AT THE TRIAL.

YEAH.

THAT'S RIGHT. OKAY. I GET YA.

I GOTTA EXPLAIN IT TO YA?

YOU'RE A COMER. YER ON TRACK.

THIS IS HOW WE FIND OUT IF YOU GOT *ALL* THE GOODS.

LADY, THIS IS A *GIMME.*

IN THAT *THEY* GOT IT COMIN' AND *YOU'RE* THE ONE CALLED TO DO IT.

(UNLESS YA AIN'T.)

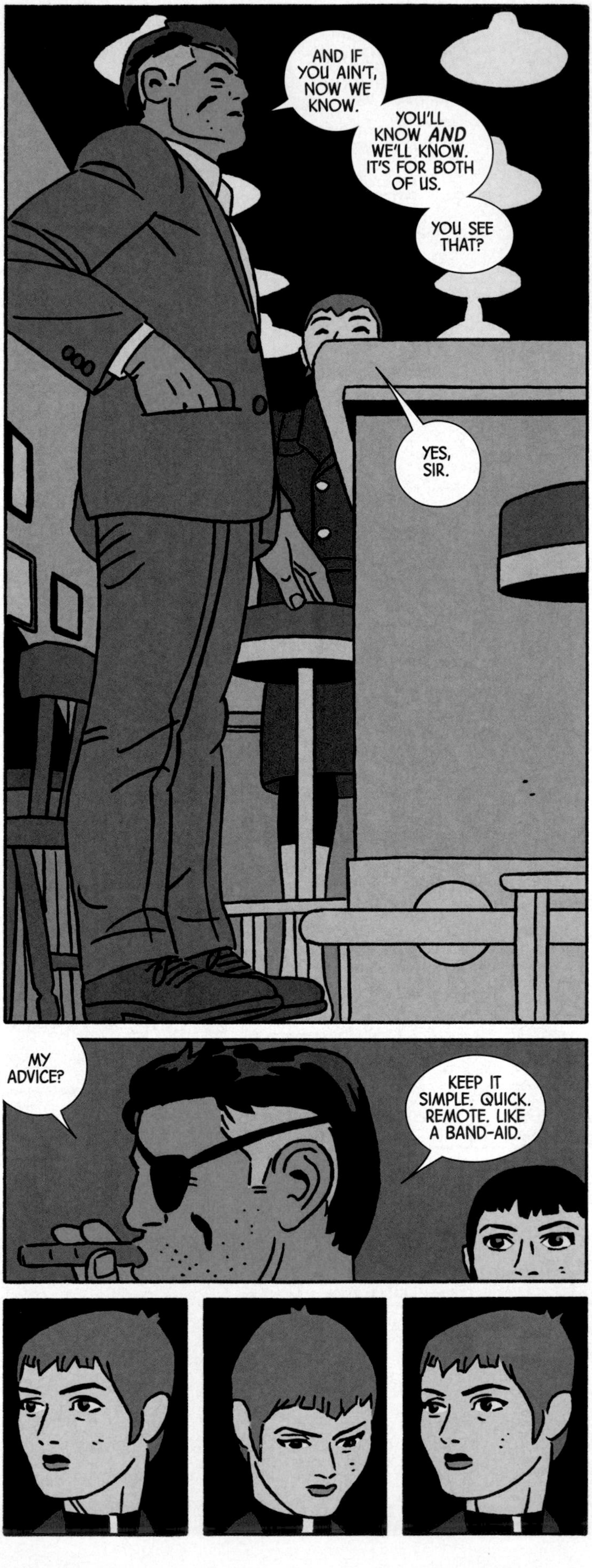
AND IF YOU AIN'T, NOW WE KNOW.
YOU'LL KNOW *AND* WE'LL KNOW. IT'S FOR BOTH OF US.
YOU SEE THAT?
YES, SIR.
MY ADVICE?
KEEP IT SIMPLE. QUICK. REMOTE. LIKE A BAND-AID.

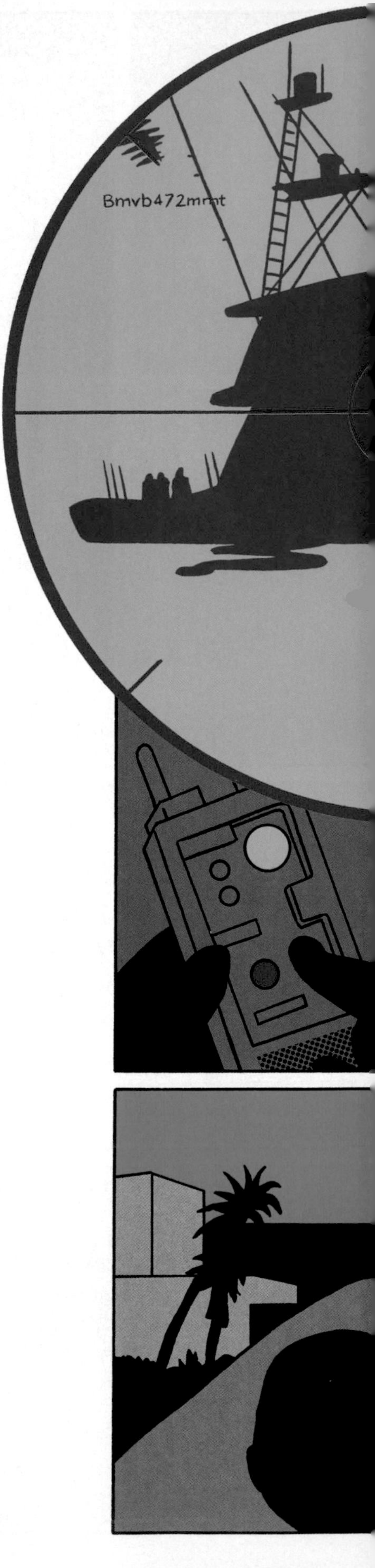
Bmvb472mmt

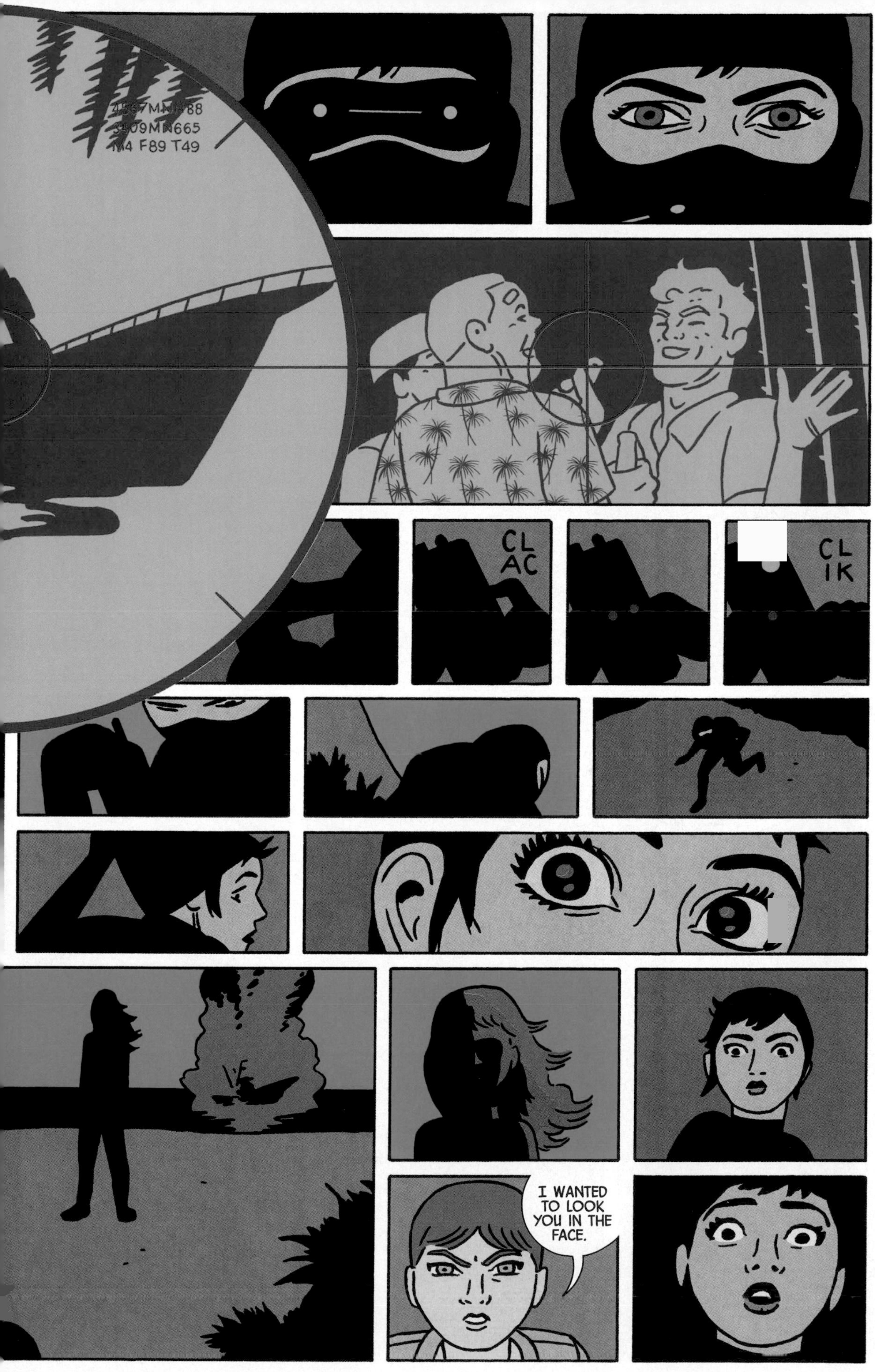
CL
AC
CL
IK
I WANTED TO LOOK YOU IN THE FACE.

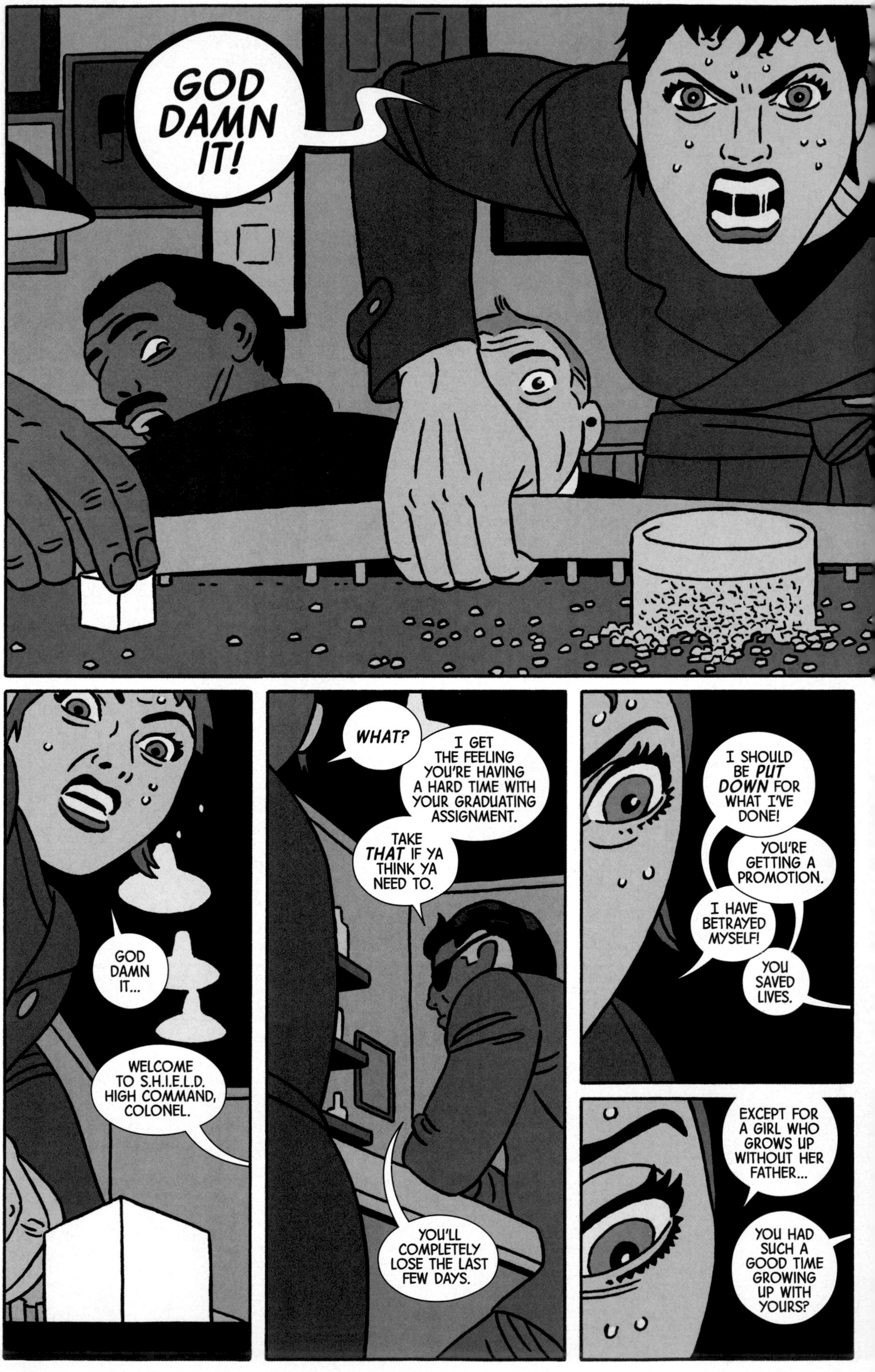
GOD DAMN IT!
GOD DAMN IT...
WELCOME TO S.H.I.E.L.D. HIGH COMMAND, COLONEL.
WHAT?
I GET THE FEELING YOU'RE HAVING A HARD TIME WITH YOUR GRADUATING ASSIGNMENT.
TAKE THAT IF YA THINK YA NEED TO.
YOU'LL COMPLETELY LOSE THE LAST FEW DAYS.
I SHOULD BE PUT DOWN FOR WHAT I'VE DONE!
YOU'RE GETTING A PROMOTION.
I HAVE BETRAYED MYSELF!
YOU SAVED LIVES.
EXCEPT FOR A GIRL WHO GROWS UP WITHOUT HER FATHER...
YOU HAD SUCH A GOOD TIME GROWING UP WITH YOURS?

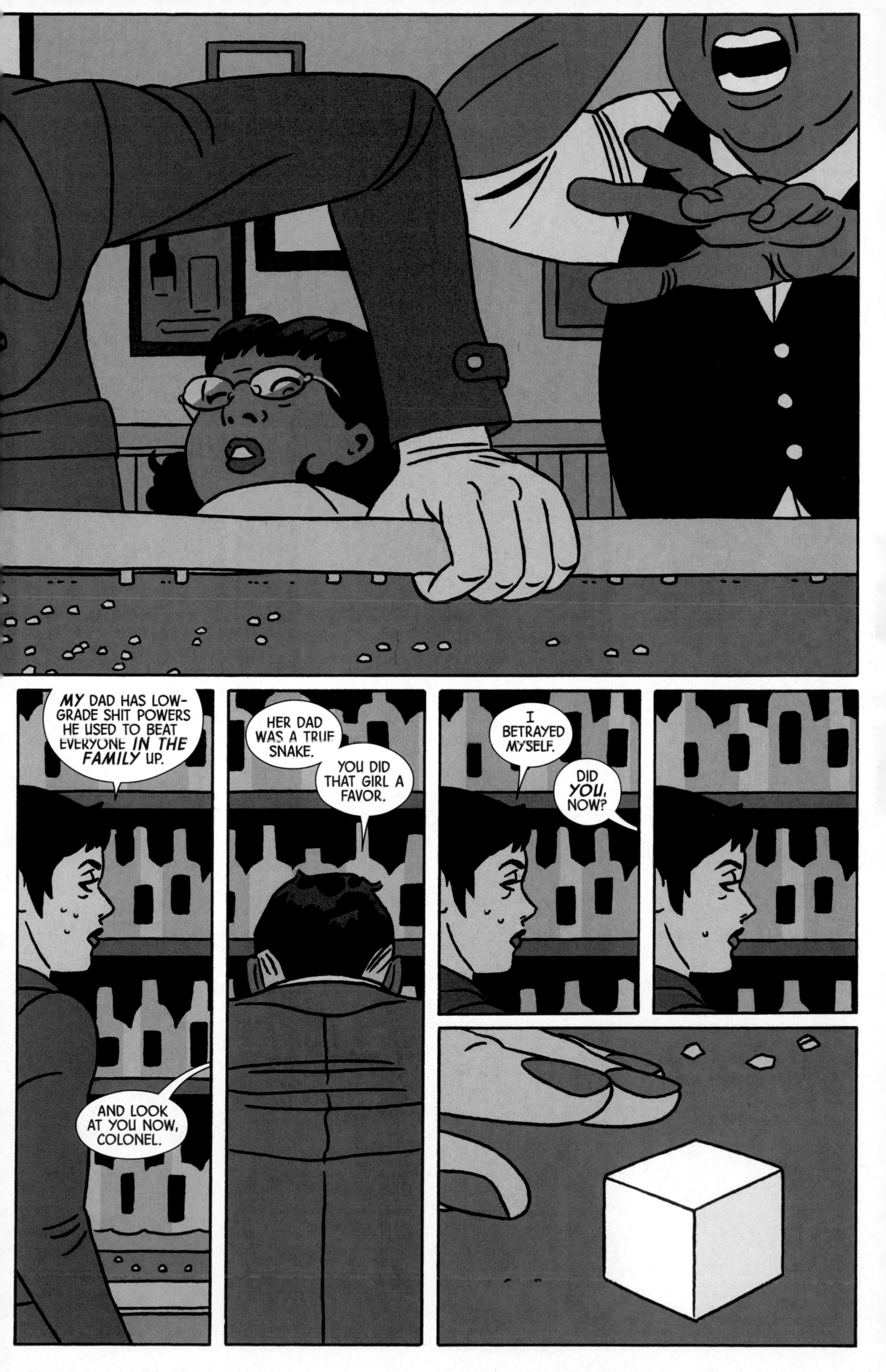
MY DAD HAS LOW-GRADE SHIT POWERS HE USED TO BEAT EVERYONE IN THE FAMILY UP.
AND LOOK AT YOU NOW, COLONEL.
HER DAD WAS A TRUE SNAKE.
YOU DID THAT GIRL A FAVOR.
I BETRAYED MYSELF.
DID YOU, NOW?

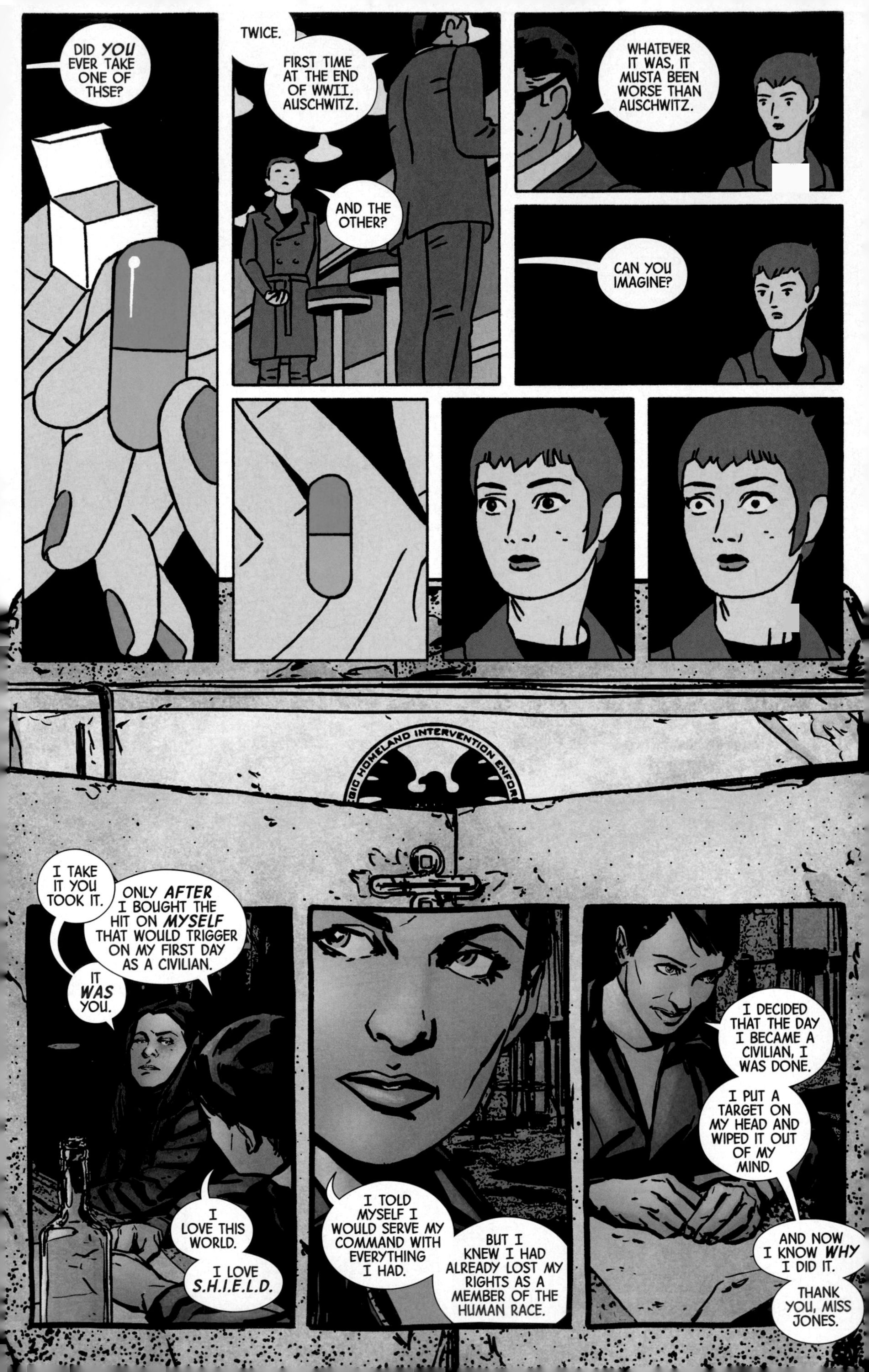
DID YOU EVER TAKE ONE OF THSE?
TWICE.
FIRST TIME AT THE END OF WWII. AUSCHWITZ.
AND THE OTHER?
WHATEVER IT WAS, IT MUSTA BEEN WORSE THAN AUSCHWITZ.
CAN YOU IMAGINE?
SHIELD HOMELAND INTERVENTION ENFOR
I TAKE IT YOU TOOK IT.
ONLY AFTER I BOUGHT THE HIT ON MYSELF THAT WOULD TRIGGER ON MY FIRST DAY AS A CIVILIAN.
IT WAS YOU.
I LOVE THIS WORLD.
I LOVE S.H.I.E.L.D.
I TOLD MYSELF I WOULD SERVE MY COMMAND WITH EVERYTHING I HAD.
BUT I KNEW I HAD ALREADY LOST MY RIGHTS AS A MEMBER OF THE HUMAN RACE.
I DECIDED THAT THE DAY I BECAME A CIVILIAN, I WAS DONE.
I PUT A TARGET ON MY HEAD AND WIPED IT OUT OF MY MIND.
AND NOW I KNOW WHY I DID IT.
THANK YOU, MISS JONES.

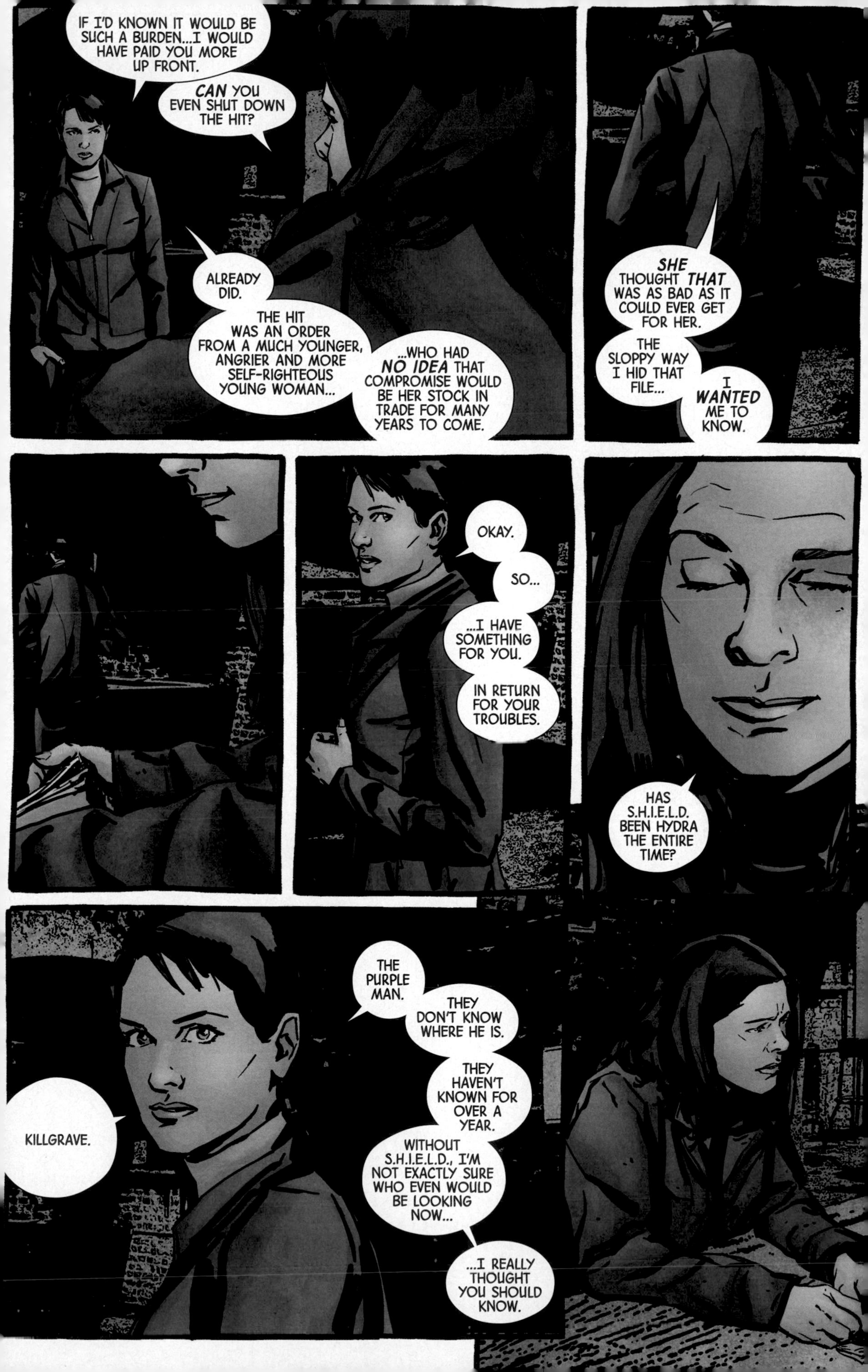
IF I'D KNOWN IT WOULD BE SUCH A BURDEN...I WOULD HAVE PAID YOU MORE UP FRONT.
CAN YOU EVEN SHUT DOWN THE HIT?
ALREADY DID.
THE HIT WAS AN ORDER FROM A MUCH YOUNGER, ANGRIER AND MORE SELF-RIGHTEOUS YOUNG WOMAN...
...WHO HAD NO IDEA THAT COMPROMISE WOULD BE HER STOCK IN TRADE FOR MANY YEARS TO COME.
SHE THOUGHT THAT WAS AS BAD AS IT COULD EVER GET FOR HER.
THE SLOPPY WAY I HID THAT FILE...
I WANTED ME TO KNOW.
OKAY.
SO...
...I HAVE SOMETHING FOR YOU.
IN RETURN FOR YOUR TROUBLES.
HAS S.H.I.E.L.D. BEEN HYDRA THE ENTIRE TIME?
KILLGRAVE.
THE PURPLE MAN.
THEY DON'T KNOW WHERE HE IS.
THEY HAVEN'T KNOWN FOR OVER A YEAR.
WITHOUT S.H.I.E.L.D., I'M NOT EXACTLY SURE WHO EVEN WOULD BE LOOKING NOW...
...I REALLY THOUGHT YOU SHOULD KNOW.

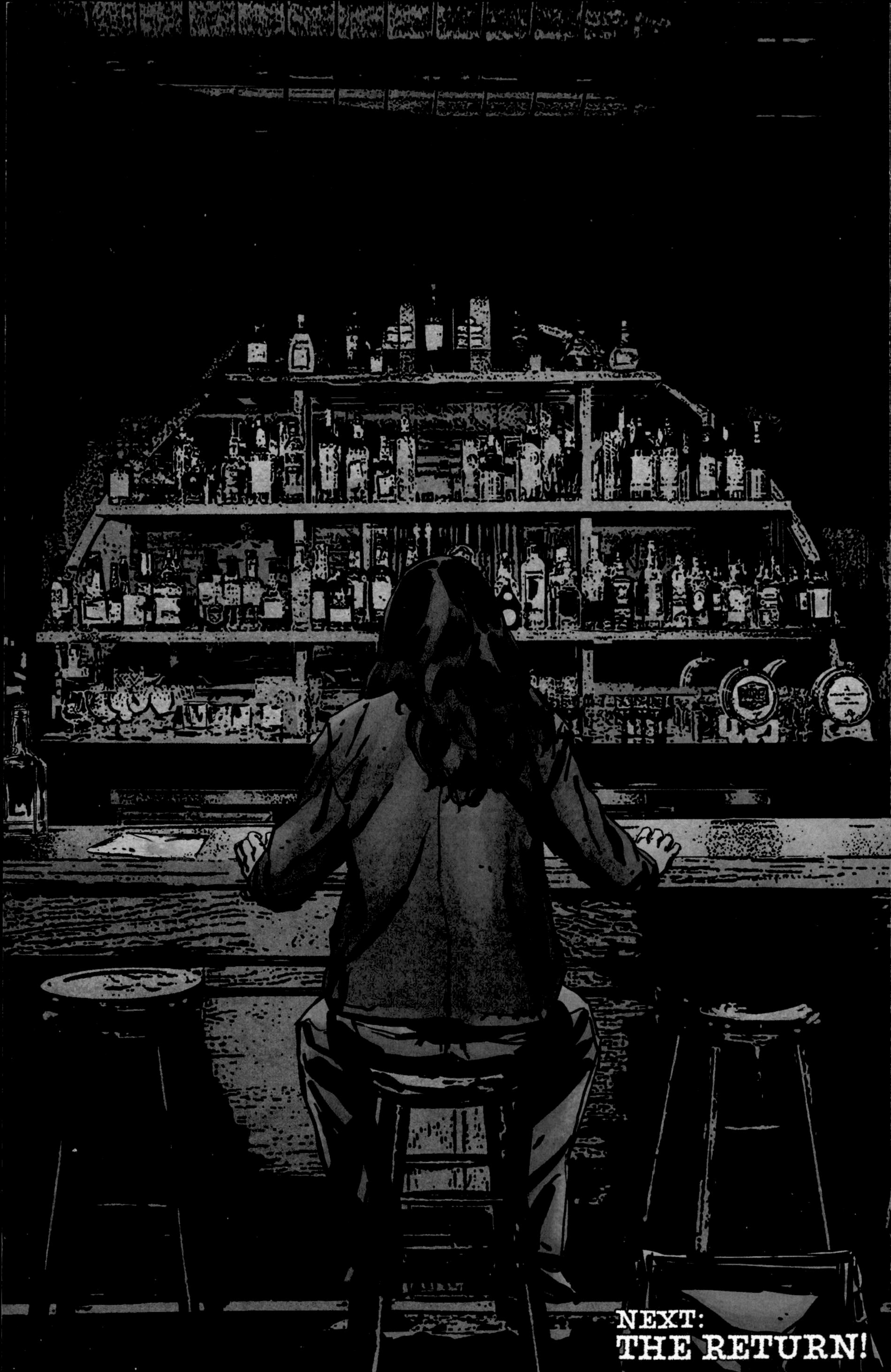
NEXT:
THE RETURN!